Lecture Notes in Computer Science   1678

Edited by G. Goos, J. Hartmanis and J. van Leeuwen

Springer

Berlin
Heidelberg
New York
Barcelona
Hong Kong
London
Milan
Paris
Singapore
Tokyo

Michael H. Böhlen   Christian S. Jensen
Michel O. Scholl (Eds.)

Spatio-Temporal Database Management

International Workshop STDBM'99
Edinburgh, Scotland, September 10-11, 1999
Proceedings

 Springer

Series Editors

Gerhard Goos, Karlsruhe University, Germany
Juris Hartmanis, Cornell University, NY, USA
Jan van Leeuwen, Utrecht University, The Netherlands

Volume Editors

Michael H. Böhlen
Christian S. Jensen
Aalborg University, Department of Computer Science
Fredrik Bajers Vej 7E, DK-9220 Aalborg Ost, Denmark
E-mail: {boehlen/csj}@cs.auc.dk

Michel O. Scholl
CNAM and INRIA
F-78153 Le Chesnay Cedex, France
E-mail: Michel.Scholl@inria.fr

Cataloging-in-Publication data applied for

Die Deutsche Bibliothek - CIP-Einheitsaufnahme

Spatio-temporal database management : proceedings / International
Workshop STDBM '99, Edinburgh, Scotland, September 10 - 11,
1999. Michael H. Böhlen ... (ed.). - Berlin ; Heidelberg ; New York ;
Barcelona ; Hong Kong ; London ; Milan ; Paris ; Singapore ; Tokyo
: Springer, 1999
(Lecture notes in computer science ; Vol. 1678)
ISBN 3-540-66401-7

CR Subject Classification (1998): H.2, H.3

ISSN 0302-9743
ISBN 3-540-66401-7 Springer-Verlag Berlin Heidelberg New York

© Springer-Verlag Berlin Heidelberg 1999
Printed in Germany

Typesetting: Camera-ready by author
SPIN: 10704266   06/3142 – 5 4 3 2 1 0   Printed on acid-free paper

Preface

The 1999 Workshop on Spatio-Temporal Database Management, held in Edinburgh, Scotland, September 10–11, 1999, brought together leading researchers and developers in the area of spatio-temporal databases to discuss the state-of-the-art in spatio-temporal research and applications and to understand the new challenges and future research directions in this emerging and rapidly advancing area. The workshop served as a forum for disseminating research and experience in spatio-temporal databases and for maximizing interchange of knowledge among researchers from the established spatial and temporal database communities. The exchange of research ideas and results not only contributes to the academic arena, but also benefits the user and commercial communities.

These proceedings contain the research papers selected for presentation at the workshop. The workshop was conceived from the outset to have a general scope within its area and to be international in participation. The call for papers aimed to attract the highest quality and most up-to-date research contributions from around the world, and the workshop was co-located with VLDB'99, enabling many participants to conveniently attend both events and thereby facilitating the widest possible international participation.

The call for papers attracted 30 research papers, which were submitted by authors from 14 countries and five continents, clearly indicating the truly international nature of the emerging area of spatio-temporal databases. A program committee consisting of 25 researchers from four continents conducted four reviews of each paper and selected 13 outstanding papers for presentation and discussion at the workshop and inclusion in the proceedings.

Spatio-temporal databases manage spatially and temporally referenced data. The papers included in this volume cover diverse aspects of the management of such data, and they have been organized into five groups: understanding and manipulating spatio-temporal data; integration, exchange, and visualization; query processing; index evaluation; and constraints and dependencies.

The first group of papers contribute to the foundations for understanding spatio-temporal data, by offering a taxonomy for the evolving, travel-related behaviors of sets of geographical entities, by giving an algebraic framework for the changes in identities of spatially-referenced objects, and by introducing a model of spatio-temporal partitions.

The second group covers the ontology-based integration of independently produced spatial data sets based on three different notions of semantic similarity among spatial objects; it describes the Italian cadastral information system, which supports the exchange of cadastral data, offers web-based access, and currently has some 15 000 end users; and it provides extensions to VRML that aim at enabling the exploration of spatio-temporal data based on interactive, web-based visualization.

The third and fourth groups of papers are closely related. These papers concern the efficient implementation of operations on spatio-temporal data, and indexing plays a central role in all of them. Efficient techniques for performing nearest-neighbor queries are presented, as is an implementation in the CONCERT system of a generic index for spatio-temporal data. Two papers concern the benchmarking of spatial and spatio-temporal indices. The BASIS system, which supports the benchmarking of spatial indices, is presented, and a performance comparison of three spatio-temporal indices is reported.

The last group of papers is more theoretical in nature and covers dependencies as well as the constraint-based approach to spatio-temporal data management. Specifically, the first paper generalizes temporal dependencies to also apply to other dimensions, including the spatial dimensions and those used in the more general multi-dimensional databases. The remaining two papers concern constraints, providing new insights into the use of so-called indefinite constraint databases for spatio-temporal data management, and exploring the animation of spatio-temporal databases defined in terms of constraints.

Many people played a role in putting together this workshop. The workshop grew out of the European spatio-temporal database project Chorochronos. We would like to thank all the direct and indirect participants in this project for their support. In particular, the project coordinator, Timos Sellis, deserves special thanks for his thoughtful and consistent assistance in the preparation of the workshop. We also thank Christiane Bernard of the European Commission for her support.

Special thanks go to the members of the program committee and the external reviewers they enlisted for their hard and diligent work. As a reflection of their dedication, more than 95% of the reviews arrived on time, with the last few reviews following quickly thereafter. A discussion phase after the initial reviewing aimed to understand and possibly resolve diverging reviews; this phase proceeded effortlessly, with each program committee member taking active part. Giedrius Slivinskas managed the technical aspects of the fully electronic reviewing process with care and dedication; he handled the receiving of submitted papers and their subsequent distribution to the reviewers; and he customized and managed the software for receiving reviews, which was originally developed for EDBT'98 and was kindly provided by Bettina Kemme and Guy Pardon. Michael Böhlen served as the proceedings editor. He managed the interaction with Springer-Verlag and lent his time and expertise to putting together this volume. Alfred Hofmann and Antje Endemann at Springer-Verlag lent us their professional help. Finally, we would like to thank Babis Theodoulidis and his team of workshop organizers at UMIST for their help. We appreciate their efforts in maintaining the workshop's Web page and distributing the call for papers.

September 1999   Christian S. Jensen and Michel Scholl
                                                               Program Chairs

Organization

STDBM'99 is organized and sponsored by the Chorochronos project, which is funded by the European Commission DG XII Science, Research and Development, as a Networks Activity of the Training and Mobility of Researchers Programme.

Executive Committee

General Chair:	Babis Theodoulidis, UMIST
Program Chairs:	Christian S. Jensen, Aalborg University
	Michel Scholl, CNAM and INRIA
Finance:	Yannis Kakoudakis, UMIST
Organization:	Ilias Petrounias, UMIST
Publication:	Michael H. Böhlen, Aalborg University
Publicity:	Alex Vakaloudis, UMIST
Registration:	Joann Slater, UMIST
Technical Coordination:	Giedrius Slivinskas, Aalborg University

Program Committee

Lars Arge, Duke University, USA
Elisa Bertino, Università di Milano, Italy
Jan Chomicki, Monmouth University, USA
Max Egenhofer, University of Maine, USA
Andrew U. Frank, Technical University of Vienna, Austria
Stéphane Grumbach, INRIA, France
Oliver Günther, Humboldt University of Berlin, Germany
Ralf H. Güting, FernUniversität Hagen, Germany
Manolis Koubarakis, UMIST, UK
Nikos Lorentzos, Agricultural University of Athens, Greece
Yannis Manolopoulos, Aristotle University of Thessaloniki, Greece
Enrico Nardelli, Università di L'Aquila, Italy
Mario Nascimento, Unicamp, Brazil
Barbara Pernici, Politecnico di Milano, Italy
Philippe Rigaux, CNAM Paris, France
John Roddick, University of South Australia, Australia
Hans-Jörg Schek, ETH Zürich, Switzerland
Timos Sellis, National Technical University of Athens, Greece
Stefano Spaccapietra, EPFL Lausanne, Switzerland
Yannis Theodoridis, National Technical University of Athens, Greece
Babis Theodoulidis, UMIST, UK
Nectaria Tryfona, Aalborg University, Denmark

Vassilis Tsotras, University of California at Riverside, USA
Ouri Wolfson, University of Illinois, USA
Michael Worboys, Keele University, UK

External Referees

Bernd Amann	Nikos Karayannidis	Guido Proietti
Julien Basch	Manolis Kazantzides	Lukas Relly
Klemens Bohm	Marinos Kavouras	Spiros Skiadopoulos
Barbara Catania	Claudia Bauzer Medeiros	Jamal Syed
Luca Forlizzi	Isabelle Mirbel	Alex Vakaloudis
Baigal Gongor	Apostolos Papadopoulos	Michael Vassilakopoulos
Kathleen Hornsby	Christine Parent	Dan Vodislav

Table of Contents

Constraints and Dependencies

A Spatio-Temporal Taxonomy for the Representation of Spatial Set Behaviours

Marius Thériault[1], Christophe Claramunt[2], and Paul Y. Villeneuve[1]

[1] Laval University, Planning and Development Research Centre,
FAS 16th floor, Quebec, G1K 7P4, Canada
{Marius.Theriault@ggr.ulaval.ca, Paul.Villeneuve@crad.ulaval.ca}

[2] The Nottingham Trent University, Department of Computing,
Burton Street, Nottingham, NG1 4BU, UK
clac@doc.ntu.ac.uk

Abstract. Currently, most models proposed for spatio-temporal databases describe changes that involve independent entities. However, many dynamic applications need new models to relate evolution of spatial entities linked by common properties and constraints or relationships. In transportation GIS, an activity-event matrix describes individual entity behaviours, travel activities and routes on a transportation network. On the other hand, modelling disaggregate travel choices behaviour for several entities implies the identification of new mechanisms to describe the evolution of their joint spatial distribution. This paper introduces and describes the concept of sets of geographical entities needed for the analysis of travel behaviour in metropolitan areas. We propose a taxonomy for the description of the evolution of entity sets in space and the selection of appropriate statistical indexes to analyse their geographical patterns. Such a framework may become a reference for the development of spatio-temporal database representations of spatial patterns evolution.

1 Introduction

The philosophical revolution of the 18th century introduced a new paradigm of the universe where space and time are perceived as relative components allowing experimentation and perception of the environment. That complements the classical absolute space and time concepts of reality. Locating transformations into their spatio-temporal context is often an essential condition for the full understanding of the real world evolution. Spatio-temporal measurements complement the description of facts and changes, as well as they are used to formulate hypotheses about events and processes, a mandatory requirement to explain evolution using scientific models. These models use abstractions to describe processes that involve and, possibly, transform real world entities (e.g., individuals or phenomena). Changes are measured from the analysis of facts (comparison of successive status) and/or events (results of transformation). Those entities are not independent and isolated individuals. They are related in space and time, and define their spatial configuration. In fact, they form networks and patterns based on their behavioural, functional and institutional links. Furthermore, these networks and patterns define geographical structures that constrain spatial processes [27]. Providing appropriate concepts, data structures and analysis procedures to handle those complex spatio-temporal relationships is a key issue for their full integration within spatio-temporal databases.

Such spatio-temporal complexity is typical of transportation modelling. This application field provides interesting examples of key issues that impede its full integration within GIS and stresses the need for improvements in spatial and temporal reasoning [21]. Disaggregate modelling of travel choices is of particular interest. Resulting processes integrate behavioural components (e.g., discrete choices) while they are constrained in space (e.g., by land use and by transportation network) and time (e.g., by the time needed to travel from A to B, using a given technology). In a recent paper dealing with strategies for integrating GIS and transportation modelling, Goodchild [22] stresses the need for the development of a dynamic modelling paradigm in order to link extended models of transportation networks with efficient representation of changes and movements. Although some transportation features are temporally stable (e.g., roads), many other entities, like vehicles and passengers, are dynamic as they change their location. Analysis and display of spatial changes are critical to applications such as transit and emergency vehicle dispatching, travel behaviour analysis and traffic management. Therefore, GIS models and software have to develop new spatio-temporal models and display mechanisms to fulfil these transportation applications needs [42].

These applications are of particular interest as the results they yield can significantly improve land planning studies. On the other hand, new models and technologies oriented to the management and manipulation of spatio-temporal data are emerging. For example, using differential GPS (DGPS) and travel diaries, it is now feasible to record movement of entities in space, while collecting data on the trip purpose and the decision mechanism leading to travel choices [34, 1, 4, 14, 48, 40]. Moreover, there is a strong interest of the transportation community in temporal GIS that can improve simulation capabilities and that may enhance the analysis of travel behaviour [46, 23, 20, 19, 25].

Two complementary scientific approaches can be used to study the semantic properties and the evolution of entities in geographical space:

- Deductive methods, that are based on a mathematical representation of spatial entity relationships and changes. These formal approaches are mainly based on a Euclidean space and/or on a topological description of space and time. This search for an ontology of space, usually named qualitative reasoning in the artificial intelligence domain, attempts to identify relative relationships in space and the identification of possible changes. This leads to some a priori knowledge of possible spatial entity relationships [15, 12, 13] and changes [17, 11].

- Inductive methods, that are based on observation and analysis of spatio-temporal data. Spatial analysis studies the properties and trends of the distribution of entities located in space. Among various spatial statistical methods that can be used to analyse travel behaviour and spatial diffusion processes, let us mention point pattern analysis, spatial autocorrelation, weighted centrographic analysis, spatial interaction and path analysis of individual routes [28, 6, 36, 35, 47, 3, 18, 26, 33].

These methods are applied to a large set of disciplines from environmental to urban and biological studies. Due to the mathematical complexity of the definition of models and proofs, qualitative reasoning methods are currently limited to the representation of a small number of geographical entities. On the other hand, inductive methods apply statistical techniques and consider large sets of spatial data. Consequently, as the purpose of this paper concerns integrated modelling of moving entities and sets of entities, the proposed framework is based on two components:

- A description of the underlying evolution of geographical entities using a description of possible changes (i.e., processes modelled using a deductive approach). The development of our model is based on the following simplification: (1) any geographical entity is located in a geographical space using a point reference; (2) We also consider that the size and orientation of a geographical entity are negligible by comparison with inter-entity distances and shapes. Consequently, for the purpose of this framework, spatio-temporal evolution of entities is restricted to point changes (i.e., appearance, stability, translation and disappearance).

- A representation of the joint spatial evolution of a set of entities that summarises entity locations and movements. These transformations are described using appropriate statistical parameters to characterise the overall spatial patterns and their evolution (combining deductive and inductive methods).

In the GIS community, research on modelling spatio-temporal processes and changes is still in progress [8, 38, 9, 16]. However, some extensions are still needed to develop efficient spatio-temporal models oriented toward the full understanding of the evolution of physical and human systems. Particularly, existing frameworks must be improved in order to describe joint evolution of entities forming sets at various abstraction levels. Current proposals are generally limited to the study of entity evolution without considering the networks of several entities sharing common properties and/or functional relationships. This hinders efficient use of many spatial statistics methods due to restrictive data structures that forbid querying spatio-temporal data through appropriate linkage networks (e.g., social network, individuals constraining their own travel choices to satisfy the needs of people living with them).

This paper identifies a set of spatio-temporal properties that characterise the geographical evolution of sets of entities, and allows for their analysis using statistical methods. From the identification of a set of the basic evolution processes of geographical entities, we propose a classification of spatio-temporal transformations among sets of entities. The proposed framework aims at the identification of modelling and computational operators for spatio-temporal databases. We will not target the analysis of specific spatio-temporal causal relationships and/or consequences. They are only relevant to various scientific disciplines and far away beyond the scope of this paper. However, we will use real data that describe travel choices and activities of individuals living in single-parent families to illustrate some of the benefits of the proposed framework. These data come from an extended origin-destination survey realised within the Quebec metropolitan region [45].

The remainder of this paper is organised as follows. Related literature about temporal GIS is summarised in Section 2. The semantics of the evolution of spatial entities (entities located in space) and sets of spatial entities is introduced in Section 3. A taxonomy of spatio-temporal processes that involve several spatial entities is introduced in Section 4. Section 5 introduces some application examples. They use actual disaggregate activity travel behaviour diaries and the activity events data structure proposed by Goodchild [22]. Finally, Section 6 concludes the paper and presents some further development avenues.

2 Related work

GIS provides computing solutions for the management and analysis of geographical data. It integrates, manipulates and visualises large sets of geographical data at various scales. However, studying the evolution of real-world systems implies the extension of the GIS paradigm by the integration of the temporal dimension. Temporal functions of current GIS are based on basic database operations with dates and/or building of time stamped snapshots using standard spatial data models (either in raster mode or in vector format). For example, overlaying remote sensing images or aerial photographs successfully compares successive land uses patterns in a region. These operations are widely used to monitor the evolution of natural systems, as well as urban and landscape transformations, and global changes [24]. GIS is also combined with statistical or numerical analysis methods for the study of local and regional changes [38, 44, 43, 32]. However, and despite the progress already made in the integration of the temporal dimension within GIS and its application to many fields, current GIS cannot handle explicit information about the changes linking several entities and the processes generating evolution [10]. This is a strong limitation for the analysis of real world phenomena at a detailed level that require a disaggregate representation of changes. GIS does not keep track of temporal networks between successive states of an entities, of spatio-temporal processes that lead to these changes, and of linkages among entities acting together to define a process. Thus, GIS models are still considered as not completely appropriate for a semantic description of geographical changes [31, 38, 37].

Recent advances in GIS research attempt to identify discrete spatial models for a database representation of evolving entities in space. The first generation of models for temporal GIS was mostly map-oriented: successive time slices being merged within the geometrical structure already used to handle geographical location [31]. These methods are generally constrained by current GIS technology. They use the concept of "amendment vectors": successive geometric primitives are time stamped and incrementally registered within the spatial database. However, a cartographic view of time leads to various semantic limitations. Space and time are merged within a single structure that does not provide efficient mechanisms in order to identify and link successive states of evolving entities [38].

In order to provide a new paradigm that integrates space and time as complementary components, more research is needed to identify a theoretical framework that may act as a foundation for the development of spatio-temporal models. Particularly, time has to be integrated as an additional dimension to provide a clear conceptual and operational separation, in computational terms, from the spatial dimension. Recent progress in the development of spatio-temporal databases include the development of conceptual and physical models and have been recently surveyed [2]. However, the representation of spatio-temporal processes has to be integrated to fulfil the needs of scientific and planning studies [39, 10, 7, 49]. Several attempts have been proposed to identify a taxonomy of changes within GIS. Current researches make a distinction between the life and motion of spatial entities [16]. Hornsby and Egenhofer [29] develop a spatial database model based on the identity of a spatial entity and its possible changes at the local and composite levels. Galton [17] proposes a formalism which uses the fluent concept to define a theory of movement. This approach defines the possible positions of a region by reference to two other fixed regions. Galton's work gives rise to an important interest of the AI community in both computational and representational issues in spatial reasoning.

Together, these studies provide a strong theoretical and mathematical background for the description of the evolution of geographical entities. However, they are still oriented to the analysis of the evolution of entities or small sets of independent geographical entities. No attempts have been made, to the best of our knowledge, to extend these models to represent the geographical evolution of sets of entities within GIS. With the exception of Cheylan and Lardon's [8] early proposal for describing movement strategy within flocks, a comprehensive model dealing with the semantics of moving sets, and of sets of moving entities, is not yet available for GIS.

3 Semantics of geographical entities

For the purpose of our research, we define a set of entities as a collection of entities that share some relevant thematic or functional attributes. The semantic extent of that definition is inclusive and suitable for many application fields. However, as our purpose is the study of the evolution of geographical entities (GE), we must add a spatial constraint: a set of geographical entities (SGE) is a set of entities in which all the members are located in a geographical space. This semantics provides a basis for the description of homogeneous and/or heterogeneous sets (e.g., individuals of different kinds sharing a habitat) of entities involved in common real world phenomena. The properties of any SGE is derived from those of its entities using application dependant strategies. This permits the spatial analysis of the geographical structure and global behaviour of SGEs. Then, spatial statistics can be used to compute indexes to compare their evolution.

Therefore, scientific models can be explored by specifying the appropriate state and linkage attributes that define the SGE. It is even possible to rely on numerical taxonomy to characterise the SGE. Nevertheless the identification of rules for the propagation of properties between entities and their communities is not always straightforward. Mainly, it is an application dependent task. Firstly, a set of entities, that have a simple behaviour, can show a complex set behaviour (e.g., models of animal behaviour). Secondly, the definition of homogeneous spatial properties for sets is a complex issue. Spatial statistic methods provide indexes for describing spatial patterns and structures. These measures are useful for comparing spatio-temporal trends of SGEs [37, 41, 43]. Consequently, our model aims at the integration of the properties of geographical entities at the local (i.e., entity) and set levels. In other words, these properties are represented as computed attributes for any SGE, using statistical aggregation methods.

This framework is based on a set of temporal and spatial basic assumptions. We assume a partial ordering of geographical entities in the time dimension. Time is defined as the set of measured times that is isomorphic to the set of real numbers. Life of geographical entities is delimited by temporal intervals. Space is considered as a positional reference system to locate geographical entities (absolute view of space). It also expresses their mutual relationships and linkages (relative view of space). The model assumes a discrete representation of geographical entities in space and time (i.e., spatially located and historically bounded entities). Spatio-temporal measurement units are chosen according to the geographical scale and temporal granularity needed by the application. This paper will not attempt to identify propagation rules across geographical scales and temporal granularities. Finally, the model does not represent fluid movements which must be studied using continuous mathematical functions (e.g., instantaneous variation of traffic flows).

In previous papers, we propose a spatio-temporal model to describe and classify basic spatio-temporal processes [9, 10, 11]. A process is defined as an action that modifies one to many entities (emphasis on the action) [5]. The concept of change represents an alteration of the properties of an entity. Our framework provides a topological structure for representing entity-based events and networks of spatio-temporal processes. It identifies a set of minimal basic processes that includes the spatial evolution of a single entity (life and motion), functional relationships (replacement and diffusion) and restructuring processes involving many entities. For the purpose of this paper, the model presented retains only the taxonomy of spatio-temporal changes for a single entity that is located using a point:

- It has a geographical location which is defined by the co-ordinates of the centre of gravity of the entity's body (no size, no shape and no orientation).

- It has an intensity that represents the importance of the phenomenon under study (e.g. duration of the activity, estimated number of persons in a vehicle).

A SGE represents a set of entities that share some thematic or functional relationships (e.g., a set of people living in the same house). Moreover, this model can be extended using higher abstraction levels (e.g., the set of all people living in any single-parent family headed by a woman). At the root of the hierarchy, an entity type characterises an overall set of entities being under study (e.g., all the commuters or people that may travel). This higher level of abstraction provides a distinction between a local or episodic disappearance and the permanent extinction of a type (e.g., commuters travelling on horseback, pupils going to school at midnight). These behaviours remain possible. However, they may define an empty set at a given place and/or during a specific period.

For the purpose of our model, we need to measure and compare patterns that represent the geographical distribution of a set of points. Depending on the application needs, these points may represent location of entities belonging to a specific SGE at any moment or during any time interval (e.g., disaggregate location of people engaged in some activity, or position of those travelling to their work place). Computing statistical indexes to express structural attributes of these patterns enable their analysis and comparison among social sets or time intervals. That defines a spatial profile (time is controlled and location is measured). However, the same strategy may be used to analyse successive locations visited by entities, during a fixed period of time (e.g., during a day or a week). Then the points may show representative locations on the travelling route of an entity (e.g., one every minute, measuring with a DGPS). This operation defines a spatio-temporal profile (time and location are measured). It may be summarised using the same spatial statistics indexes. Therefore, they could be combined with usual movement measures (e.g. trip duration, travelling speed) and used to compare spatio-temporal behaviours of entities or sets of entities.

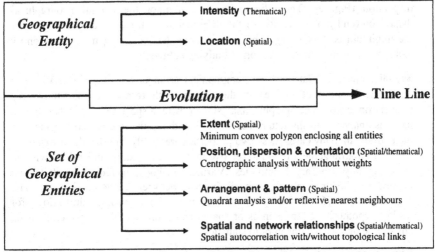

Fig. 1. Evolution components for geographical entities and sets of geographical entities

During a time interval, a single geographical entity that is assimilated to a point can only experience life cycle transformations (e.g., appearance, disappearance), translation (e.g., move to another location) and/or modify its thematic attributes (e.g., intensity change). During the same period, a set of geographical entities will combine all of the basic processes of its entities. This may modify the life cycle of the SGE (appearance or disappearance of the set, extinction of the type). Otherwise, that could modify the spatial pattern defined by all entity locations that belong to the SGE. Without any attempt to be exhaustive, we can distinguish four basic components of spatial evolution that can be measured using well known statistical methods and that are of particular interest for the modelling of disaggregate activity-travel behaviour (Fig. 1). They are as follows:

- Territorial extent of the SGE can expand or contract. Its coverage is measured using the minimum convex polygon (Fig. 2) that is sufficient to contain all the entity locations (i.e., points). It has a shape and a size. This spatial coverage is easily computed in the GIS by aggregating Delaunay triangles defined from entities in the set [47]. For transportation purpose, this convex polygon measures the overall maximum extent of the region that is visited by any entity of the SGE.

- Spatial distribution of SGE members is summarised using centrographic analysis methods [33]. That is the spatial counterpart of classical descriptive statistics computed from X and Y co-ordinates. Additionally, each point can be weighted to reflect its importance (intensity of the phenomenon). The centre of gravity (CG) indicates the equilibrium point of the distribution (Fig. 2). It expresses the central position of the SGE. The standard distance (SD) is the extension of the standard deviation of univariate statistics to the 2-D space. It is defined as the minimal second moment of the point-series and summarises distances to the CG. The orientation is obtained using principal axis extraction techniques. It defines the azimuth angle of a cross that presents the major directions of the point series (maximum and minimum dispersion). Finally, these two axes define an ellipse of dispersion (Fig. 2). The ellipse area can monitor the overall geographical dispersion (and global density) of the SGE members. It has clear advantage over the minimum convex polygon because it integrates weighting from every entity and is less sensitive to the location of outlying entities.

- Spatial pattern is related to the geographical arrangement of entities. We may study the location of entities in the pattern with respect to the study area (dispersion using centrographic analysis) or with respect to each other (using patterns analysis). In the latter case, we are studying the internal arrangement of the entities. In many cases these two properties are highly correlated. However, as the internal arrangement refers to relative locations, its study can be done without imposing any arbitrary boundaries. Various methods, including quadrats and nearest neighbour analyses, can distinguish between random, clustered and regular patterns [6]. Counting the number of entities in each quadrat allows for testing hypothesis of randomness or spatial co-occurrence of two patterns, using chi-square or variance/mean ratio statistics.

- When a phenomenon exhibits an association in which intensity values at a set of places depend on values of the same attribute at other neighbouring locations, there is a spatial autocorrelation. It is present, for example, when similar values cluster together. Spatial autocorrelation provides statistical methods to measure the dependence among nearby values on the same attribute. Moran's I and Geary's c coefficients are among widely spread measures of spatial autocorrelation. They lead to tests of hypotheses that can verify the existence of spatial structure in the data. Are similar entities concentrated in space? That is a central question to every geographical study. Analysing spatial organisation of people having similar travel or activity behaviour is a prerequisite to its use for any regional transportation modelling. One can use Euclidean distances among neighbours, topological links of a road network as well as the existence of common boundaries, in order to define an interaction matrix. Actually, the structure of this interaction matrix is very similar to an origin-destination matrix, and plays the same role. It contains weights for every pair of locations. These weights can be adjusted as required, in order to test effects of a functional relationship on the intensity of a phenomenon in geographical space. Using weighted spatial autocorrelation, it is even possible to mix traffic flows and network characteristics to assess the effects of the transportation network on the actual geographical relationships [36, 18, 26].

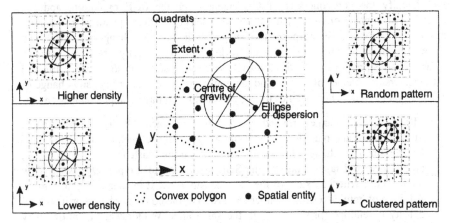

Fig. 2. Statistical parameters to assess spatial distribution within sets of geographical entities

4 Spatio-temporal processes involving sets of geographical entities

The above statistical methods provide efficient tools to measure the evolution of the location of geographical entities, taking into account proximity or network relationships among entities, at a more or less local scale. However, describing the evolution of a set needs an extension to identify mechanisms that combine evolution of entities, members of a set, and to define the evolution of the entire set. Therefore, this section is aimed at the identification of spatio-temporal processes which involve sets of geographical entities. However, due to space limitation, this paper does not attempt to build a formal taxonomy of spatio-temporal processes that apply to SGEs. As well, we will not attempt to portray the transfer and aggregation of properties from entities to the set they form. This is far beyond the purpose of this paper and that issue will be addressed in a forthcoming research. Therefore, the following paragraphs describe a selection of spatio-temporal processes (STPs) involving SGEs which are relevant for disaggregate travel and activity behaviour. Particularly, we will analyse the combined evolution of entities for the interpretation of aggregation mechanisms responsible for the overall evolution of sets.

Our approach combines a deductive identification of the evolution of a SGE from the evolution of the component GE, with an inductive calculation of these changes based on the previously identified spatial statistics indexes. Therefore, this framework will identify the consequences of GE changes for the SGE evolution, and the quantitative impacts on some parameters like density, pattern, position, orientation and territorial extent. The purpose is to categorise the possible changes of a SGE and to model these changes using real world data on activity travel behaviour. Characteristics previously identified for GE and SGE lead to the study of the life and set membership changes of a SGE, and the impact of movement or intensity change of each GE on its SGE. These lead us to study the following three complementary cases:

- The first are changes related to the life of each GE (i.e., appearance, disappearance and mutation). Obviously, they modify set membership. They may be combined to change the life of the SGE, if its existence is affected (e.g., appearance or disappearance of the SGE, extinction of a type). Otherwise, they modify the territorial extent or the local density of SGE in space (Fig. 3, Part I). Addition of entities results in either expansion of the convex polygon or increased density of entities (progression) in the same area. Withdrawal of entities may contract the polygon, or else result in lower densities (regression), if GEs in outlying positions are kept (Fig. 3-a and 3-b).

- The second are changes related to movement of entities (Fig. 3, Part II). Results depend on the actual paths followed by every travelling entity and the existence of any intersection with the convex polygon boundary. If an entity goes outside of the convex polygon (centrifuge move), a territory spread will result (Fig. 3-c). Conversely, if movement is directed toward the centre of the polygon (centripetal force), a concentration will result; the dispersion ellipse will shrink, and eventually, the convex polygon may become smaller. If all trips stay inside the convex polygon, then only the dispersion ellipse, the CG location and the SD can change. Therefore, there is some internal restructuring within the SGE (Fig. 3-e). Otherwise, if any outlying entity that defines the convex polygon border is displaced, the territory shape must change, leading to a deformation of the SGE's spatial extent (Fig. 3-d).

- The last are changes related to movement of the entire SGE (Fig. 3, Part III). They involve co-ordinated movements of all entities included in the SGE. If all members move to the same direction, at the same speed, then we observe an overall translation of the SGE (Fig. 3-f). If people move at different speeds, turning around a central point and keeping their relative positions, then there is an overall rotation of the SGE (Fig. 3-g). These co-ordinated moves have few applications for urban travel modelling. However, they may be required to model activities such as aerial or maritime navigation.

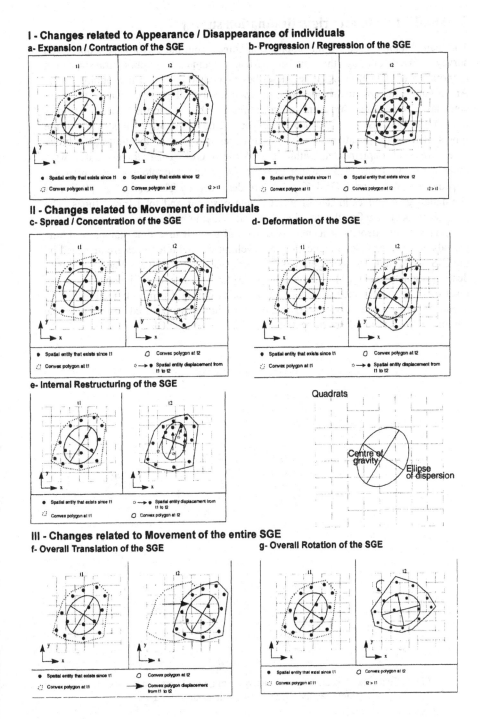

Fig. 3. Taxonomy for the evolution of sets of geographical entities (SGE)

5 Application to an origin destination survey

The main database used for this application comes from the origin destination (OD) survey carried out by the Quebec Urban Community's public transportation corporation (STCUQ). This survey describes individual trips in a metropolitan area. An origin-destination matrix describes trips made by all persons during a typical weekday. This takes the form of a mobility table. Descriptive data resumes households, persons, trips and activities. The spatial properties of this database are represented using Canadian six-digit postal codes that provide location at the block face level and implemented within the MapInfo GIS. Then, travel routes were modelled using TransCAD (Caliper Corporation), using a topological road network, impedance values, and a GISDK procedure described by Thériault *et al.* [45]. This simulation gave fair estimates of intermediate positions and total travel times. The latter were used to define the duration of the stays and to build an activity-events table [22]. This matrix depicts sequences of stays and trips. It uses time-stamps to define periods of activity, either at a location or travelling. Spatial references are managed by the GIS, using points to locate entities (at their places of activity) and line segments to describe their trips (Fig. 4). The model can display spatio-temporal behaviours at any level of detail (e.g., every road segment travelled during a trip is defined as a sub-event). Using such a structure, statistical procedures can be used to compute the parameters required to describe spatial characteristics of the SGEs.

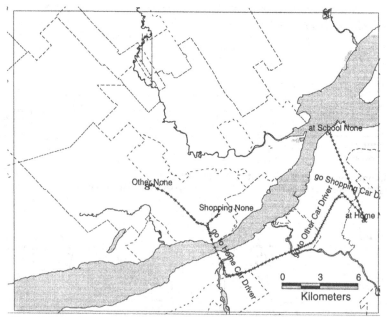

Fig. 4. Example of a daily trips and activities of all members of a four persons single-family selected using a thematic criteria

The following demonstration will analyse the geographical distribution of single-family mothers aged between 20 and 40, employed full time and still at work at 5PM. We will compare the working places of those having one child at home with those having more than one child. Working places of mothers having only one child at home show a territorial extent which is more than twice as large as that of mothers having children. However, that dispersion is largely related to positions in remote places, far from the city centre. Dispersion ellipses have about the same sizes. This means that the overall spatial dispersions are mostly similar. That is confirmed by similar standard and mean distances statistics. The difference in their orientation (major axis azimuth) is more significant (72 / -42 degrees measured from the map grid North). The elongation of both ellipses is also rather similar (oblongitude ratio). Using co-ordinates of their centres of gravity, it is even possible to measure Euclidean distance between the points of equilibrium of both distributions (839 metres). This provides a rather classical way to compare the geographical distributions of two SGEs at a given time.

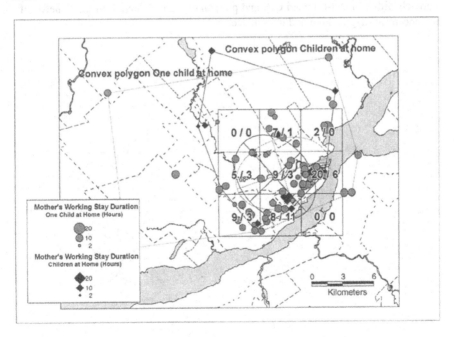

Fig. 5. Spatial analysis of working places Mother of single-parent family employed full time and still at work at 5PM Grey: one child at home; Black: children at home Centrographic analyses are weighted using the working stay duration (hours) Figures in quadrats (4x4 Kilometres) indicates the total number of families with one child / children

To measure change, the procedure is modified to compare sets of locations at successive times (or time periods). For example, it can follow moves over an entire day cycle (Fig. 6). The kind of results shown on Fig. 6 would be better expressed using map animation. However, using spatial statistics computed with an SGE having its membership redefined at various hours (e.g., Women working at 8AM, noon, 4 PM and 8 PM), it is possible to analyse trends, movements and spatial transformations. In the worked example, we can see that concentration and dispersion trends are not linked to the variations in membership. And more interestingly, between 8 AM and noon, the distribution of women's working places is concentrating (ellipse area from 89 to 83 sq. Km), at the same time as it is extending its overall territorial coverage (convex polygons from 386 to 400 sq. Km). This application example should clearly illustrate the usefulness of the approach initiated in this paper. Using spatial statistics, one can also measure global movements of a group of individuals. Having all this information, a user can derive a good understanding of the transformation of geographical distributions involving any SGE. The approach is suited for SGE having a stable membership (fixed set of entities) or defining it dynamically using membership criteria. The worked example uses current GIS technology (MapInfo and its geo-relational query operators). Current work includes the integration of our approach within object-oriented GIS and particularly the evaluation of the benefits of the concepts of aggregation and inheritance.

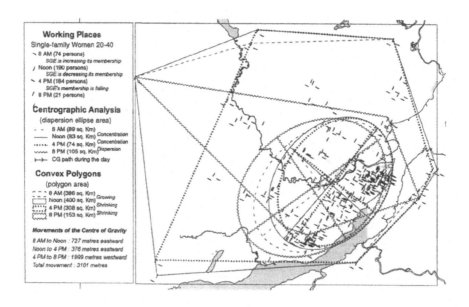

Fig. 6. Spatio-temporal comparison of working places. Dynamically defined sets of single-family women aged 20-40 and working at 8 AM, noon, 4 PM and 8 PM Changes and evolution trends are italicised.

6 Conclusion

This paper demonstrates that the study of the evolution of geographical entities can be realised at complementary abstraction levels. Such an approach is based on the analysis of dynamic geographical phenomena, and illustrated with the analysis of activity-travel behaviours. We propose a model that integrates the motion and life of entities within a representation of changes at a higher level of abstraction. Accordingly, a concept of geographical entity set is introduced and qualified with a set of geographical and thematical parameters derived from the entity level using thematical and statistical parameters. The application and the theoretical fundamentals presented in this paper complement the method of analysis of displacement structures introduced by Janelle, Klinkenberg and Goodchild [30]. This later approach uses the three dimensional factorial analysis in order to generate aggregated structures of space and daily activity patterns within an urban system. Our approach complements this work with spatial statistic methods that support the description of entity displacement patterns, and social set activities. This allows the description of relevant spatio-temporal attributes and their comparison. Such a model can be implemented using current GIS capabilities. However, a complete application of this spatio-temporal framework to the study of travel-activity behaviours leads to some additional requirements and observations:

- The integration of spatial statistics methods within spatio-temporal databases is of particular importance for the successful development of urban and environmental studies, because they require analyses of spatio-temporal patterns.

- Current conceptual spatio-temporal models still need to be extended toward a more complete representation of spatio-temporal processes. That is particularly true for dynamic applications in the transport or traffic monitoring domains, where networks are of great importance.

- New query languages and interfaces are required in order to adapt these models to a flexible representation and manipulation of time within spatio-temporal databases (including the relative and chronological visions of time).

- New mapping languages adapted to an interactive visualisation of these phenomena. They can also improve the communication with novice database users.

More experimental studies are also needed to validate our model, particularly, applications that combine entity actions and aggregated behaviours. Transport modelling is strongly related to the analysis of individual activities.

Acknowledgements

This project was funded by the Quebec Province's FCAR research teams program, the Canadian SSHRC, the Canadian NSERC and the Canadian GEOID Network. It was realised in close co-operation with the STCUQ (Quebec Urban Region Transit Society) and the Quebec provincial Ministère des transports.

References

1. Abdel-Aty, M., R. Kitamura, P. Jovanis, R. Reddy and K. Vaughn, 1995. New approach to route choice data collection: Multiphase, computer-aided telephone interview panel surveys using geographical information systems data base. *Transportation Research Record 1493*, TRB, NRC, Washington, D. C., 159-169.

2. Abraham, T. and Roddick, J. F., 1999. Survey of Spatio-Temporal Databases. *Geoinformatica*, 3(2), pp. 61-99.

3. Anselin, L. and A. Getis, 1992. Spatial statistical analysis and geographic information systems. *The Annals of Regional Science*, 26: 19-33.

4. Ben-Akiva, M. E. and J. L. Bowman, 1995. Activity-based disaggregate travel demand model system with daily activity schedules. in *Proceedings of the Conference on Activity-Based Approaches: Activity Scheduling and the Analysis of Activity Patterns*, Eindhoven, The Netherlands.

5. Bestougeff, H., and Ligozat, G., 1992, *Logical Tools for Temporal Knowledge Representation*, Ellis Horwood, United-Kingdom, 311p.

6. Boots, B. N. and A. Getis, 1988. *Point Pattern Analysis*. Scientific Geography Series, Sage, Newbury Park.

7. Cheng, T. and M. Molenaar, 1998. A process-oriented spatio-temporal data model to support physical environmental modeling, in *Proceedings of the 8th International Symposium on Spatial Data Handling*, Vancouver, July 11-15, 418-430.

8. Cheylan, J. P. and S. Lardon, 1993. Toward a conceptual model for the analysis of spatio-temporal processes. In *Spatial Information Theory*, Frank, A. and Campari, I. Eds., Springer-Verlag, Berlin, 158-176.

9. Claramunt, C. and M. Thériault, 1995. Managing time in GIS: An event-oriented approach. In *Recent Advances in Temporal Databases*, Clifford, J. and Tuzhilin, A. Eds., Berlin, Springer-Verlag, 23-42.

10. Claramunt, C. and M. Thériault, 1996. Toward semantics for modelling spatio-temporal processes within GIS. In *Advances in GIS Research*, Kraak, M. J. and Molenaar, M. Eds., Delft, Taylor & Francis, 47-63.

11. Claramunt, C., M. Thériault and C. Parent, 1997. A qualitative representation of evolving spatial entities in two-dimensional topological spaces. In *Innovations in GIS V*, Carver S. Ed., London, Taylor & Francis, 119-129.

12. Clementini, E., P. Di Felice and P. van Oosterom, 1993. A small set of topological relationships suitable for end-user interaction. In *Advances in Spatial Databases*, D. J. Abel and B. C. Ooi Eds., Berlin, Springer-Verlag, 277-295.

13. Cui, Z., A. Cohn and D. Randell, 1993. Qualitative and topological relationships in spatial databases. In *Advances in Spatial Databases*, Abel D. and Ooi B. Eds., LNCS 692, Springer-Verlag, Berlin, 293-315.

14. Doherty, S. T. and E. J. Miller, 1997. Tracing the household activity scheduling process using one-week computer-based survey. In *Proceedings of the Eight Meeting of the International Association of Travel Behaviour Research*, Austin, Texas.

15. Egenhofer, M., 1991. Reasoning about binary topological relations. In *Advances in Spatial Databases*, edited by O. Günther and H.-J. Schek, Berlin: Springer-Verlag, 143-160.

16. Frank, A. U., 1996. Socio-economic units: Their life and motions. in *GIS Data European Workshop*, Napflion, Greece.

17. Galton, A., 1995. Towards a qualitative theory of movement. In *Spatial Information Theory: A Theoretical Basis for GIS*, Frank, A. U. and Kuhn, W. Eds., Berlin, Springer-Verlag, 377-396.

18. Getis, A. and J. K. Ord, 1992. The analysis of spatial association by use of distance statistics. *Geographical Analysis*, 24-3: 206.

19. Golledge, R. G., 1998. The relationship between geographical information systems and disaggregate behavioral travel modeling, *Geographical Systems*, 5: 9-17.

20. Golledge, R. G., M. P. Kwan and T. Gärling, 1994. Computational process modeling of household travel decision using a geographical information system. *Papers in Regional Science*, 73-2: 99-117.

21. Golledge, R. and M. Egenhofer, 1998. Guest editors' preface, GIS and disaggregate behavioral travel modeling. Special issue of *Geographical Systems*, 5: 1-7.

22. Goodchild, M. F., 1998. Geographic information systems and disaggregate transportation modelling. *Geographical Systems*, 5: 19-44.

23. Goodchild, M. F., B. Klinkenberg and D. G. Janelle, 1993. A factorial model of aggregate spatio-temporal behavior: application to the diurnal cycle. *Geographical Analysis*, 25-4: 277-294.

24. Goodchild, M. F., L. T. Steyaert, B. O. Parks *et al.* Eds., 1996. *GIS and Environmental Modelling: Progress and Research Issues*, Fort Collins, GIS World Books.

25. Greaves, S. and P. Stopher, 1998. A synthesis of GIS and activity-based travel-forecasting. *Geographical Systems*, 5: 59-89.

26. Griffith, D. A., 1993. Advanced spatial statistics for analysing and visualising geo-referenced data. *International Journal of Geographical Information Systems*, 7(2): 107-123.

27. Hägerstrand, T., 1967. *Innovation Diffusion as a Spatial Process*, Chicago, The University of Chicago Press.

28. Haynes, K. E. and A. S. Fotheringham, 1984. *Gravity and Spatial Interaction Models*. Scientific Geography Series, Newbury Park, Sage.

29. Hornsby, K. and M. Egenhofer, 1997. Qualitative representation of change. In *Proceedings of the Conference on Spatial Information Theory COSIT'97*, Frank, A.U. and Mark, D. Eds., Springer-Verlag, LNCS 1329.

30. Janelle, D. G., B. Klinkenberg and M. F. Goodchild, 1998. The temporal ordering of urban space and daily activity patterns for population role groups. *Geographical Systems*, 5: 117-137.

31. Langran, G., 1992. *Time in Geographic Information Systems*, London, Taylor & Francis.

32. Lee, H. and Z. Kemp, 1998. Supporting complex spatiotemporal analysis in GIS. In S. Carver Ed., *Innovations in GIS 5*, London, Taylor & Francis, 151-160.

33. Levine, N., 1996. Spatial statistics and GIS: Software tools to quantify spatial patterns. *Journal of the American Planning Association*, 62(3): 381-391.

34. Mahmassani, H., T. Joseph and R. C. Jou, 1993. Survey approach for study of urban commuter choice dynamics. *Transportation Research Record 1412*, TRB, National Research Council, Washington, D. C., 80-89.

35. Morril, R., G. L. Gaile and G. I. Thrall, 1988. *Spatial Diffusion*. Scientific Geography Series, Newbury Park, Sage.

36. Odland, J., 1988. *Spatial Autocorrelation*, Scientific Geography Series, Sage, Newbury Park.

37. Openshaw, S., 1994, Two exploratory space-time-attribute pattern analysers relevant to GIS. In *Spatial Analysis and GIS*, Fotheringham, S. and Rogerson, P. Eds., London, Taylor & Francis, 83-104.

38. Peuquet, D. J., 1994. It's about time: A conceptual framework for the representation of temporal dynamics in geographic information systems. *Annals of the Association of the American Geographers*, 84(3): 441-461.

39. Peuquet, D. J., and N. Duan, 1995. An Event-based spatiotemporal data model (ESTDM) for temporal analysis of geographical data. *International Journal of Geographical Information Systems*, 9(1): 7-24.

40. Quiroga, C. A. and D. Bullock, 1999. Travel time information using GPS and dynamic segmentation techniques. *Proceedings of the Transportation Research Board 78th Annual Meeting*, Washington D. C., January 10-14, 1999.

41. Shibasiki, R. and S. Huang, 1996. Spatio-temporal interpolation by integrating observational data and a behavioral model. In *Advances in GIS Research*, Kraak, M. J. and Molenaar, M. Eds., Delft, Taylor & Francis, 655-666.

42. Spear, B. D. and T. R. Lakshmanan, 1998. The role of GIS in transportation planning and analysis. *Geographical Systems*, 5: 45-58.

43. Takeyama, M. and H. Couclelis, 1997. Map dynamics: Integrating cellular automata and GIS through geo-algebra. *International Journal Geographical Information Science*, 11(1): 73-91.

44. Thériault, M. and F. Des Rosiers, 1995. Combining hedonic modelling, GIS and spatial statistics to analyse the residential markets in the Quebec Urban Community. In *Proceedings of the Joint European*, March 26-31, EGIS Foundation, The Hague, The Netherlands, 2:131-136.

45. Thériault, M., D. Leroux and M. H. Vandersmissen, 1998. Modelling travel route and time within GIS: its use for planning. In A. Bargiela and E. Kerckhoffs eds. *Simulation Technology Science and Art. Proceedings of the 10th European Simulation Symposium*, The Nottingham-Trent University, October 26-28, Society for Computer Simulation International, Ghent, Belgium, 402-407.

46. Thill, J. C. and J. L. Horowitz, 1997. Travel-time constraints on destination choice sets. *Geographical Analysis*, 29-2: 108-123.S

47. Upton, G. J. G. and B. Fingleton, 1989. *Spatial Data Analysis by Example*, John Wiley & Sons, Chichester.

48. Wolf, J., S. Hallmark, M. Oliveira, R. Guensler and W. Sarasua, 1999. Accuracy issues with route choice data collection using GPS. *Proceedings of the Transportation Research Board 78th Annual Meeting*, Washington, D. C., January 10-14, 1999.

49. Yuan, M., 1998. Representing spatiotemporal processes to support knowledge discovery in GIS databases. In *Proceedings of the 8th International Symposium on Spatial Data Handling*, Vancouver, July 11-15.

Lifestyles - An Algebraic Approach to Change in Identity

Damir Medak

Department of Geoinformation
Technical University Vienna
Gusshausstrasse 27-29, E127
A-1040 Vienna, Austria
medak@geoinfo.tuwien.ac.at

Abstract. This paper proposes a unified formal environment for spatiotemporal databases and modeling the change in identity of objects. The real world is represented as a set of snapshots consisting of identifiable objects and relations among objects. A database needs transaction time for the consistent management of temporal links among identifiers. Four basic operations affecting object identity are proposed: *create, destroy, suspend,* and *resume*. Their compositions are either applicable on a single object (*evolve*), or on a group of objects (constructive and weak *fusion, fission, aggregate* and *segregate*). These operations build a finite set of identity affecting operations - lifestyles. Executable algebraic specifications, written in the functional programming language Haskell, are provided both for the database model and for lifestyles. The specifications of typical lifestyles can be re-used for various application domains.

1 Introduction

The question "under what conditions does an object persist through time as one and the same object" has attracted the attention of philosophers since antiquity. The idea was described by Plutarch in his writings about the Greek hero Theseus. A paraphrased version of the Plutarch's story is:

> Theseus started his voyage in a simple wooden ship. During the journey, he replaced the wooden planks of the ship with new ones, throwing the old planks over board. At the same time, another ship sailed parallel to the ship of Theseus. The sailors of the second ship were collecting the planks thrown by Theseus and using them to replace their own planks. Until the end of the journey, Theseus replaced all parts of his ship, and the escort ship consisted of all parts of the ship Theseus started the journey. *(Plutarch "Vita Thesei", 22-23)*

The puzzling questions are: Which of the two ships is identical to the original? If it is the second ship, when it got the new identity? Is it possible that both ships are identical to the original ship? Alternatively, could neither of them be identical to the original?

In this paper, we are concerned with representations of the real world for constructing database systems, which can track change in identity of objects, and provide formal solutions. We are not concerned with change in attributes of objects. Thus, different processes involving deformations and movements are not covered here.

Special attention is paid to the needs in geographic information systems (GIS). Early GIS dealt only with spatially referenced information. Such atemporal GIS describe only a single state of the data. Thus, expressiveness of GIS was reduced to a snapshot view of the selected phenomena: an update replaced and destroyed the previously stored data. Historical states were lost and could not be recovered. Such limitation was due to the lack of readily available hardware. The problem of storage and fast retrieving of data was dominating the efforts to build GIS software.

The previous work on formal modeling of change is discussed in Sect. 2. In Sect. 3, we enumerate ontological assumptions about the real world and build a representation model on top of it. A short introduction in functional notation and categorical, point-free style of writing algebraic specifications is given as well. In Sect. 4 we present the main topic of this study: a small set of primitive operations affecting identity of objects and their compositions. It includes the examples how lifestyles can be used to model various application domains, including small-scale physical objects and abstract non-tangible concepts. An executable specification of the fusion lifestyle, written in functional programming language Haskell, is given in Sect. 5. Conclusions are given in Sect. 6.

2   Previous Work

The first efforts in formal modeling of change were undertaken in the field of artificial intelligence. Situation calculus, developed by John McCarthy, is a first order language designed to represent dynamically changing worlds in which all changes are the result of named actions [16], [17]. A situation or a state is a snapshot of the world at a given moment. The world is conceived as being in some state s, and this state can change only in consequence of some agent (human, robot, or nature) performing an action. The management of facts that remain valid after each change - the frame problem - was not solvable in a first order language. Recently, Reiter has applied the situation calculus for solving database problems [19].

The research in temporal databases has been intensified in last decades, both in relational and object-oriented model [20], [21]. Temporal database designs applicable to GIS applications are presented in [13]. In the relational database model, the change is captured by creating new versions. Langran compares three methods of database versioning in respect to GIS: table, tuple, and attribute versioning. She emphasized the recognition of different versions of a changing object as a fundamental problem for temporal databases. The semantic problem of what magnitude of change causes an entity to get a new identity and not another version of the old, depends on the application.

A similar problem emerges in an integrated GIS when several thematic databases, related to the same geographical domain, are used simultaneously [1]. Namely, an old house can be represented as residential area in the local cadastre database, and as a national monument in the state monuments database. They enumerated a set of temporal constructs, see Fig. 1.

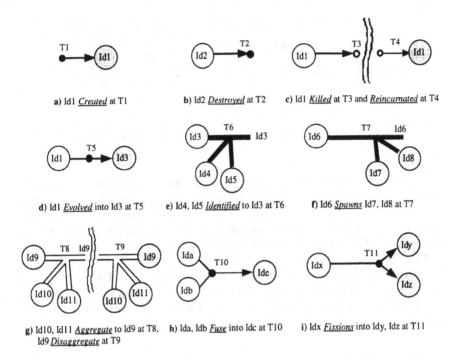

a) Id1 *Created* at T1

b) Id2 *Destroyed* at T2

c) Id1 *Killed* at T3 and *Reincarnated* at T4

d) Id1 *Evolved* into Id3 at T5

e) Id4, Id5 *Identified* to Id3 at T6

f) Id6 *Spawns* Id7, Id8 at T7

g) Id10, Id11 *Aggregate* to Id9 at T8, Id9 *Disaggregate* at T9

h) Ida, Idb *Fuse* into Idc at T10

i) Idx *Fissions* into Idy, Idz at T11

Fig. 1. Temporal constructs of identities according to [1].

Al-Taha and Barrera proposed the three criteria for the identity: uniqueness, immutability and non-reusability. Further, they proposed three capabilities for manipulating identities in a GIS: interrogation of a feature for its identity, using identity as a handle for the feature itself, and, finally, the comparison operation to decide if two identities correspond to the same feature. They also proposed the definition of identity as an abstract data type that hides the actual structure of the identifying mechanism from the user and shows only relevant usage operations: for comparing identities, assigning an identity to a null element, constructing a null element, and for destroying the identity. The transaction time perspective was discussed only.

Hornsby and Egenhofer discerned the following operations that either preserve or change object identity: *create, destruct, reincarnate, issue, continue existence, continue non-existence, spawn, metamorphose, merge, generate, mix, aggregate, compound, unite, amalgamate, combine, separate, splinter, divide, se-*

cede, dissolve, and *select.* The change description language (CDL) was proposed for qualitative graphical representation of operations on identity of objects [10]. Several operations affecting single objects are represented in Fig. 2: dotted arrows represent the operation *issue* (creating new objects) and normal arrows represent the operation *continue existence* from one state to the next.

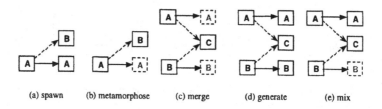

    (a) spawn   (b) metamorphose   (c) merge   (d) generate   (e) mix

Fig. 2. Object identity operations on single objects from [10].

The effects of change on the object properties and the relationships between objects were analyzed with an emphasis on topological relations between spatial objects. This work is extended to operations for composite objects in [11], where two types of composite objects are distinguished: aggregation (based on the relation *part-of*), and association (based on the relation *member-of*).

Claramunt and Thèriault proposed another taxonomy of change for spatial entities, also including deformations and movements [7] . They divided the change in three groups according to the number of entities involved: evolution of a single entity, functional relationships between entities, and evolution of several entities.

3 Framework for Spatiotemporal Databases

Before we begin with the discussion about change in identity of objects, we must provide an environment for our objects to live in. The conceptual model of the database is developed on top of ontological assumptions about the real world. Basic functional notation necessary for implementation of the model is explained and the elements of the database are formally defined.

3.1 Ontology of Spatiotemporal Databases

We borrow assumptions about the real world from Bunge's ontology [5]. According to Bunge, the world is composed of things and forms are properties of things. Things are grouped into systems or aggregates of interacting components. Every thing changes. The world is viewed as composed of things of two kinds: concrete things that are called entities or substantial individuals, and conceptual things. An individual may be either simple or composite, namely, composed of other individuals.

Properties of substantial individuals are called substantial properties. A distinction is made between attributes and properties. An individual may have a property that is unknown to us. In contrast, an attribute is a feature assigned by us to an object. Indeed, we recognize properties only through attributes. A known property must have at least one attribute representing it.

Properties do not exist on their own but are "attached" to entities. On the other hand, entities are not bundles of properties. Thus, it might be said that the fundamental components of the world are entities, that entities are "known" to us through their properties, and their properties materialize in terms of attributes.

It is important that no two concrete things can be the same. No two substantial individuals have exactly the same properties. If we perceive that two entities are identical, it is just because we do not assign attributes to all their substantial properties.

3.2   Epistemology of Spatiotemporal Databases

Features in the real world are represented as objects in the database. Identities of features are represented by identifiers. Properties of features are represented as attributes. The real world at the particular moment is represented as a snapshot: a set of selected objects and a set of relations among represented objects. Objects in a database have life spans; their lives begin when they are entered in the database and end when they are removed from the database. Between these two points the objects are updated: changes in their attributes are recorded. Both the static and the dynamic sides of an object are common for a particular class or type of objects.

The static aspect of an object is expressed by a collection of named attributes, each of which may take a value from a pre-specified domain [24]. A car object might have color, manufacturer name, and engine power among its attributes. A particular car might take the value red for the color attribute. All attribute values for a given object in a particular moment constitute its state.

Objects in the database are connected through relations. Relations are defined by object types; they are valid only if the related objects are of the proper type. Binary relationships involve two object types, ternary relations involve three object types, and so on. A binary relationship may be *one-to-one*, *one-to-many*, or *many-to-many*, depending on how many instances of each type participate in the relationship [6].

The changing world is represented as a series of snapshots. An update operation can be applied on the latest snapshot only and a new snapshot is appended for each change. Time is assumed to be linear and a new timestamp is issued for each new snapshot.

3.3   Algebraic Specifications and Functional Notation

Algebraic specifications represent the necessary step between a conceptual model and its implementation, used to formally prove the correctness of the latter, [14].

Algebraic specifications are based on solid mathematical foundations (category theory) and mathematical methods can be applied to them. An algebra consists of three parts: types, operations on types and axioms that define the behavior. The most familiar example of an algebra is the an algebra of numbers (Abelian group). Category theory is the algebra of functions; the principal operation on functions is taken to be composition [23]. Category theory can be used in defining the basic building blocks of datatypes in programming, and it offers economy in definitions and proofs. In a categorical setting, algorithmic strategies can be formulated without reference to specific datatypes, [4]. This leads to the point-free style of programming, which is free of the complications involved in manipulating formula dealing with bound variables introduced by explicit quantifications.

Functional programming languages are formally defined: a compiler checks the syntax, completeness and other formal aspects of a program. Such programs are executable and can be used as a prototype. Furthermore, functional programming languages and algebraic specifications use a similar syntax and have similar mathematical foundations [2]. Functional languages can express semantics and are easy to understand, which are the essential requirements for formal specification languages [9].

Basic notions from category theory (functional domain, range, composition, and identity) are expressed in the formalism of functional programming language Haskell,[18], as follows. In an expression $f :: a \rightarrow b$, f is a function with the domain in a and range in b. Functional composition is denoted with a "dot" symbol "." and binds to the right: if $h = f.g$ then $h\,x$ is equal to: $f(g(x))$. The identity function id returns its argument unchanged: $id\,x = x$.

The most fundamental datatype in functional programming is a list. Elements of a list can be of any type provided that all of them are of the same type. In the functional programming language Haskell, lists are denoted with square brackets: *[]* is an empty list, *[1,2,3]* is a list of integers. Many functions for lists are predefined. For example, the function *head* gives the first element of a list: *head [1,2,3]=1*.

The most important function over lists is the general purpose function *foldr* that accumulates the results of a function applied on a starting value and each element of a list in turn. For example: *foldr (+) 0 [1,2,3,5] = 11*. Here, the function (+) with the starting value 0 (zero) is used to sum up a list of integers. An application of *foldr* with (∗) and 1 as arguments would give us the product of a list of integers.

Another function over lists that is used in this paper is the function *filter* for selection of elements from the list that satisfy the given condition. For example, *filter (¡4) [3, 7, 2, 5] = [3, 2]*. Both *filter* and *foldr* are used in a slightly modified forms, *filter'* and *foldr'*, that take their arguments as pairs:

```
foldr' f (xs, a) = foldr f a xs
filter' (p, xs) = filter p xs
```

A detailed introduction in functional programming and its mathematical background can be found in the textbooks [3] and [22].

3.4 Data Model for a Spatiotemporal Database

A series of snapshots is represented as an ordered list. Each snapshot consists of a list of objects, a list of relations, and a timestamp. An object consist of its identifier, its object type and a list of attributes. Each attribute consists of a value set (e.g., color, area) and a value (e.g., "blue", 200). Relations consist of a relation type and two identifiers connected with a relation. Each of these concepts is modeled as an abstract datatype in a functional setting with implementation dependent operations for information retrieval. An additional level of abstraction is achieved by parameterization of classes. An example is the specification of the abstract datatype *Objects*:

```
class Objects o ot a where
     makeObj    :: (ID, ot) -> o ot a   -- constructor
     getID      :: o ot a -> ID         -- observer
     getObjType :: o ot a -> ot         -- observer
     getAttribs :: o ot a -> [a]        -- observer
     select' :: (ID,[o ot a]) -> o ot a
```

Any implementation of the abstract datatype *Objects* must provide the instantiation of a constructor (*makeObj*) and observers for the identifier, the object type and the list of attributes. The function *select'* finds an object with the given identifier in a list of objects.

The abstract datatype for snapshots is defined in the same manner. The part of its specification shows the constructor (*empty*) and three observers.

```
class Objects o ot a => Snapshots s o ot a r rt where
     empty      :: s o ot a r rt
     getLastID  :: s o ot a r rt -> ID
     getObjs    :: s o ot a r rt -> [o ot a]
     getRels    :: s o ot a r rt -> [r rt]
     select     :: (ID, db o ot a r rt) -> o ot a
     select = select' . cross (id, getObjs)
```

The function *select* is predefined and implementation independent. It is expressed as a functional composition without naming its arguments (point-free). The method *select'* is inherited from the class *Objects*. Standard categorical combinator *cross* is defined as *cross (f, g) (a,b) = (f a , g b)*.

The class Snapshots has five parameters: *o, ot, a, r, rt*, that is, datatypes for objects, object types, attributes, relations, and relation types respectively. Thus, it can be implemented independently of specification for objects and relations, and a single implementation of snapshots can be re-used for any type of objects and relations.

4 Lifestyles

We propose four basic operations affecting the identity of a single object: *create, destroy, suspend,* and *resume*. Basic operations are known under different names in literature: as *create, destroy, kill*, and *reincarnate* in [8], as *create, destruct,* and *reincarnate* in [10]. The effects of primitive operations on the existence of an object are shown in Fig. 3. The value of the predicate *exists* changes after each operation.

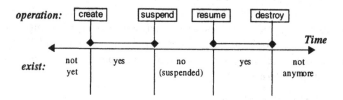

Fig. 3. Possible episodes in the life of an object.

4.1 Create

The existence of an object in the database begins with the creation of its identifier in the database. In Fig. 4 an identity labeled "Id1" is created at the time point t_1. The operation *create* is essential for both the static and the temporal databases, since the unique identity is needed for distinguishing objects in static databases.

Fig. 4. Identity operation create (at t1) and destroy (at t2).

When an identifier is created in a database, it is chosen from an infinite abstract set Ω. Therefore, the domain of the operation *create* is the set Ω, and the range is the set of identifiers. For a particular creation, the result type is an identifier (ID). Creating a specified identifier is not allowed, because such operation might violate the properties of uniqueness and non-reusability of identifiers. Note that the label ID for an identifier has different meaning from the label *id* for the identity function.

Using functional notation, the signature of the function *create* is written: *create* :: $\Omega \to ID$. The effect of the creation on a database is explained using the standard technique in program verification of state-oriented specifications: precondition and postcondition, [15]. Verification consists of a set of assertions of the form: $\varphi P \psi$, where φ and ψ are formulas of predicate logic and P is the piece of program to be specified. If the precondition φ holds before execution of P, then this execution terminates and the postcondition ψ holds.

In our example, creation of a new objects takes the database from one state to another. The precondition for the initial state is that the object with the identifier i does not yet exist. The postcondition for the final state after the execution of the operation *create* is that the object with the identifier i exists. Formally, this reads as:

```
Pre/Post - conditions:        Code:
{exist (i) = 'not yet'}       create
{exist (i) = 'exist'}
```

The concept of predecessors, inevitable in temporal databases, is inherently tied with the creation of an object. The creation is the only basic identity operation involving predecessors. A set of predecessors is empty if the object is created independently from other objects. Therefore, there is no special notation in Fig. 4.

4.2 Destroy

The existence of an object in the database is terminated by destroying its identifier from the database (see Fig. 4 right). For the database, it means that, from the moment of destruction, it is not possible to use the object by calling its identifier. An object is required to exist if it is to be destroyed; *destroy* takes an identifier as an argument. The identifiers of destroyed objects are not forgotten, because the non-reusability is required. In addition, the database may be queried about the past existence of a destroyed object. When an identifier is destroyed, i.e. removed from a database, it is disposed to an undefined space. Therefore, the domain of the operation *destroy* is the set of identifiers, and the range is infinity Ω. For a particular destruction, the argument type is an identifier ID. Using functional notation, the signature of the function *destroy* is written: $destroy :: ID \to \Omega$.

The precondition for the operation *destroy* is the existence of the identifier to be destroyed in the database. The postcondition is the non-existence of the destroyed identifier. In formal language:

```
Pre/Post - conditions:        Code:
{exist (i) = 'yes'}           destroy (i)
{exist (i) = 'not any more'}
```

4.3 Suspend and Resume

An object may have multiple episodes of its existence. A well-known example from history is the state of Austria, which disappeared and reappeared during this century. Temporary loss of existence is modeled with two operations: *suspend* and *resume*. The first operation requires an active (not-suspended) identifier, while the second requires a suspended identifier. In Fig. 5, the shadowed box with the struck label represent the suspended identifier. The operation *suspend* freezes an object by preserving it from other operations until it is resumed. Appropriateness of this pair of operations is the matter of user's choice: living beings are mortal, but one could assume that sleeping appears to be equivalent to suspended state.

Fig. 5. Identity operations suspend (at t1) and resume (at t2).

The type of arguments and results of the operations suspend and resume is the same: an identifier (ID). The signature of both operations is written: $suspend, resume :: ID \rightarrow ID$.

The precondition for the operation suspend is the existence of the object. The postcondition is that the object is suspended.

```
Pre/Post - conditions:              Code:
{exist (i) = 'yes'}                 suspend (i)
{exist (i) = 'no (suspended)'}
```

The precondition for the operation resume is that the object is suspended. The postcondition is that the object exists again.

```
Pre/Post - conditions:              Code:
{exist (i) = 'no (suspended)'}      resume (i)
{exist (i) = 'yes'}
```

This pair of operations, *suspend/resume*, reflects the pair *kill/reincarnate* first introduced in [8]. Hornsby and Egenhofer define reincarnation as a *destruct* operation (equivalent to *destroy* in our notation) followed by a *create* of an object with the same identity [10]. In our model, destroyed identifiers cannot be recreated.

4.4   Evolve

Basic operations presented so far could be composed in various ways. In this section, we analyze compositions of two basic operations applied subsequently to the same object. Since the order of composed operations matter, there are 16 different compositions (see Table 1). A composition yielding undefined results is marked with ⊥. A composition yielding the state that is the same as the original is the identity function (*id*).

Table 1. Compositions of two operations on a single identifier.

g f	create	destroy	suspend	resume
create	⊥	evolve	⊥	⊥
destroy	id	⊥	destroy	destroy
suspend	suspend	⊥	⊥	id
resume	⊥	⊥	id	⊥

The results in Table 1 are calculated as $g.f$. That is, the operations from the row f are applied first. Then, the operations from the column g are applied to the results of the first operation (f).

A composition as *create.create* is undefined, because the postcondition of the first creation is the existence of the identifier i. Thus, it cannot be created again, since the precondition for the operation create is the non-existence of the object. Formally:

```
Pre/Post - conditions:              Code:
{exist (i) = 'not yet'}             create
{exist (i) = 'exist'}               create
not fulfilled since \\
{exist (i) = 'exist'} /= {exist (i) = 'not yet'}
```

The same conclusion can be proved for the composition *destroy.destroy*. The precondition for the second application of *destroy* is not fulfilled, because the identifier is already destroyed:

```
Pre/Post - conditions:              Code:
{exist (i) = 'yes'}                 destroy
{exist (i) = 'not anymore'}         destroy
not fulfilled since
{exist (i) = 'not anymore'} /= {exist (i) = 'yes'}
```

If an identity is destroyed immediately after its creation, the result is the identity function *id* (under assumption that the value 'not yet' is identical to 'not anymore' if the object is destroyed at the same time it was created):

```
Pre/Post - conditions:              Code:
{exist (i) = 'not yet'}             create
{exist (i) = 'yes'}                 destroy
{exist (i) = 'not anymore'}
```

Both possible compositions of *suspend* and *resume* yield the identity function. We show the case of the composition *resume.suspend*:

```
Pre/Post - conditions:              Code:
{exist (i) = 'yes'}                 suspend
{exist (i) = 'no (suspended)'}      resume
{exist (i) = 'yes'}
```

The composition of the operations *suspend* or *resume* with *destroy* result in *destroy* if the former is performed last. If the opposite is the case, i.e. if *destroy* is performed first, the result is undefined, because the destroyed identifier is not available for suspend or resume.

The compositions *create.suspend* and *create.resume* are undefined, because the object must not exist in order to be created (precondition for create). The composition *resume.create* fails because the precondition for resume is not fulfilled after the creation. Finally, *suspend.create* results in suspend.

A composition of creation and destroying where the destroying comes first is the most important result - a new operation *evolve*, having the following signature: *evolve* :: $ID \rightarrow ID$.

Because of the identity properties, the newly created identifier is denoted j in the following verification. In addition, the old identifier i is the argument of the operation *create* in order to maintain a temporal link with its predecessor.

```
Pre/Post - conditions:              Code:
{exist (i) = 'yes'}                 destroy (i)
{exist (i) = 'not anymore'}         create (i)
{exist (j) = 'yes'}
```

The concept of identity evolution allows an object to change its identity under conditions that a temporal link with the previous identity is established. An example for such an operation is a country suddenly changing its constitution from a monarchy to a republic (like Italy during the Second World War).

A state diagram represents possible arrows on the single object identity (Fig. 6). The evolve arrow yields the same result as the combination of destroy and create. The temporal chain is represented with the label "(1)" in the box of Id2: the identity Id1 is the predecessor of the identity Id2.

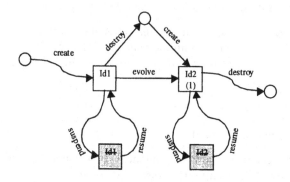

Fig. 6. State diagram for operations affecting identity of a single object.

A short explanation of the difference between static and temporal database with respect to the operation destroy, and of the difference between destroying and removing of the history of an object is necessary. If an object is destroyed from a static database, there is no way to recall it later: the object is gone forever. In a temporal database, the object is not present in the database from the time of destruction onwards, while its past states may be referred to. If we want to remove an object from all snapshots of the database, we need another type of operation, which neglects the historical concept of temporal databases. Such an operation is dangerous because it can cause an irrecoverable loss of data. It gives the opportunity to forge the history in an arbitrary way (see Fig. 7).

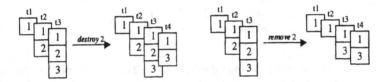

Fig. 7. Destroying (left) vs. removing histories (right).

The left-hand side of Fig. 7 shows the effect of the destroy operation: from the time-point t_4 onwards, the object with the identifier 2 is not available, but its existence before t_4 is preserved. The right-hand side of the same figure shows what happens if the objects with the identifier 2 are removed completely from the database: every track of its existence vanishes. All we may conclude is that the object with the identifier 2 existed, but the object with that identifier can not be retrieved.

4.5   Operations Affecting Multiple Objects

Basic identity operations and their simple composition *evolve* operate on a single object. Yet, there are many examples of change taking more than one object as arguments, or producing several objects as a result. Merging of two cadastral parcels produces a new, third parcel. On the other hand, a single cadastral parcel, if divided, produces two or more parcels with new identifiers. Assembling all car parts produces a new object - a car. Disassembling the car produces, in general, the original parts with their old existence.

All possible combinations of basic operations are shown in Table 2. The operations affecting two or more identities come from the column g, and these are marked with the suffix "PL" (plural). The operations affecting single identity come from the row f. Operations are applied in such order that the creation is performed at the end, because it takes identifiers for predecessors.

Table 2. Compositions of operations affecting multiple identities.

g(many) f(one)	create	destroy	resume	suspend
createPL	$\perp$	fission	$\perp$	w-fission
destroyPL	fusion	$\perp$	w-fusion	$\perp$
resumePL	$\perp$	segregation	$\perp$	w-segregation
suspendPL	aggregation	$\perp$	w-aggregation	$\perp$

Signatures for "PL" operations are given as follows ([ID] stands for a set of identifiers):

$$createPL :: \Omega \rightarrow [ID]$$

$$destroyPL :: [ID] \rightarrow \Omega$$
$$suspendPL :: [ID] \rightarrow [ID]$$
$$resumePL :: [ID] \rightarrow [ID]$$

The compositions on the left-hand side of Table 2 are "constructive", because the object on the one-side is created or destroyed. The compositions on the right-hand side are "non-constructive" or weak, because the one-side object is neither destroyed nor created. Non-constructive compositions are marked with the prefix "w-" for weak.

Depending on the operations applied on the PL-side, two groups of operations are distinguished: fusion/fission and aggregate/segregate group. In what follows, the details of these two lifestyles are analyzed.

4.6   Fission and Fusion

A (constructive) fission is the composition of destroying an object and creating a set of its successors at the same time. Emerging objects maintain a temporal link with the original object. A weak fission does not destroy the original object, but only suspend it.

A (constructive) fusion is the composition of destroying several objects and creating a new single object at the same time. The emerging object maintains a temporal link with the set of destroyed objects. A weak fusion does not create the new objects, but resumes an already existing one. The precondition for a weak fusion is a weak fission.

An example from a cadastral database involving fission and fusion of parcels is shown in Fig. 8. The parcel 1 is destroyed and the new parcels (2 and 3) emerge. Both new parcels maintain a temporal link to the parcel 1. At some later point, the two parcels are united again. The identifiers 2 and 3 are destroyed. The new parcel gets the new identity (4), maintaining the temporal link with both of its predecessors.

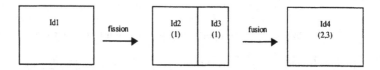

Fig. 8. Fission and fusion of cadastral parcels.

It is questionable whether the identity resulting from the fusion of a complete set of identities should be the same as the original identity which fissioned before. The original identity must be suspended (instead of destroyed) to be resumed. This is modeled by weak fission and fusion (w-fission and w-fusion). As an example, consider a carafe full of water whose content is poured into two glasses. When the water is poured back to the carafe, the original liquid object with the identifier Id1 is resumed (see Fig. 9).

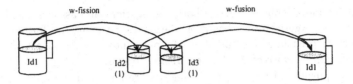

Fig. 9. Weak fission and fusion of liquid objects.

Common to both types of fusion is the irreversibility of the fusion operation: fused identities are destroyed and cannot be re-used. Hence, identities of two cadastral parcels fused into one cannot be re-established; liquid objects in two glasses cannot be distinguished after having been poured into the carafe. The complete set of possible fusions and fissions is shown in Fig. 10.

Fig. 10. The lifestyle of fusions (D - destroy, C - create, S - suspend, R - resume).

The four distinctive operations are shown with the arrows indicating the order of their application to the set of objects: First, the two (or more) objects are destroyed (DD) and a new object is created (C) in a constructive fusion (DD-C). Next, the resulting fused object can be suspended by a weak fission (S-CC), or destroyed by an immediate constructive fission (D-CC) - the longest arrow in Fig. 10. In the former case, emerging objects may fuse again resuming the original object by a weak fusion (DD-R). At the end, the life of the fused object ends with a constructive fission.

4.7   Aggregation and Segregation

Discussion about the identity and aggregation is connected with the *part/whole* relation. From the perspective of operations affecting object identity explained so far, only such aggregations (and segregations) matter, which change identities of involved objects, i.e. perform one of the four basic operations. The relation *member-of* without influence on the identity is not considered as an aggregation in this paper. Such link is usually called association [12].

An example of association is the membership of a person in a sport club: neither the identity of the person nor the identity of the club changes if the person leaves the club. The same goes for the associations of the states based on certain regional groupings (e.g., Scandinavian countries, Mediterranean states, etc.).

Hornsby and Egenhofer refer to both aggregations and associations as composite objects. Aggregations, based on the relation *part-of*, are formed from a framework - a predefined method of placing parts into "slots". Collections, based on the relation *member-of*, are formed without framework [11].

For the purpose of this paper, aggregates are based on the relation part-of only. In addition, an object can be a part of exactly one object (the engine of one car cannot be in another car at the same time). The multiple levels of parthood can be modeled as hierarchies.

The example of constructive aggregation is a federation of several states. It is created by the political contract among the states in question. The federal government takes over all representing functions (foreign policy) from the member-states. In that respect, member-states are suspended. Now, suppose that the federation breaks apart: its identity is destroyed, while the identities of member-states are resumed. A later re-union would have produced the new object (see Fig. 11.

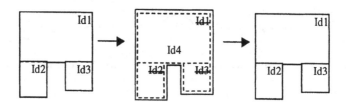

Fig. 11. Constructive aggregation: the aggregate is a new object dependent on its parts.

An example of a weak aggregation (w-aggregate and w-segregate) is an episode in the life of a car. The identity of the particular car emerges when all necessary parts are produced and properly connected. As long as the car functions, its parts do not have meaning outside the aggregate (car). If a part of the car is broken and needs to be repaired, the identity of the car is suspended (since the car does not function) and the identity of the parts are resumed. The broken part is repaired and all parts are aggregated again, resuming the original identity of the car.

The fundamental criteria for an aggregation to qualify for an identity affecting operation is the dependence of aggregated objects on the aggregate. If the aggregated objects are suspended and the aggregate is created for the first time, it is a constructive aggregation. If the aggregate already exists, it is a weak aggregation: the objects and the aggregate are mutually suspended and resumed. The complete set of possible aggregate and segregate operations is shown in Fig. 12.

It starts with a constructive aggregate when the parts are suspended giving birth to the new object. The new object could be destroyed in the next step (the long arrow) or suspended (weak segregation). The difference in respect to

Fig. 12. The lifestyle of aggregates (D - destroy, C - create, S - suspend, R - resume).

the previously explained fusion lifestyles is in the reversibility of weak aggregation/segregation. In the case of a weak fusion, objects on the many-side were destroyed and therefore not resumable. In the case of weak segregation, objects on the many side are resumed, and can be suspended and resumed again.

4.8 Lifestyles are Algebras

We claim that lifestyles are the operations of an algebra affecting object identifiers. Basic identity operations are: create, destroy, suspend, and resume. These operations build an algebra with the following axioms:

```
create . destroy = evolve
destroy . create = id
suspend . resume = id
resume . suspend = id
```

Further, compositions of basic operations define eight new operations (the suffix "PL" means that the operation is applied to the group of two or more identifiers) and three additional axioms. All axioms are independent of the arguments (types of objects involved).

```
destroy . createPL = fission
create . destroyPL = fusion
suspend . createPL = w-fission
resume . destroyPL = w-fusion
create . suspendPL = aggregate
destroy . resumePL = segregate
resume . suspendPL = w-aggregate
suspend . resumePL = w-segregate
w-fusion . w-fission = id
w-aggregate . w-segregate = id
w-segregate. w-aggregate = id
```

5   Formalization of Lifestyles

In this section, we give an abstraction of constructive and weak fusion lifestyles that is completely implementation independent, because all operations have default definitions. Functional notation necessary for reading the specification are standard categorical combinators based on the categorical product [4], with the following semantics:

```
pair (f, g) a = (f a, g a)
cross (f, g) (a,b) = (f a, g b)
outl (a, b) = a
outr (a, b) = b
wrap a = [a]
```

Fusions are represented in two classes: the class *Fusions* for constructive fusion and fission and the class *Wfusions* for weak fusion and fission. The essential difference is in inherited operations: the class *Wfusions* needs the operation suspend, provided by the class *Suspendable*.

```
class (Snapshots s o ot a r rt, Creatable s o ot a r rt) =>
    Fusions s o ot a r rt where
  fusion :: ([ID],(ot, s o ot a r rt)) -> s o ot a r rt
  fusion = foldr' destroy . pair (outl, create)
  fissionN :: (Int, (ID, s o ot a r rt)) -> s o ot a r rt
  fissionN = createN . cross (id, pair (wrap.outl, f))
    where f = pair (getObjType . select, destroy)
class (Snapshots s o ot a r rt, Creatable s o ot a r rt,
    Suspendable s o ot a r rt) =>
    Wfusions s o ot a r rt where
  wFusion :: ([ID], (ID,s o ot a r rt)) -> s o ot a r rt
  wFusion = foldr' destroy . cross (id, resume)
  wFissionN :: (Int, (ID, s o ot a r rt)) -> s o ot a r rt
  wFissionN = createN . cross (id, pair (wrap.outl, f))
    where f = pair (getObjType . select, suspend)
```

The specification for fusions is completely independent of implementation of the underlying classes. If an abstract datatype, (e.g., for parcels) needs an implementation of fusion lifestyle, it is sufficient to add the class *Fusions* in the context of the class *Parcels*:

```
class Fusions s o ot a r rt => Parcels s o ot a r rt where
    newParcel :: ...
    getValue  :: ...
    getArea   :: ...
```

The fusion-like behavior is automatically inherited from the class fusion and need not to be defined again. If an application domain would have allowed the fissioned parcels to be fusioned again, resuming the original parcel at the same time, the class *Parcels* would have needed the class *Wfusions* in the context.

6   Conclusions

In this paper, we presented a formal model for unified treatment of identity change in object-oriented spatiotemporal databases.

We used the entity-relationship model (ER-model) for representation of the real world. Identifiable features are represented as objects, which are distinguishable by unique identifiers. Properties of features are represented as attributes (functions from objects to values). Relationships among features are modeled as relations among objects.

Objects and relations are changing over time. We used linear, discrete, and totally ordered model of time. All objects and relations at a single point of time build a snapshot. For each change, a new snapshot is appended to the database. The whole spatiotemporal database consists of a number of snapshots.

Objects are metaphorically perceived as having life: an object has its birth or creation, its life or existence, its death or destroying. The central concept in the life of an object is its identifier, which is unchanged from the birth to the death of the object. Identifiers are system constructs and they are maintained by the database independently of the user.

Four basic operations affecting object identity are proposed: *create, destroy, suspend*, and *resume*. Their compositions are either applicable on a single object (*evolve*), or on a group of objects (constructive and weak fusion, fission, aggregate and segregate). Altogether, these operations build a finite set of identity affecting operations. Depending on the applicability of operations on identity, objects can be divided into two main lifestyles: fusions and aggregates.

The theory of lifestyles reduces the efforts for constructing the applications that need temporal database models. In order to build an application (e.g., for temporal GIS), the designer must only instantiate his objects to appropriate lifestyles classes, and all necessary properties will be automatically deduced using the inheritance mechanism.

References

1. Khaled Al-Taha and Roberto Barrera. Identities through Time. In Ehlers, editor, *International Workshop on Requirements for Integrated Geographic Information Systems*, pages 1–12, New Orleans, Louisiana, 1994.

2. John Backus. Can Programming Be Liberated from the von Neumann Style? A Functional Style and Its Algebra of Programs. 21:613–641, 1978.

3. Richard Bird. *Introduction to Functional Programming Using Haskell*. Prentice Hall Series in Computer Science. Prentice Hall Europe, Hemel Hempstead, UK, second edition, 1998.

4. Richard Bird and Oege de Moore. *Algebra of Programming*. Prentice Hall, London, 1997.

5. Mario Augusto Bunge. *Treatise on Basic Philosophy: Vol. 3: Ontology I: The Furniture of the World*, volume 3. Reidel, Boston, 1977.

6. Peter Pin-Shan Chen. The Entity-Relationship Model - Toward a Unified View of Data. *ACM Transactions on Database Systems*, 1(1):9 – 36, 1976.

7. Christophe Claramunt and Marius Thèriault. Toward Semantics for Modelling Spatio-Temporal Processes within GIS. In Menno-Jan Kraak and Martien Molenaar, editors, *7th International Symposium on Spatial Data Handling*, volume 2, pages 2.27–2.43, Delft,The Netherlands, 1996. International Geographical Union.

8. James Clifford and Albert Croker. Objects in Time. *Database Engineering*, 7(4):189–196, 1988.
9. Andrew U. Frank and Werner Kuhn. Specifying Open GIS with Functional Languages. In Max J. Egenhofer and John R. Herring, editors, *Advances in Spatial Databases (4th Int. Symposium on Large Spatial Databases, SSD'95, in Portland, USA)*, volume 951 of *Lecture Notes in Computer Science*, pages 184–195. Springer-Verlag, 1995.
10. Kathleen Hornsby and Max J. Egenhofer. Qualitative Representation of Change. In S. C. Hirtle and A. U. Frank, editors, *Spatial Information Theory - A Theoretical Basis for GIS (International Conference COSIT'97)*, volume 1329 of *Lecture Notes in Computer Science Vol.1329*, pages 15–33. Springer-Verlag, Berlin-Heidelberg, 1997.
11. Kathleen Hornsby and Max J. Egenhofer. Identity-Based Change Operations for Composite Objects. In Thomas K. Poiker and Nicholas Chrisman, editors, *8th Internal Symposium on Spatial Data Handling*, pages 202–213, Vancouver, 1998. International Geographical Union.
12. Setrag Khoshafian and Razmik Abnous. *Object Orientation - Concepts, Languages, Databases, User Interfaces*. John Wiley and Sons, New York, NY, 1990.
13. Gail Langran. A review of temporal database research and its use in GIS applications. *IJGIS*, 3(3):215–232, 1989.
14. Barbara Liskov and John Guttag. *Abstraction and Specification in Program Development*. The MIT Electrical Engineering and Computer Science Series. MIT Press, Cambridge, MA, 1986.
15. Jacques Loeckx, Hans-Dieter Ehrich, and Markus Wolf. *Specification of Abstract Data Types*. Wiley, Teubner, 1996.
16. John McCarthy. Situations, actions and causal laws. Artificial Intelligence Project AI-Memo 1, Stanford University, 1957.
17. John McCarthy and Patrick J. Hayes. Some Philosophical Problems from the Standpoint of Artificial Intelligence. In B. Meltzer and D. Michie, editors, *Machine Intelligence 4*, pages 463–502. Edinburgh University Press, Edinburgh, 1969.
18. John Peterson, Kevin Hammond, Lennart Augustsson, Brian Boutel, Warren Burton, Joseph Fasel, Andrew D. Gordon, John Hughes, Paul Hudak, Thomas Johnsson, Mark Jones, Erik Meijer, Simon Peyton Jones, Alastair Reid, and Philip Wadler. The Haskell 1.4 Report. 1997.
19. Raymond Reiter. On Specifying Database Updates. *The Journal of Logic Programming*, 19(20), 1994.
20. Richard T. Snodgrass. Temporal Databases. In A.U. Frank, I. Campari, and U. Formentini, editors, *Theories and Methods of Spatio-Temporal Reasoning in Geographic Space*, volume 639 of *Lecture Notes in Computer Science*, pages 22–64. Springer-Verlag, Heidelberg-Berlin, 1992.
21. Richard T. Snodgrass. Temporal Object-Oriented Databases: A Critical Comparison. In Won Kim, editor, *Modern Database Systems - The Object Model, Interoperability, and Beyond*, pages 386–408. Addison-Wesley, New York, 1995.
22. Simon Thompson. *Haskell - The Craft of Functional Programming*. International Computer Science Series. Addison-Wesley, Harlow, UK, second edition, 1999.
23. R.F.C. Walters. *Categories and computer science*, volume 1 of *Cambridge Computer Science Texts*. Carslaw Publications, Cambridge, UK, 1991.
24. Michael F. Worboys. *GIS: A Computing Perspective*. Taylor and Francis, London, 1995.

The Honeycomb Model of Spatio-Temporal Partitions*

Martin Erwig and Markus Schneider

FernUniversität Hagen, Praktische Informatik IV
58084 Hagen, Germany
[erwig|markus.schneider]@fernuni-hagen.de

Abstract. We define a formal model of spatio-temporal partitions which can be used to model temporally changing maps. We investigate new applications and generalizations of operations that are well-known for static spatial maps. We then define a small set of operations on spatio-temporal partitions that are powerful enough to express all these tasks and more. Spatio-temporal partitions combine the general notion of temporal objects and the powerful spatial partition abstraction into a new, highly expressive spatio-temporal data modeling tool.

1 Introduction

The subject of this paper is the *temporal evolution of maps*. The metaphor of a *map* has turned out to be a fundamental and ubiquitous spatial concept in many spatially-oriented disciplines like geography and cartography as well as in computer-assisted systems like geographical informations systems (GIS), spatial database systems, and image database systems, but also simply for human's spatial orientation in everyday life. A map is a widely recognized geometric structure that is capable of carrying a large amount of information and that can be well displayed in visual form.

The central elements of maps are so-called *partitions* whose importance is already reflected by the fact that the notion "map" is frequently used as a synonym for "partition". The mathematical understanding of a partition differs slightly (but decisively) from its spatial interpretation. In [6], we have motivated and formally defined the notion of *spatial partition*. Spatial partitions are proposed as a generic data type that can be used to model arbitrary maps and to support spatial analysis tasks. Three fundamental, powerful operations on partitions have been identified that allow one to express and even to generalize all known application-specific operations on maps. Examples of spatial partitions are the subdivision of the world map into countries, classification of rural areas according to their agricultural use, areas of different degrees of air pollution, distribution of ethnic groups, areas with different spoken languages, etc.

---

* This research was partially supported by the CHOROCHRONOS project, funded by the EU under the Training and Mobility of Researchers Programme, Contract No. ERB FMRX-CT96-0056.

A spatial partition is a subdivision of the plane into pairwise disjoint *regions* where regions are separated from each other by *boundaries* and where each region is associated with an attribute having simple or even complex structure. That is, a region (possibly composed of several components) with an attribute incorporates all points of a spatial partition having this attribute. A spatial partition implicitly models topological relationships between the participating regions which can be regarded as integrity constraints. First, it expresses neighborhood relationships for different regions that have common boundaries. This property is immediately visible on a map. A second related aspect is that different regions of a partition are always disjoint (if we neglect common boundaries) so that a visual representation of a partition has a very simple structure and is easy to grasp. Both topological properties of spatial partitions will be denoted as *partition constraints*.

As a purely geometric structure, a map yields only a *static* description of spatial entities and required constraints between them. Recently, strong research efforts have been made in spatial and temporal data modeling to integrate both directions into a common research branch, called *spatio-temporal modeling*, and to construct *spatio-temporal databases*. The central aim is to observe and to model evolutions of spatial phenomena over time. Spatio-temporal data models for single, self-contained entities like *moving points* or *evolving regions* have already been studied in [4, 5]. But so far, data models for spatial partitions changing over time have not been considered.

The main objectives of this paper are twofold. First, we give some examples of interesting application scenarios for spatial partitions evolving over time and illustrate their characteristic features. Using a *three-dimensional (3D) view*, we will see that temporally changing spatial partitions can be well visualized by *three-dimensional spatial partitions* where each temporally changing region develops into a volume. Partition constraints adapted to the 3D case are maintained by the volumes. Additionally, application-specific operations on two-dimensional partitions can be "lifted" to the spatio-temporal case. The interesting aspect here is that these operations can be even further generalized. We will demonstrate this by examples.

Second, we study the temporal development of spatial partitions thoroughly and give a formal semantics to them and to their operations. This leads us to so-called *spatio-temporal partitions*, that is, to collections of regions satisfying the partition constraints for each time of their lifespan and maintaining these constraints over time. Temporal changes of spatial partitions can occur either continuously (for example, distribution of air pollution or temperature zones) or in discrete and stepwise constant steps (for example, reunification of West and East Germany, splitting of Yugoslavia). If we imagine a spatio-temporal partition and a time axis perpendicular to the Euclidean plane, for each time slice parallel to the xy-axis, we obtain a stationary, two-dimensional spatial partition which changes over time due to altering shapes, sizes, or attribute values of regions. This imagination corresponds to the *temporal object view* already described in [8]; it is based on the observation that everything that changes over time can be considered as a function over time. In the context here, spatio-temporal partitions can be viewed as functions from time to a two-dimensional spatial partition.

The remainder of the paper is structured as follows. Section 2 recalls related work with respect to spatial partitions and spatio-temporal objects. Section 3 informally describes the structure of and operations on spatio-temporal partitions from an application point of view. In Section 4 our formal model of spatial partitions is briefly reviewed which serves as the foundation for a formal model of spatio-temporal partitions which is then given in Section 5. Additionally, some more operations are introduced emphasizing the temporal aspect of spatio-temporal partitions. Section 6 draws some conclusions.

2   Related Work

In this section we will briefly review related work on spatial partitions and on spatio-temporal data modeling as far as it is relevant for this paper. We are not aware of any work on the combination of both research aspects.

2.1   Spatial Partitions

Spatial partitions or maps have been identified as a basic *spatial concept* to organize and conceptualize our perception and understanding of space. They correspond to humans' cognitive experience and knowledge of areal phenomena in the real world. If we consider the same space with respect to two different thematic or cognitive aspects (for example, districts and cereals) modeled as two partitions, their overlay is a partition again.

Maps arising from classifying space according to some aspect are frequently called *thematic maps* or *categorical coverages* [10, 21]. But these concepts mainly focus on partitions of attribute values alone – spatial operations are completely ignored. In particular, *boundaries* are not considered which play an important role in connection with geometric intersection.

In geographic applications and systems spatial partitions are regarded as a fundamental and user-friendly data modeling tool offering a powerful basis for coping with spatial analysis and cartographical tasks [1, 9, 10, 14, 20, 21]. Distinct features over the same space can be combined and evaluated under different requirements. Partition-based spatial analysis functions include operations like overlay, generalization, and reclassification. They all produce a new partition as a result.

From a data type perspective there have been some unsatisfactory proposals in the past to model partitions. In [12] a spatial data type *area* is suggested to model the partition constraints. Within the framework of an extended relational data model the set of polygons occurring in a relation as a column of an attribute of type *area* has to fulfill the integrity constraint that all polygons are adjacent or disjoint to each other. Unfortunately, the maintenance of this property is not supported by the data model, rather it is up to the user's responsibility. A generic data type for partitions, called *tessellation*, is informally introduced in [14] as a specialized type for sets of polygons; this type can be parametrized with an attribute of a yet unspecified type. In [13] so-called *restriction types* have been proposed. This concept allows one to restrict the general type for regions to subtypes whose values all satisfy a specific topological predicate (like *disjoint*) and which nevertheless inherit the properties and operations of the more general type for regions.

A rigorous and thorough formal definition of spatial partitions and of application-specific operations defined on them is given in [6]. The basic idea is that a spatial partition is a mapping from the Euclidean space $\mathbb{R}^2$ to some *label type*, that is, regions of a partition are assigned single labels (see Section 4.1). Adjacent regions have different labels in their interior, and a boundary is assigned the pair of labels of both adjacent regions.

In [6] all application-specific operations have been reduced to the three fundamental and powerful operations *intersection, relabel,* and *refine* (see Section 4.2). Intersecting two spatial partitions means to compute the geometric intersection of all regions and to produce a new spatial partition; each resulting region is labeled with the pair of labels of the original two intersecting regions, and the values on the boundaries are derived from these. Relabeling a spatial partition has the effect of changing the labels of its regions. This can happen by simply renaming the label of each region. Or, in particular, distinct labels of two or more regions are mapped to the same new label. If some of these regions are adjacent in the partition, the border between them disappears, and the regions are fused in the result partition. Relabeling has then a coarsening effect. Refining a partition means to look with a finer granularity on regions and to reveal and to enumerate the connected components of regions.

All of the following application-specific operations are covered by these three operations:

- *Overlay.* This most important application operation on maps [1, 9, 13, 12, 14–17, 20] allows to lay two partitions with different attribute categories on top of each other and to combine them through geometric intersection into a new partition of disjoint and adjacent regions. The attributes from the input partitions are then either distributed to each region of the result partition or appropriately mapped to a new attribute. The underlying basic operation is obviously intersection.
- *Reclassify* [1, 14] retains the geometric structure of the spatial partition and transforms all or some partition attributes to new or modified attributes. It is a special case of relabeling.
- *Fusion* [13–17] is a kind of grouping operation with subsequent geometric union. It merges neighbored regions of a partition with respect to partially identical attributes and is also a special case of relabeling.
- *Cover* [17] forms the geometric union of all regions of a partition and yields a result partition consisting of one region. Since *cover* is a special case of *fusion*, it can again be realized by relabeling.
- *Clipping* [17] computes the intersection of a partition and a given rectangular window. As a special case of *overlay*, it can be expressed by intersection. We

have generalized this operation and allow general so-called "unit partitions" as clipping windows [6].

- *Difference* [14] takes two spatial partitions defined over the same attribute domain and computes the geometric difference of their point sets. All the regions of the first partition are maintained in the result partition except for those parts that have the same attributes in both partitions. We have generalized this operation in several ways; it can be reduced to a combination of intersecting and relabeling [6].

- *Superimposition* [17] allows to superimpose the regions of a partition onto another partition and to cover and erase parts of the other partition. It is a special case of intersection.

- *Window* [17] retrieves those complete regions of a spatial partition whose intersection with a given window is not empty. Its definition, which was generalized in [6], is based on all three fundamental operations. In particular, this is the only operation that requires the partition operation *refine*.

2.2 Spatio-Temporal Objects

So far, only a few data models for spatio-temporal data have been proposed. They all focus on describing the temporal development of single, self-contained spatial objects but do not take into account collections of evolving spatial objects possibly satisfying some constraints over time. Either spatial data models [22] or temporal data models [11, 2] have been extended to become spatio-temporal. The main drawback of all these approaches is that they are incapable of modeling *continuous* changes of spatial objects over time.

Our approach to dealing with spatio-temporal data supports an integrated view of space and time and incorporates the treatment of continuous spatial changes. It is based on the concept of *spatio-temporal data types* [4, 5]. These data types are designed as abstract data types whose values can be integrated as complex entities into databases and whose definition and integration into databases is independent of a particular DBMS data model.

A temporal version of an object of type α is given by a function from *time* to α. Spatio-temporal objects like *moving points* or *evolving regions* are regarded as special instances of temporal objects where α is a spatial data type like *point* or *region*. A moving point describes a point changing its location in the Euclidean plane over time. An evolving region is a temporally changing region that can move and/or grow/shrink. It can even disappear or reappear, and its components can either split or merge.

A straightforward and very instructive view of spatio-temporal objects is to conceptualize and visualize their temporal evolution as purely geometric, *three-dimensional* objects, that is, the time axis is regarded as a third geometric dimension. An evolving region is then represented as a *volume* in 3D space (with z-monotonic surfaces), and a moving point is then visualized as a (z-monotonic) *3D curve*. Any intersection parallel to the xy-plane yields a spatial object, that is, a region or a point. These two views, the *temporal object view* and the *three-dimensional object view*, together with the concept of 2D spatial partitions described in Section 2.1 will serve as the main design guidelines for modeling spatio-temporal partitions.

Note that in the same way as spatial partitions cannot be modeled adequately with a type of spatial regions, evolving regions are insufficient to capture the inherent constraints of spatio-temporal partitions.

3   Applications of Spatio-Temporal Partitions

Spatio-temporal partitions or "temporal maps" have a wide range of interesting applications. In this section we will have a look at some of these applications and demonstrate the essence and power of spatio-temporal partitions and operations defined on them. Section 3.1 introduces selected applications for temporal maps and uses them to explain the structure of spatio-temporal partitions. Section 3.2 briefly deals with a possible visualization of spatio-temporal partitions in user interfaces. Finally, Section 3.3 considers applications that combine spatio-temporal partitions through operations.

3.1   Structure of Spatio-Temporal Partitions

The following examples comprise time-dependent spatial mapping and analysis tasks as they are relevant for cartography, GIS, and other spatially-related application areas. Their actual power is later revealed when two partitions are combined appropriately (see Section 3.3).

From an application point of view, we can generally distinguish two categories of temporal maps. The first category incorporates applications whose temporal changes are discrete. For example, consider the temporal development of any hierarchical decomposition of space into administrative or cadastral units like the world map into countries or districts into land parcels. Another application is the classification of rural areas according to their agricultural use (like the cultivation of cereals) over time. A further example is a chronology of ruling parties in countries.

A characteristic feature of applications of this first category is that the number of discrete temporal changes is finite and that there is no change between any two subsequent *temporal change points*, that is, the development is stepwise constant which is a special form of (semi-)continuity. For each time between two temporal change points we expect and obtain a unique and correct spatial partition.

The open issue now is what happens at temporal change points with their abrupt transition from one spatial partition to another. If we consider the time point when West and East Germany were reunified, did the spatial partition before or after the reunification belong to this time point? Since we cannot come to an objective decision but only know that not both spatial partitions can simultaneously belong to the temporal change point, we have to decide arbitrarily and to assign one of both spatial partitions to it. This, in particular, maintains the functional character of our temporal object view. We have chosen to ascribe the temporally later spatial partition to a temporal change point. Mathematically this means that we permit a finite set of time points where the temporal function is not continuous.

The examples reveal that after a temporal change point the continuity of the temporal function proceeds for some time interval up to the next temporal change point; there are no "thin, isolated slices" containing single spatial partitions at temporal change points. Consider the result of the reunification of West and East Germany which after that event has lasted up to now. Hence, we have to tighten our requirement in the sense that mathematically the temporal function has to be (*upper*) *semicontinuous* at each time. Intuitively, this means that the temporal function has to be continuous from the upper side.

The second category includes applications whose temporal changes are continuous or smooth. Consider the temporal evolution of climatic phenomena like temperature zones or high/low pressure areas, areas of air pollution with distinct degrees of intensity, or developments of forest fires in space and time. They all show a very dynamic and attribute-varying behavior over time. Application examples which have by far slower temporal changes are the increasing spread of ethnic or religious groups, the decreasing extent of mineral resources like oil fields during the course of time due to exploitation, or the subdivision of space into areas with different sets of spoken languages over time.

So far, we have intuitively described the *temporal object view* of spatio-temporal partitions. An alternative imagination of spatio-temporal partitions is given by the *three-dimensional object view*. The idea is to regard the time axis as a third geometric dimension, the z-axis, and to represent the temporal evolution of regions of a spatial partition as solid 3D volumes. This leads to *three-dimensional partitions* where any two volumes are either disjoint, or they are adjacent and have common boundary parts. The predicates "disjoint" and "adjacent" denote topological relationships in three-dimensional space. We will denote these 3D volumes as *partition volumes*.

An interesting observation is that partition volumes cannot be shaped arbitrarily. They must reflect the functional character of spatio-temporal partitions. That implies that the boundaries with respect to the z-axis are somewhat "strictly monotonic". A suitable metaphor illustrating this feature is a *honeycomb*. The partition volumes correspond to the cells, and borders correspond to the cell walls.

3.2   Visualization of Spatio-Temporal Partitions

The three-dimensional object view suggests an obvious method to visualize spatio-temporal partitions, namely by three-dimensional pictures. In particular, it views spatio-temporal partitions from a global perspective since one can completely see the whole evolution of a spatial partition. Nevertheless, it seems that 3D pictures are too static and that they are only adequate for simple spatio-temporal partitions with a small number of regions and little changes.

An alternative which can be especially used to grasp complex application scenarios like weather reports are methods of virtual reality like cyber gloves which allow to migrate through space and time. Another technique is to record snapshots in temporal order like on a film and to play the film. This is already used, for example, in weather forecasting where the development of temperature zones is displayed in a film. The disadvantage is that the user has no control of how the film is played.

An improvement of the snapshot approach is to admit user interaction when the film is displayed. A user interface could, for example, contain a time slider which allows to exert influence on the time interval, on the speed, and on the temporal direction of display and which gives an immediate feedback with respect to space and time.

A more sophisticated strategy could take a layered approach. The idea is to visualize two or more snapshots of the same scenario at different time points in parallel. For that purpose, the representations of these snapshots have to be slightly bent in the same way and to be positioned one on top of the other in temporal order. The spatial distance between two subsequent snapshot layers should visualize their temporal distance. This strategy allows to simultaneously compare the development of a spatial partition at different times. Each snapshot can be either controlled individually by its own time slider or altogether with the others to maintain selected temporal distances between subsequent snapshots.

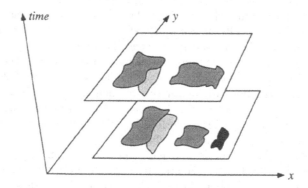

3.3   Operations on Spatio-Temporal Partitions

In this section we focus on the transfer of the two basic spatial partition operations *intersection* and *relabel* to the spatio-temporal case and additionally introduce some new operations that are more directed to the time dimension. All operations are discussed informally and illustrated with query examples. A spatio-temporal *refine* poses problems, as we will see later, and is thus omitted. Moreover, in [6] *refine* was mainly employed to define the *window* operation.

Overlay. Similar to the spatial case, temporal overlays are based on a spatio-temporal *intersection* operation and turn out to be the most important operations on spatio-temporal partitions. They can be used to analyze the temporal evolution of two (or more) different attribute categories.

For example, consider a temporal map indicating the extent of mineral resources like oil fields or coal deposits and another temporal map showing the country map over time. Then an overlay of both temporal maps can, for instance, reveal the countries that had or still have the richest mineral resources, it can show the grade of decline of mineral deposits in the different countries, and it can expose the countries which most exploited their mineral resources.

Another application refers to social analysis and assumes temporal maps about average income, about the countries of the world, and about ethnic groups. If we overlay these three temporal maps (by two intersections), we can, for instance, recognize which ethnic groups in which countries belong to the richest or poorest social strata and whether the same ethnic groups have the same social status in different countries.

A further example for overlay supports weather forecasting and gale warning. Suppose that we are given three temporal maps, one about temperature distributions, one about high/low pressure areas, and one about spatial and temporal occurrences of storms and hurricanes. An overlay of these three temporal maps gives information about the influence of temperature and air pressure on the formation of hurricanes.

Clipping. An interesting special case of *intersection* is the *clipping* operation. We transfer the 2D operation to the spatio-temporal case but admit not only constant *spatio-temporal unit partitions* as "clipping volumes" but also general, that is, time-varying, ones. An application is a temporal map about the development of diseases. As a clipping window we use a temporal map of urban areas developing in space over time. The task is to analyze whether there is a connection between the increase or decrease of urban space and the development of certain diseases. Hence, all areas of disease outside of urban regions are excluded from consideration. The clipping works as a *spatio-temporal filter*. Another example is a temporal map about animal species that predominantly populate certain areas. As a clipping window we use a temporal map of forests and ask for the development of animal species in growing and shrinking forests.

Reclassification. As an application of a spatio-temporal *relabel* operation we take a temporal map marking all countries of the world with their population numbers. This allows to pose a ranking of countries with regard to their population number for each time and especially over time. A query can now ask for the proportion of each country's population on the world population over time, a task that can be performed by temporal relabeling. This corresponds to a reclassification of attribute categories over time without changing geometry.

Fusion. Assume that a temporal map of districts with their land use is given. The task is to identify regions with the same land use over time. At each time neighboring districts with the same land use are replaced by a single region, that is, their common boundary line is erased. We obtain a temporal fusion operator which is based on relabeling.

Static and Dynamic Relabeling. In the two previous examples the relabeling function did not change over time, that is, it was constant. We call this *static relabeling*. But we can generalize even this and look at applications requiring temporally changing relabeling functions. It can often be used if the semantics of attribute classifications alters over time. An example of *dynamic relabeling* is the classification of income to show poor and rich areas over time. Due to the changing value of money, due to inflation, and due to social changes, the understanding of wealthy and poorness varies over time. Hence, we need different and appropriate relabeling functions that are applied to distinct time intervals.

Dynamic relabeling can also be used for temperature maps. Imagine we have two relabeling functions, the first function mapping different temperature zones to distinct warm colors (orange, red, yellow, etc.) and a second function mapping temperatures less than five degrees to dark blue and the other temperatures to light blue. A visualization of temperature maps could now use the first relabeling (presentation) function for daytime and the second relabeling function for the night.

Domain. The two operations *intersection* and *relabel* are motivated by spatial aspects. In order to also emphasize temporal aspects, we add a few more operations addressing the time dimension. The operation *dom* determines the domain of a temporal map, that is, all times where the map does not yield the completely undefined partition. An example is a temporal map of earthquakes and volcanic eruptions in the world as they are interesting for seismological investigations. Applying the operation *dom* on this map returns the time periods of earthquake and volcanic activity in the world.

Temporal restriction. The operation *restrict* realizes a function restriction on spatio-temporal partitions and computes a new partition. As parameters it obtains a temporal map and a set of (right half-open) time intervals describing the time periods of interest. Imagine that we have a temporal map of birth rates, and we are only interested in the birth rates between 1989 and 1991 and between 1999 and 2001 ("millennium baby"). Then we can exclude all the other time periods and compare the change of birth rates in these two time intervals.

Temporal selection. The operation *select* is also a very powerful operation. It allows to scan spatio-temporal partitions over time and to check for each time whether a specified predicate is fulfilled or not. Consider a map showing the spread of fires. We could be interested in when and where the spread of fires occupied an area larger than 300 km^2. The operation *select* takes the temporal map and an appropriate predicate as arguments and computes the resulting temporal map (whose domain is, in general, reduced). Other applications are when and in which districts the birth rates exceeded the death rates, or when and in which countries socialist/conservative parties ruled.

Temporal aggregation. The operation *aggregate* collects all labels of a point over time and combines them with the aid of a binary function into one label. The result is a two-dimensional spatial partition. If, for example, the population numbers, the birth rates, the death rates, the population density, the average income, etc. of the countries in the world are available, we can aggregate over them and compute the maximum or minimum value each country ever had for one of these attributes.

Temporal projection. A special kind of aggregation is realized by the *project* operation which computes the projection of a spatio-temporal partition onto the Euclidean space and which yields a spatial partition. For each point in space, all labels, except for the undefined label denoting the outside, are collected over time. That is, if a point has always had the same single label over its lifetime, this single label will appear in the resulting partition and indicate a place that has never changed. On the other hand, points of the resulting partition with a collection of labels describe places where changes occurred.

Another application is the projection of a temporal map showing which countries were ruled by which parties. The result reveals those countries that were always ruled by the same party and those countries that had to accept changes of ruling parties. A further example is the projection of a temporal map illustrating the water levels of lakes onto the Euclidean plane. The result shows those parts of lakes that have always, sometimes, and never been covered with water.

4   A Formal Model of Spatial Partitions

In this section we briefly repeat some definitions of our model for two-dimensional spatial partitions. First, we provide a precise definition for the type of two-dimensional partitions in Section 4.1 since the snapshot of a spatio-temporal partition at a certain point in time (that is, the application of a spatio-temporal partition to a time point) yields a two-dimensional partition. After that we define the operations on two-dimensional partitions in Section 4.2. These operations are used in Section 5.2 to define operations on spatio-temporal partitions. Three-dimensional spatial partitions can be defined as a generalization of two-dimensional ones; they provide a helpful model to understand spatio-temporal partitions, and they can actually serve as a specification for an implementation of spatio-temporal partitions. Exhibiting the precise relationships between spatio-temporal partitions and 3D partitions will be a topic of future research.

Before we start giving mathematical definitions for partitions, we shortly summarize the employed notation. The application of a function $f : A \to B$ to a set of values $S \subseteq A$ is defined as $f(S) := \{f(x) \mid x \in S\} \subseteq B$. If we are sure that $f(S)$ yields a singleton set, we write $f^!(S)$ to denote this single element (instead of the singleton set), that is, $f(S) = \{y\} \implies f^!(S) = y$. ($f^!(S)$ is undefined if $|f(S)| \neq 1$.) Similarly, for doubly-nested singleton sets we use $f^{!!}$ to extract elements, that is, $f(S) = \{\{y\}\} \implies f^{!!}(S) = y$. The *inverse function* $f^{-1} : B \to 2^A$ of f is defined by $f^{-1}(y) := \{x \in S \mid f(x) = y\}$. Note that, in general, f^{-1} is a partial function and that f^{-1} applied to a set yields a set of sets. The *range* of a function $f : A \to B$ is defined as $rng(f) := f(A)$. We also introduce a notation for power sets containing sets of constrained size: for $\triangleright \in \{>, \geq, =\}$ and $k \in \mathbb{N}$ we define $S^{\triangleright k} := \{s \in S \mid |s| \triangleright k\}$.

Let (X, T) be a topological space with topology $T \subseteq 2^X$, and let $S \subseteq X$.[1] The *interior* of S is defined as the union of all open sets that are contained in S and is denoted by $\operatorname{Int} S$, and the *closure* of S is defined as the intersection of all closed sets that contain S and is denoted by $\overline{S}$. The *exterior* of S is given by $\operatorname{Ext} S := \operatorname{Int}(X - S)$, and the *boundary* (or *frontier*) of S is defined as $\operatorname{Fr} S := \overline{S} \cap \overline{X - S}$. An open set is called *regular* if $A = \operatorname{Int} \overline{A}$. Regular open sets are closed under intersection. A topological space we need in this paper is $\mathbb{R}^2$.

A *partition* of a set S can be viewed as a total function $f : S \to I$ into an index set I. f induces an equivalence relationship $\equiv_f$ on S that is defined by $x \equiv_f y \iff f(x) = f(y)$. The equivalence classes $S/\equiv_f$ are called *blocks*. The block S_i that corresponds to an index i is given by $S_i := f^{-1}(i)$, and the whole partition $\{S_i \mid i \in I\}$ ($= S/\equiv_f$) is also given by $f^{-1}(I)$ if f is surjective.

4.1   Two-Dimensional Spatial Partitions

A spatial partition is not just defined as a function $f : \mathbb{R}^2 \to I$ for two reasons: first, in most applications f cannot be assumed to be total, and second, f cannot be uniquely defined on borders between adjacent subsets of $\mathbb{R}^2$. Moreover, it is desirable from an application point of view to require blocks (modeling regions of a common label) to be regular open sets [19].

Therefore, we have defined spatial partitions in several steps [6]: first, a *spatial mapping* of type A is a total function $\pi : \mathbb{R}^2 \to 2^A$. We require the existence of an undefined element $\perp_A \in A$, which is used to represent undefined labels, that is, the "exterior" or "outside" of a partition is the block $b \subseteq \mathbb{R}^2$ with $\pi'(p) = \perp_A$ for all $p \in b$. The power set range type is used to model labels on region borders: a *region* of π is a block that is mapped to a singleton set whereas a *border* of π is a block that is mapped to a subset of A containing two or more elements. Then the *interior* of π is defined as the union of π's regions, and the *boundary* of π is defined as the union of π's borders.

Definition 1. Let π be a spatial mapping of type A.

   (i) $\rho(\pi) := \pi^{-1}(rng(\pi)^{=1})$ (*regions*)

   (ii) $\omega(\pi) := \pi^{-1}(rng(\pi)^{>1})$ (*borders*)

   (iii) $\iota(\pi) := \bigcup_{r \in \rho(\pi)} r$ (*interior*)

   (iv) $\beta(\pi) := \bigcup_{b \in \omega(\pi)} b$ (*boundary*)

Finally, a *spatial partition* of type A is a spatial mapping of type A whose regions are regular open sets and whose borders are labeled with the union of labels of all adjacent regions:

---

[1] Recall that in a topological space the following three axioms hold [3]: (i) $U, V \in T \implies U \cap V \in T$, (ii) $S \subseteq T \implies \bigcup_{U \in S} U \in T$, and (iii) $x \in T$, $\emptyset \in T$. The elements of T are called *open sets*, their complements in X are called *closed sets*, and the elements of X are called *points*.

Definition 2. A *spatial partition* of type A is a spatial mapping π of type A with:

(i) $\forall r \in \rho(\pi) : r = \text{Int}\,\bar{r}$

(ii) $\forall b \in \omega(\pi) : \pi^!(b) = \{\pi^{!!}(r) \mid r \in \rho(\pi) \wedge b \subseteq \bar{r}\}$

The type of all partitions of type A is denoted by $[A]$.

The reader might wonder why in the above definition (and in some of the following) we have used $\pi^!(b)$ on the left hand side and $\pi^{!!}(r)$ on the right hand side in (ii). This is explained in the following remark to which we will refer quite a few times later:

Remark 1

Consider a block of a partition π, for example, a region r or a border b. For each point p that is contained in r or in b, $\pi(p)$ yields as a label a set of values. For $p \in r$, this is a singleton set, say $\{a_1\}$, and for $p \in b$, this is a set $\{a_1, a_2, \dots\}$ of two or more elements. Now when we apply π to the whole set r (or b), we obtain the set of all labels for all points. By definition these are all equal, so the results of $\pi(r)$ and $\pi(b)$ are $\{\{a_1\}\}$ and $\{\{a_1, a_2, \dots\}\}$, respectively. Thus, if we want to denote the common label of all points of a block, this is given by $\pi^!(r) = \{a_1\}$ or $\pi^!(b) = \{a_1, a_2, \dots\}$, respectively. Likewise, $\pi^{!!}(r) = a_1$.

Hence, $\pi^!(b)$ denotes the common label, a set $\{a_1, a_2, \dots\}$, of border block b, and $\pi^{!!}(r)$ gives the label a_i of each touching region.

In the following we will sometimes need the notion of a *constant partition* which is a partition that yields one and the same label for all points:

$$\pi_x = \lambda p{:}\mathbb{R}^2.x$$

As a special case, the undefined partition of type A is given by $\pi_{\perp_A}$. Note that the lambda-notation $\lambda x{:}S.e(x)$ is just a shorthand for the set expression $\{(x, e(x)) \mid x \in S\}$ (which actually represents a function).

4.2   Operations on 2D-Partitions

We have defined three basic operations on spatial partitions: *intersection*, *relabel*, and *refine*. The intersection of two partitions π_1 and π_2 of types A and B, respectively, is again a spatial partition (of type $A \times B$) where each interior point p is mapped to the pair of values $(\pi_1^!(p), \pi_2^!(p))$, and all border points are mapped to the set of labels of all adjacent regions (as required by the second part of the definition of partition). Formally, we can define the intersection of two partitions $\pi_1 : [A]$ and $\pi_2 : [B]$ in several steps: first, we compute the regions of the resulting partition. This can be done by simple set intersection since regions are, by definition, regular open sets and since $\cap$ is closed on regular open sets:

$$\rho_\cap(\pi_1, \pi_2) := \{r \cap r' \mid r \in \rho(\pi_1) \wedge r' \in \rho(\pi_2)\}$$

Second, the union of all these regions gives the interior of the resulting partition:

$$\iota_\cap(\pi_1, \pi_2) := \bigcup_{r \in \rho_\cap(\pi_1, \pi_2)} r$$

Now the spatial mapping restricted to the interior can be just obtained by mapping each interior point $p \in I := \iota_\cap(\pi_1, \pi_2)$ to the pair of labels given by π_1 and π_2, respectively:

$$\pi_I := \lambda p : I.\{(\pi_1^!(p), \pi_2^!(p))\}$$

Third, the boundary labels can be derived from the labels of all adjacent regions. Let $R := \rho_\cap(\pi_1, \pi_2)$, $I := \iota_\cap(\pi_1, \pi_2)$, and $F := \mathbb{R}^2 - I$. Then we have:

$$\text{intersection} : [A] \times [B] \to [A \times B]$$
$$\text{intersection}(\pi_1, \pi_2) := \pi_I \cup \lambda p : F.\{\pi_I^{!!}(r) \mid r \in R \wedge p \in \bar{r}\}$$

To understand the use of $\pi^{!!}$ in the above definition, recall Remark 1: since we have to place pairs of labels in the result set and since $\pi(r) = \{\{(a_1, a_2)\}\}$, we obtain (a_1, a_2) by application of $\pi^{!!}$.

The fact that *intersection* indeed yields a spatial partition is captured by the following lemma:

Lemma 1. *If $\pi_1 : [A]$ and $\pi_2 : [B]$, then intersection$(\pi_1, \pi_2) : [A \times B]$.* $\square$

The proof can be found in [6].

Relabeling a partition π of type A by a function $f : A \to B$ is defined as $f \circ \pi$, that is, in the resulting partition of type B each point p, interior as well as boundary, is mapped to $f(\pi(p))$:

$$\text{relabel} : [A] \times (A \to B) \to [B]$$
$$\text{relabel}(\pi, f) := \lambda p : \mathbb{R}^2.f(\pi(p))$$

The fact that *relabel* is well-defined and always yields a spatial partition can be proved in several steps culminating in

Lemma 2. *If $\pi : [A]$ and $f : A \to B$, then relabel$(\pi, f) : [B]$.* $\square$

Again, the proof is given in [6].

Finally, the refinement of a partition means the identification of connected components. This is achieved by attaching consecutive numbers to the components. We omit the formal definition here (see [6] for details) since we are not going to define spatio-temporal refinement anyhow.

5 Spatio-Temporal Partitions

In the following we have to work with different kinds of partitions. We therefore add the subscripts 2D and ST to disambiguate notations. For example, π_{2D} denotes a two-dimensional partition, and $[A]_{ST}$ denotes the set of all spatio-temporal partitions of type A. When no subscript is given, we assume by default spatio-temporal partitions, that is, π is a shorthand for π_{ST}.

5.1 The Type of Spatio-Temporal Partitions

In order to define temporally changing partitions we need a type for time. Since we are dealing with continuously changing information, we use *time* $= \mathbb{R}$ as a model of time.

Next we define a spatio-temporal partition as a function of two-dimensional spatial partitions over time. A *spatio-temporal mapping* of type A is a total function $\pi_{ST} : time \rightarrow [A]_{2D}$. Spatio-temporal mappings are too general to be used as a partition model since they can have an undesired structure: consider, for example, two different two-dimensional partitions π_{2D} and π'_{2D} and the following spatio-temporal mapping:

$$\pi_{ST}(t) = \begin{cases} \pi_{2D} & \text{if } t \text{ is rational} \\ \pi'_{2D} & \text{otherwise} \end{cases}$$

Here π_{ST} describes a completely discontinuous, rather pathological, change of partitions; we would like to rule out such spatio-temporal mappings as spatio-temporal partitions.

What we require is a kind of (semi-)continuity of spatio-temporal mappings. More precisely, we regard only *upper semicontinuous* spatial mappings as spatio-temporal partitions. To formally define continuity we employ a difference measure for 2D spatial partitions. A measure of "nearness" or "equality" is given by the size of the total area that is labeled equally in both partitions (that is, the corresponding set of points). We can now define an operator $\delta : [A]_{2D} \times [A]_{2D} \rightarrow \mathbb{R}$ that computes the size of the regions that are labeled differently.

$$\delta(\pi, \pi') := \int_{\{p \in \mathbb{R}^2 | \pi(p) \neq \pi'(p)\}} dx\, dy$$

Using δ we can define the notion of upper semicontinuity of a spatial mapping.

Definition 3. Let π be a spatio-temporal mapping and $t \in$ *time*. π is *upper semicontinuous* at t if $\lim_{\epsilon \to 0} \delta(\pi(t), \pi(t + \epsilon)) = 0$. Moreover, π is *upper semicontinuous* (everywhere) if it is upper semicontinuous at each $t \in$ *time*.

Now we accept as spatio-temporal partitions only upper semicontinuous spatio-temporal mappings.

Definition 4. A *spatio-temporal partition* of type A is an upper semicontinuous spatio-temporal mapping of type A.

The type of spatio-temporal partitions with labels of type A is denoted by $[A]_{ST}$.

5.2 Basic Operations on Spatio-Temporal Partitions

Next we define the two partition operations *intersection* and *relabel*. We omit a definition of spatio-temporal *refine*, since it leads to a somewhat unpleasant behavior of the numbering of blocks. For example, a spatial partition $\pi_{2D} = \pi_{ST}(t)$

obtained by a refined spatio-temporal partition π_{ST} contains, in general, non-consecutive numberings of labels. Moreover, we need *refine* mainly for completeness reasons (that is, to be able to define the application-specific operation "window", see [6]). Instead, we are considering some operations that take the time dimension more explicitly into account, namely, operations for temporal selection and for temporal projection/aggregation.

Since spatio-temporal partitions are defined as temporal functions of 2D partitions, we can simply reduce the definitions to the two-dimensional case. For example, for intersection we obtain:

$$intersection_{ST} : [A]_{ST} \times [B]_{ST} \to [A \times B]_{ST}$$
$$intersection_{ST}(\pi, \pi') := \lambda t{:}time.intersection_{2D}(\pi(t), \pi'(t))$$

We have to prove that this definition indeed yields a spatio-temporal partition as a result.

Lemma 3. *If* $\pi : [A]_{ST}$ *and* $\pi' : [B]_{ST}$, *then* $intersection_{ST}(\pi, \pi') : [A \times B]_{ST}$.

Proof. Let $\pi_I = intersection_{ST}(\pi, \pi')$. First, it is obvious from the definition that π_I is a spatio-temporal mapping (of type $A \times B$). It remains to be shown that π_I is upper semicontinuous, which means to show that $\lim_{\epsilon \to 0} \delta(\pi_I(t), \pi_I(t+\epsilon)) = 0$. We call the points that are labeled differently by $\pi_I(t)$ and $\pi_I(t+\epsilon)$ the *difference region* for π_I (on the interval $[t, t + \epsilon]$). We next show that a difference region for π_I is always covered by the difference regions for π and for π'.

Consider an arbitrary point $p \in \mathbb{R}^2$, a time value $t \in time$, and an $\epsilon > 0$. By definition of δ, p is in the difference region for π_I if $\pi_I(t)(p) \neq \pi_I(t + \epsilon)(p)$. By the definition of $intersection_{ST}$ we know $\pi_I(t) = intersection_{2D}(\pi(t), \pi'(t))$, and thus we have:

$$\pi_I(t)(p) \neq \pi_I(t + \epsilon)(p) \iff$$
$$intersection_{2D}(\pi(t), \pi'(t))(p) \neq intersection_{2D}(\pi(t + \epsilon), \pi'(t + \epsilon))(p)$$

Now the definition of $intersection_{2D}$ depends on whether p is an interior or a boundary point. We can ignore boundary points, since they do not contribute to the value of the integral in δ. (This is because the area (2D) integral of lines (1D) is always 0.) Since p can be an interior point of $\pi_I(t)$ only if it is an interior point of both $\pi(t)$ and $\pi'(t)$, we need to consider the definition of $intersection_{2D}$ only for interior points. Therefore, we can substitute the definition for interior points into the above condition:

$$\pi_I(t)(p) \neq \pi_I(t + \epsilon)(p) \iff (\pi(t)(p), \pi'(t)(p)) \neq (\pi(t + \epsilon)(p), \pi'(t + \epsilon)(p))$$

Next we observe that the inequality on the right hand side holds if either of the pairs' components are not equal, that is,

$$\pi_I(t)(p) \neq \pi_I(t + \epsilon)(p) \iff \pi(t)(p) \neq \pi(t + \epsilon)(p) \vee \pi'(t)(p) \neq \pi'(t + \epsilon)(p)$$

Now this is nothing but the condition that p is either contained in the difference region for π or for π'.

We can conclude that if the difference region for π_I is covered by the difference regions for π and for π', the value of $\lim_{\epsilon \to 0} \delta(\pi_I(t), \pi_I(t + \epsilon))$ is bounded by

$$\lim_{\epsilon \to 0} \delta(\pi(t), \pi(t + \epsilon)) + \lim_{\epsilon \to 0} \delta(\pi'(t), \pi'(t + \epsilon))$$

Since both terms are 0, we also know that $\lim_{\epsilon \to 0} \delta(\pi_I(t), \pi_I(t + \epsilon)) = 0$. □

Next we define the relabeling operation. A first attempt is to simply "lift" the two-dimensional function as follows.

$$relabel_{ST} : [A]_{ST} \times (A \to B) \to [B]_{ST}$$
$$relabel_{ST}(\pi, f) := \lambda t{:}time.relabel_{2D}(\pi(t), f))$$

Note that the relabeling function f must be total. We can generalize this definition considerably by allowing a temporally changing relabeling function. Thus, we could try the slightly changed definition shown below:[2]

$$relabel_{ST} : [A]_{ST} \times (time \to A \to B) \to [B]_{ST}$$
$$relabel_{ST}(\pi, f) := \lambda t{:}time.relabel_{2D}(\pi(t), f(t)))$$

Unfortunately, with this definition, we can construct spatio-temporal mappings that are not spatio-temporal partitions. As a simple example consider the "universal partition" π_a $(= \lambda t{:}time.\lambda p{:}\mathbb{R}^2.a)$ that maps every point at every time to $a \in A := \{a, b, \perp_A\}$. We relabel $\underline{\pi_a}$ with the function $f : time \to A \to A$ that is defined by:

$$f(t)(x) = \begin{cases} b & \text{if } t = t_0 \\ a & \text{otherwise} \end{cases}$$

so that $relabel(\pi_a, f)$ yields a spatio-temporal mapping π° which is defined by:

$$\pi^\circ(t)(p) = \begin{cases} b & \text{if } t = t_0 \\ a & \text{otherwise} \end{cases}$$

Now it is obvious that π° is not upper semicontinuous at t_0 and is thus not a spatio-temporal partition. Therefore, the above definition for *relabel* is too general.

Fortunately, by adding a simple condition we can ensure that *relabel* again yields spatio-temporal partitions: we require f to be what we call *upper semiconstant*, that is, we demand $\forall t \in time : \exists \epsilon > 0 : \forall 0 \le \delta \le \epsilon : f(t + \delta) = f(t)$. This means that after each change, f must be constant for some short period of time. (This rules out dynamic changes of relabeling function that would, in principle, also be possible. However, to define the more general version we need a quite complex topological continuity definition for function spaces requiring A and B to be topological spaces, too, which is not needed otherwise. In summary, it seems that there are not very many highly important applications for the general case so that the complex definition does not seem to be justified.)

---

[2] Note that the function type constructor associates to the right, that is, $X \to Y \to Z = X \to (Y \to Z)$.

5.3   More Operations on Spatio-Temporal Partitions

Beyond the "classical" partition operations there are some more operations that address the time dimension more explicitly. First of all, we can determine the domain of a spatio-temporal partition π which is defined as the set of all times t when $\pi(t)$ does not yield the undefined 2D partition.

$$dom_{ST} : [A]_{ST} \to 2^{time}$$
$$dom_{ST}(\pi) := \{t \in time \mid \pi(t) \neq \pi_{\perp_A}\}$$

Related to *dom* is the operation *restrict* that restricts the domain of a spatio-temporal partition to a subset of *time*. For the same reasons as for *relabel* we cannot allow arbitrary subsets of *time*. Instead we require the set be given by *right half-open* intervals. For a totally ordered set S, right half-open intervals are defined as:

$$[s,t[:= \{x \in S \mid s \leq x < t\}$$

The set of all these intervals is then defined by $[S[:= \{[s,t[\mid s,t \in S\}$. In practice we need sets of intervals that do not overlap (to describe subsets of *time*):

$$\langle S \rangle := \{T \in 2^{[S[} \mid \forall I,J \in T : I \cap J \neq \varnothing \implies I = J\}$$

The set of values contained in an interval set S is denoted by $\cup S := \bigcup_{s \in S} s$. Now we can define the *restrict* operation precisely.

$$restrict : [A]_{ST} \times \langle time \rangle \to [A]_{ST}$$
$$restrict(\pi, T) := \lambda t{:}time. \begin{cases} \pi(t) & \text{if } t \in \cup T \\ \pi_{\perp_A} & \text{otherwise} \end{cases}$$

To prove that *restrict* indeed yields spatio-temporal partitions as results we exploit the fact that *restrict* can also be defined via *relabel*: let "id" denote the identity function, that is, $\mathrm{id}(x) = x$. We have:

Lemma 4.

Let $T : \langle time \rangle$ and $f_T := \begin{cases} \mathrm{id} & \text{if } t \in \cup T \\ \lambda x{:}A.\perp_A & \text{otherwise} \end{cases}$. *Then:*

$\quad restrict(\pi, T) = relabel(\pi, f_T)$ $\qquad\qquad\qquad\qquad\qquad\qquad\qquad$ □

Since f_T is upper semiconstant by its definition, we obtain as a corollary of Lemma 4:

Corollary 1. *If* $\pi : [A]_{ST}$ *and* $T : \langle time \rangle$, *then* $restrict(\pi, T) : [A]_{ST}$. $\qquad$ □

The notion of restriction of spatio-temporal partitions can be also viewed from a different perspective: we can restrict a partition to those times at which a predicate on the corresponding spatial partition is true. This is a kind of "temporal selection" which could be formally defined by:

$$select : [A]_{ST} \times ([A]_{2D} \to \mathbb{B}) \to [A]_{ST}$$
$$select(\pi, P) := \lambda t{:}time. \begin{cases} \pi(t) & \text{if } P(\pi(t)) \\ \pi_{\perp_A} & \text{otherwise} \end{cases}$$

Unfortunately, without any restriction on the kind of partition predicates used as arguments this definition does not, in general, yield spatio-temporal partitions as a result. As an example consider a spatio-temporal partition π that describes a constantly shrinking square labeled by a (this can be well imagined as a pyramid) and a predicate P that asks for the size of the region labeled a to be exactly x. Assuming that the square is initially greater and at the end smaller than x, an expression $select(\pi, P)$ yields a spatial mapping (much like the one described for *relabel*) that gives only at one time t a spatial partition other than $\pi_{\perp_A}$ (namely a square of size x). Thus, $select(\pi, P)$ is not upper semicontinuous at t and is therefore not a spatio-temporal partition.

How can we correct the definition? It seems to be extremely difficult to characterize the class of predicates that guarantee the above definition to deliver proper spatio-temporal partitions. Fortunately, we can take a different route: first, we determine the set of time intervals on which P is true. This is done by finding the set of time points at which P holds and then regularizing this set by restricting it to half-open intervals. The time set regularization is performed by the function *reg* (note that $\forall I, J \in \langle time \rangle : I \geq J \iff \cup I \supseteq \cup J$):

$$reg : 2^{time} \to \langle time \rangle$$
$$reg(T) := \max\{I \in \langle time \rangle \mid \cup I \subseteq T\}$$

Then we can define *select* simply via *restrict* on this regular interval set.

$$select : [A]_{ST} \times ([A]_{2D} \to \mathbb{B}) \to [A]_{ST}$$
$$select(\pi, P) := restrict(\pi, reg(\{t \in time \mid P(\pi(t))\}))$$

With this definition we again get the proof that *select* computes spatio-temporal partitions for free.

Corollary 2. *If* $\pi : [A]_{ST}$ *and* $P : [A]_{2D} \to \mathbb{B}$, *then* $select(\pi, P) : [A]_{ST}$. $\qquad \square$

Finally, we consider how to form aggregations of partitions over time. From a different point of view, a partition $\pi : [A]_{ST}$ can be also regarded as a function $\xi : \mathbb{R}^2 \to time \to A$, that is, ξ gives for each point $p \in \mathbb{R}^2$ a time-dependent label function ξ_p.[3] Aggregation now means to combine all the values delivered by ξ_p into a single label of type, say B, so that aggregation of a spatio-temporal partition yields a two-dimensional partition of type B.

We shall not give here a completely generic definition since infinite aggregations (over an infinite set of time points) lead to a quite complex definition because of several requirements on the label type. Therefore, we instead restrict to aggregating functions f of type $A \times A \to A$ that are commutative. Commutativity allows to process the labels in any order. Therefore, we can simply

---

[3] Formally, $\xi = \lambda p{:}\mathbb{R}^2.\lambda t{:}time.\pi(t)(p)$.

collect the set of all labels at a point p and aggregate them by f. For this we use the notation $agg(f, S)$ to denote the aggregation of a finite, non-empty set by a binary function:

$$agg(f, \{a\}) = a$$
$$agg(f, (\{a\} \cup S)) = f(a, agg(f, S))$$

Now we can define aggregation as follows:

$$aggregate : [A]_{ST} \times (A \times A \to A) \to [A]_{2D}$$
$$aggregate(\pi, f) := \lambda p{:}\mathbb{R}^2 . agg(f, \cup_{s \in \{\pi(t)(p) \mid t \in time\}} s)$$

Functions that can be used to get interesting aggregations are, for example, max or min. As a special case of aggregation (that actually omits aggregation altogether) we define the function *project* that simply collects all (defined) values for a point:

$$project : [A]_{ST} \to [2^A]_{2D}$$
$$project(\pi) := \lambda p{:}\mathbb{R}^2 . \{\pi(t)(p) \mid t \in time\} - \{\bot_A\}$$

This function exhibits very nicely a correspondence between spatio-temporal partitions and vagueness: assume we consider the growing/shrinking of lakes, forests, etc. over a certain period of time given by a corresponding partition π_{ST}. By computing $project(\pi_{ST})$ we obtain a two-dimensional spatial partition in which regions labeled with singleton sets like $\{\{a\}\}$ give regions that have not changed during the considered time interval, whereas labels $\{\{a\}, \{b\}, \{a, b\}\}$ indicate regions that do have changed (from $\{a\}$ to $\{b\}$). In the terminology of [7] the former regions correspond to the *kernel* and the latter to the *boundary* of a vague region.

6   Conclusions

We have investigated dynamically changing maps; in particular, we have identified and generalized operations that are of practical interest. Moreover, by formally defining spatio-temporal partitions as a generalization of spatial partitions we have provided a theoretical foundation for temporally changing maps and their operations. Thus, spatio-temporal partitions can serve as a formal backbone to dynamic maps as does the model of spatial partitions for static maps.

References

1. J. K. Berry. Fundamental Operations in Computer-Assisted Map Analysis. *Int. Journal of Geographical Information Systems*, 1(2):119–136, 1987.
2. T. S. Cheng and S. K. Gadia. A Pattern Matching Language for Spatio-Temporal Databases. In *ACM Conf. on Information and Knowledge Management*, pages 288–295, 1994.

3. J. Dugundji. *Topology*. Allyn and Bacon, 1966.
4. M. Erwig, R. H. Güting, M. Schneider, and M. Vazirgiannis. Abstract and Discrete Modeling of Spatio-Temporal Data Types. In *6th ACM Symp. on Geographic Information Systems*, pages 131–136, 1998.
5. M. Erwig, R. H. Güting, M. Schneider, and M. Vazirgiannis. Spatio-Temporal Data Types: An Approach to Modeling and Querying Moving Objects in Databases. *GeoInformatica*, 3(3), 1999. To appear.
6. M. Erwig and M. Schneider. Partition and Conquer. In *3rd Int. Conf. on Spatial Information Theory*, LNCS 1329, pages 389–408, 1997.
7. M. Erwig and M. Schneider. Vague Regions. In *5th Int. Symp. on Advances in Spatial Databases*, LNCS 1262, pages 298–320, 1997.
8. M. Erwig, M. Schneider, and R. H. Güting. Temporal Objects for Spatio-Temporal Data Models and a Comparison of Their Representations. In *Int. Workshop on Advances in Database Technologies*, LNCS 1552, pages 454–465, 1998.
9. A. U. Frank. Overlay Processing in Spatial Information Systems. In *8th Int. Symp. on Computer-Assisted Cartography*, pages 16–31, 1987.
10. A. U. Frank, G. S. Volta, and M. MacGranaghan. Formalization of Families of Categorical Coverages. *Int. Journal of Geographical Information Science*, 11(3):215–231, 1997.
11. S. K. Gadia and S. S. Nair. Temporal Databases: A Prelude to Parametric Data. In *[18]*, pages 28–66, 1993.
12. R. H. Güting. Geo-Relational Algebra: A Model and Query Language for Geometric Database Systems. In *Int. Conf. on Extending Database Technology*, LNCS 303, pages 506–527, 1988.
13. R. H. Güting and M. Schneider. Realm-Based Spatial Data Types: The ROSE Algebra. *VLDB Journal*, 4(2):100–143, 1995.
14. Z. Huang, P. Svensson, and H. Hauska. Solving Spatial Analysis Problems with GeoSAL, a Spatial Query Language. In *6th Int. Working Conf. on Scientific and Statistical Database Management*, 1992.
15. H.-P. Kriegel, T. Brinkhoff, and R. Schneider. The Combination of Spatial Access Methods and Computational Geometry in Geographic Database Systems. In *2nd Symp. on Advances in Spatial Databases*, LNCS 525, pages 5–21, 1991.
16. M. Schneider. *Spatial Data Types for Database Systems - Finite Resolution Geometry for Geographic Information Systems*. LNCS 1288. Springer-Verlag, 1997.
17. M. Scholl and A. Voisard. Thematic Map Modeling. In *1st Int. Symp. on Large Spatial Databases*, LNCS 409, pages 167–190, 1989.
18. A. U. Tansel, J. Clifford, S. Gadia, S. Jajodia, A. Segev, and R. Snodgrass. *Temporal Databases: Theory, Design, and Implementation*. The Benjamin/Cummings Publishing Company, 1993.
19. R. B. Tilove. Set Membership Classification: A Unified Approach to Geometric Intersection Problems. *The Computer Journal*, 37(1):25–34, 1994.
20. C. D. Tomlin. *Geographic Information Systems and Cartographic Modeling*. Prentice Hall, 1990.
21. G. S. Volta and M. J. Egenhofer. Interaction with Attribute Data Based on Categorical Coverages. In *1st Int. Conf. on Spatial Information Theory*, LNCS 716, pages 215–233, 1993.
22. M. F. Worboys. A Unified Model for Spatial and Temporal Information. *The Computer Journal*, 37(1):25–34, 1994.

Ontology-Based Geographic Data Set Integration

Harry T. Uitermark[1], Peter J. M. van Oosterom[1], Nicolaas J. I. Mars[2], and
Martien Molenaar[3]

[1] Kadaster (*Cadastre and Public Registry Agency*), Postbus 9046,
7300 GH Apeldoorn, The Netherlands.
{uitermark, oosterom}@kadaster.nl

[2] University of Twente, Enschede, The Netherlands.
mars@cs.utwente.nl

[3] International Institute for Aerospace Survey and Earth Sciences (ITC),
Enschede, The Netherlands.
molenaar@itc.nl

Abstract. In order to develop a system to propagate updates we investigate the semantic and spatial relationships between independently produced geographic data sets of the same region (data set integration). The goal of this system is to reduce operator intervention in update operations between corresponding (semantically similar) geographic object instances. Crucial for this reduction is certainty about the semantic similarity of different object representations. In this paper we explore a framework for ontology-based geographic data set integration, an ontology being a collection of shared concepts. Components of this formal approach are an ontology for topographic mapping (a domain ontology), an ontology for every geographic data set involved (the application ontologies), and abstraction rules (or capture criteria). Abstraction rules define at the class level the relationships between domain ontology and application ontology. Using these relationships, it is possible to locate semantic similarity at the object instance level with methods from computational geometry (like overlay operations). The components of the framework are formalized in the Prolog language, illustrated with a fictitious example, and tested on a practical example.

1 Introduction: Context, Related Work and Overview

Geographic Data Set Integration (or *Map Integration*) is the process of establishing *relationships* between *corresponding object instances* in different, autonomously produced, geographic data sets of a certain region [1]. The purpose of geographic data set integration is to share information between different geographic information sources. We are especially studying geographic data set integration in the context of *update propagation*, that is the *reuse* of updates from one geographic data set to another geographic data set ([2], [3], [4], [5]).

Geographic data set integration gets more and more attention nowadays since the digitizing of traditional map series has ended. In these map series, corresponding object instances were only linked implicitly by a common spatial reference system, e.g. the national grid. In order to make these relationships explicit geo-science researchers and computer scientists have developed various strategies. In the computer science domain, *schema integration* has been the dominant methodology for database integration [6]. That approach has been extended for geographic data sets [7]. Geoscientists on the other hand have adopted methods from communication theory like *relational matching* [8]. In our case we adopted *ontologies* from the field of Artificial Intelligence [9]. The construction and use of ontologies for geographic data sets makes it possible to check the result of the geographic data set integration process for *inconsistencies*.

The organization of the paper is as follows. A framework for ontology-based geographic data set integration is presented in Section 2. The framework of Section 2 is represented in a formal manner with Prolog-statements in Section 3 (Prolog is a logic programming language; for references see [10]). The framework is the most important part of the paper, and to our best kwoledge, has not been presented before in literature. With a simple example the construction of domain and application ontology is illustrated in Section 4. There is a test on a practical example with real data in Section 5. Section 6 finishes with a discussion of the results and our conclusions.

We want to emphasize that this paper reports the exploration of ideas. While the applied geographic data sets are real we are not addressing the efficiency of the method nor its scalability. First we want to understand the principles of ontology-based integration.

Update propagation has many *temporal aspects*. However in this paper we concentrate on the linking aspect between different data sets. The notion of *synchronizing data sets* by using their temporal attributes is crucial for geographic data set integration. That issue together with update propagation is covered in earlier work ([3], [11]).

2   A Conceptual Framework for Ontology-Based Geographic Data Set Integration

Sharing and reusing data is a *communication* problem. Any successful communication requires a language which builds on a core of shared concepts [12]. An *ontology* is such a collection of shared concepts. Ontologies can be constructed for the conceptual dimensions of geographic objects, e.g. for geometry, topology, symbology of representations, and thematic contents [13]. In our research we emphasize the thematic contents, in particular in the field of *topographic mapping*. A *domain ontology* for topographic mapping will be introduced. A domain ontology must be supplemented with an *application ontology* for every geographic data set at hand. *Abstraction rules* define the relationships between the concepts of the domain ontology and the concepts of the application ontologies.

2.1   Ontologies

An ontology is a collection of shared concepts. More formally, the definition of an ontology in this research is "a structured, limitative collection of unambiguously defined concepts" [14]. This definition contains four elements:

1. An ontology is a collection of *concepts*.
2. The concepts are to be *unambiguously* defined.
3. The collection is *limitative*. Concepts not in the ontology cannot be used.
4. The collection has *structure*. Structure means that the ontology contains relationships between the concepts.

2.2   Domain Ontologies

An ontology for a certain discipline is called a *domain ontology*. This research uses data sets from the discipline of topographic mapping. In a domain ontology for such a discipline definitions of topographic objects, like *roads, railways,* and *buildings,* are given. As an example, the concept "road" is defined as "a leveled part for traffic on land". In The Netherlands, a domain ontology for the discipline of topographic mapping is under construction (the **Geo-Information Terrain Model: GTM**; for details see [15]).

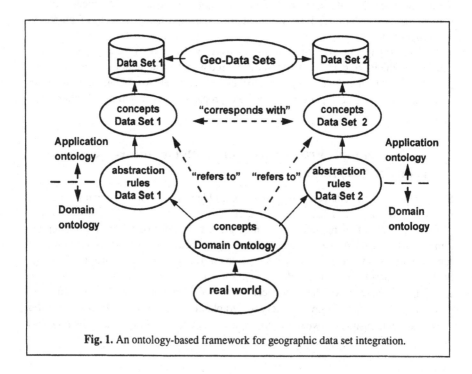

Fig. 1. An ontology-based framework for geographic data set integration.

2.3   Application Ontologies

A domain ontology (for topographic mapping, in our case) is the *first level* for the design of an ontology-based geographic data set integration framework. The *second level* concerns the actual geographic data sets. In these geographic data sets, names for mapped or surveyed concepts, such as "road" or "building" are used, but their precise meaning is not always the same as similar names for concepts in the domain ontology! That's why we must make a distinction between concepts in the domain ontology and concepts used in the data sets, by constructing an *application ontology* for every data set involved in the integration process.

2.4   Abstraction Rules

Abstraction rules describe the transformation process from topographic objects (Real World objects) to geographic data set objects. So, abstraction rules define *what* topographic objects and *how* topographic objects are represented. Abstraction rules include:

- inclusion rules: what objects are selected ("capture criteria" in [16])
- representation rules: how objects are represented
- simplification rules: how objects are simplified
- aggregation rules: how objects are merged.

2.5   A Definition of Corresponding Object Instances

The abstraction rules define the relationships between the concepts in the application ontology and the concepts in the domain ontology. Concepts from *different* application ontologies are *semantically similar* if they refer to the *same* concepts (or *related*) concepts in the domain ontology (Fig. 1). *Corresponding object instances* can now defined as semantically similar and, in addition, *share the same location* (e.g. their geometry's do overlap, or are near to each other). In the next section three types of semantic similarity will be introduced.

3   A Formal Expression of Ontologies in Prolog

3.1   Ontologies as Taxonomies

Ontologies in this research are structured like *taxonomies*. A taxonomy is like a tree with branches and leaves. It is a model for a hierarchy of classes, with concepts such as *sub*-classes and *super*-classes.

The basic taxonomy-structure is expressed and asserted as *Prolog facts* with the predicate name *taxon*:

```
taxon[SubClass, Class]
```

For example, *grassland* as a sub-class from terrain class TRN in the GTM domain ontology is expressed as:

```
taxon[grassland, trn]
```

A sub-class relationship *subClass* is recursively defined using the taxon-predicate in the following two *Prolog rules*:

```
subClass[X, X].
subClass[X, Z]:- (taxon[X, Y] && subClass[Y, Z]).¹
```

The first rule stops the recursion from the second rule that allows for sub-classes at any depth.

3.2   Semantic Relationships between Domain Ontology and Application Ontology

Relationships between the classes of the domain ontology and the classes of the application ontologies define the *semantics* of our universe of discourse. *Two relationships*, expressed as *Prolog clauses*, exist between concepts from domain ontology and application ontology:

- the *first* relationship concerns *equivalent* classes between domain ontology and application ontology:

```
refersToEquivalentClass[DomainClass, ApplClass].
```

- the *second* relationship relates (two or more) classes from the domain ontology that make up an aggregated (or composed) class in an application ontology:

```
refersToAggregateClass[DomainClass, ApplClass].
```

Note that these two relationships mean that the domain ontology should be rich enough to capture all the concepts of the application ontologies.

3.3   Semantic Relationships between Object Classes from Different Geographic Data Sets

With these two semantic relationships from the previous subsection *semantic relationships between object classes from different geographic data sets* are defined (after an idea in [19]):

1. Object classes from different application ontologies are *semantically equivalent* if they are equivalent with the *same class* in the domain ontology:

```
semanticEquivalentClass[ApplClass1, ApplClass2]:-
(refersToEquivalentClass[DomainClass, ApplClass1]
&&
 refersToEquivalentClass[DomainClass, ApplClass2]).
```

2. Object classes from different application ontologies are *semantically related* if they are equivalent with classes in the domain ontology, that are *sub-classes* or *super-classes* from each other:

```
semanticRelatedClass[ApplClass1, ApplClass2]:-
(refersToEquivalentClass[DomainClass1, ApplClass1]
```

---

¹ Prolog facts and rules are expressed in a syntax fashion compatible with a Prolog implementation in *Mathematica*® [17] made by R. E. Maeder [18].

```
&&
 refersToEquivalentClass[DomainClass2, ApplClass2])
&&
(subClass[DomainClass1, DomainClass2] ||
 subClass[DomainClass2, DomainClass1]).
```

which reads like: *semanticRelatedClass ← P1 & P2 & (P3 || P4)* where *Pi* stands for a precondition.

3. Object classes A and B from different application ontologies are *semantically relevant* if A is equivalent with a class in the domain ontology, that refers to an *aggregated class* in B, or vice versa:

```
semanticRelevantClass[ApplClass1, ApplClass2]:-
(refersToEquivalentClass[DomainClass, ApplClass1] ||
 refersToEquivalentClass[DomainClass, ApplClass2])
&&
(refersToAggregateClass[DomainClass, ApplClass2] ||
 refersToAggregateClass[DomainClass, ApplClass1]).
```

which reads like: *semanticRelevantClass ← (P1 || P2) & (P3 || P4)* where *Pi* stands for a precondition (this basic expression for *semanticRelevantClass* was extended to allow for cases where domain classes are sub-classes from each other).

In terms of *cartographic generalization* there is an analogy between semantic relatedness and *class driven* object generalization, or, semantic relevantness and *geometry driven* object generalization [20].

4   Demonstrating and Illustrating the Concepts of Ontology-Based Geographic Data Set Integration

The geographic data sets involved in this research are introduced in this section. With a simple example, highly schematic, and error free ("perfect data", with respect to semantics and geometric accuracy), the construction of domain and application ontology is illustrated.

4.1   Two Topographic Data Sets of The Netherlands

In this research, the geographic data set integration process is investigated between two different topographic data sets:

1. The first data set is a large-scale topographic data set (presentation scale 1 : 1,000), known as *GBKN*. It is usually produced by photogrammetric *stereo plotting* with field completion. It has an nation wide coverage of buildings, roads and waterways. The accuracy of the GBKN is stated in terms of *relative precision*: in built-up areas the relative precision between two well defined points should be better than $20\sqrt{2}cm$, and in rural areas better than $40\sqrt{2}cm$ [21]. The GBKN is updated continuously [11].

2. The second data set is a mid-scale topographic data set (presentation scale 1 : 10,000), known as *TOP10vector*. It is usually produced by photogrammetric *mono plotting* with field completion. It has a nation wide coverage of buildings,

roads, waterways and terrain objects. The accuracy of TOP10vector is stated in terms of *absolute precision* in relation to the *national reference system*: the location of points should be better then *two meter*. TOP10vector is updated every four years [22].

The two data sets are produced by different organizations and are an accurate representation of the terrain. There is no displacement of representations for cartographic reasons. However, in the mid-scale map, some object representations (like buildings) are simplified and aggregated.

4.2   A Simple, Highly Schematic, and Error Free Example

After this introduction of the two geographic data sets involved a simple example will be given. The simple example refers to a Real World situation explained in the following subsection.

4.2.1   The Real World

The Real World of our example, depicted in Fig. 2, consists of:

- several buildings, labeled with class label BLD. *Main building* and *annex* are subclasses from BLD
- some land parcels with different land use, labeled with TRN. *Grass land* and *arable land* are sub-classes from TRN
- a riding track between 4 and 7 meters wide, labeled with *conngt4m*, which is a subclass from *riding tracks*, with on each side
- a verge. One verge is less or equal *6m* wide (labeled with *vergele6m*); the other verge is more then *6m* wide (*vergegt6m*)
- there are also ditches, labeled with WTR. *Road ditch* is sub-class from WTR.

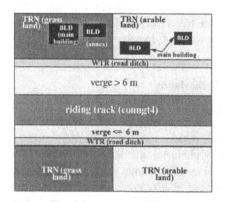
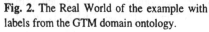
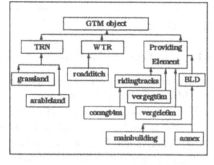

Fig. 2. The Real World of the example with labels from the GTM domain ontology.

Fig. 3. The GTM domain ontology classification.

Of course there is more present in the Real World but all the objects that are not relevant for topographic mapping are filtered out. It is as if we wear a pair of spectacles with glasses where only objects of the domain ontology are passed through.

4.2.2   The Domain Ontology of the Real World

The domain ontology of the example is based on the GTM domain ontology in [15] and depicted in a class hierarchy in Fig. 3. Riding tracks, verges and buildings are all sub-classes from *Providing Element*, which is a super-class of geographic objects, describing the terrain in more detail.

Using the classification above a taxonomy is set up with facts like:

```
taxon[grassland, trn].
taxon[arableland, trn].
taxon[trn, gtmobject].
taxon[roadditch, wtr].
taxon[wtr, gtmobject].
taxon[conngt4m, ridingtracks].
taxon[ridingtracks, providingelement].
taxon[vergele6m, providingelement].
taxon[vergegt6m, providingelement].
taxon[mainbuilding, bld].
taxon[annex, bld].
taxon[bld, providingelement].
taxon[providingelement, gtmobject].
```

4.2.3   Topographic Data Set 1: an Application Ontology of the GBKN

For the GBKN application ontology of the example seven object classes are relevant:
- buildings with a (street) address (labeled *hoofdgebouw*)
- buildings without an address (*bijgebouw*)
- verges ≤ 6 meters wide (*bermsm6m*)
- verges > 6 meters wide (*bermbr6m*)
- road ditches (*bermsloot*)
- (paved or unpaved) road surfaces (*rijbaan*)
- terrain, or anything that can not be classified according the classes mentioned before (*terrein*).

We use Dutch labels for identification of the concepts. After all, the language of these labels is not essential for understanding the concepts. The concepts get their meaning in their actual relationship with the domain ontology! The GBKN abstraction rules state that six GBKN application ontology object classes are equivalent with domain ontology object classes:

```
refersToEquivalentClass[vergele6m, bermsm6m].
refersToEquivalentClass[vergegt6m, bermbr6m].
refersToEquivalentClass[ridingtracks, rijbaan].
refersToEquivalentClass[roadditch, bermsloot].
refersToEquivalentClass[mainbuilding, hoofdgebouw].
```

```
refersToEquivalentClass[annex, bijgebouw].
```

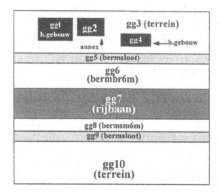 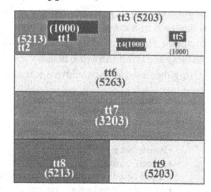

Fig. 4. The GBKN as an abstraction from the Real World (Fig. 2). gg1, gg2, ..., gg10 are object identifiers (oid's).

Fig. 5. The TOP10vector as an abstraction from the Real World (Fig. 2). tt1, tt2, ..., tt10 are object identifiers (oid's).

GBKN application ontology object class *terrein* is aggregated from two domain ontology classes *grassland* and *arableland*:

```
refersToAggregateClass[grassland, terrein].
refersToAggregateClass[arableland, terrein].
```

If the GBKN abstraction rules are applied to the Real World situation, then a map like Fig. 4 is produced. In Fig. 4 not all objects of the Real World in Fig. 2 are represented. The GBKN abstraction rules state that a *building object* will be represented in the GBKN if the building in the Real World:

- has an address, or
- is situated in urban area, and is accessible, or
- is situated in rural area, with an area > $20m^2$.

If the rightmost building in Fig. 2 is situated in rural area, with an area < $20m^2$, then it is not represented in Fig. 4.

Also, there is no distinction in different land use in the GBKN.

4.2.4   Topographic Data Set 2: an Application Ontology for TOP10vector

For the TOP10vector application ontology of the example five object classes are relevant:

- buildings (labeled *1000*)
- roads with a paved surface 4 to 7 meters wide (*3203*)
- arable land (*5203*)
- grass land (*5213*)
- land not classified in any other way (*5263*).

Here the labels are numbers (codes) that represent TOP10vector application ontology concepts. Also these concepts get their meaning in their actual relationship with the domain ontology concepts! The TOP10vector abstraction rules state that three TOP10vector application ontology object classes are equivalent with domain ontology object classes:

```
refersToEquivalentClass[grassland, 5213].
refersToEquivalentClass[arableland, 5203].
refersToEquivalentClass[bld, 1000].
```

TOP10vector application ontology object class *3203* is aggregated from domain ontology classes *vergele6m* and *conngt4m*:

```
refersToAggregateClass[vergele6m, 3203].
refersToAggregateClass[conngt4m, 3203].
```

Also, TOP10vector application ontology object class *5263* is aggregated from domain ontology object class *vergegt6m* (and other classes, not present in this example):

```
refersToAggregateClass[vergegt6m, 5263].
```

If the TOP10vector abstraction rules are applied to the Real World situation in Fig. 2 then a map like Fig. 5 is produced.

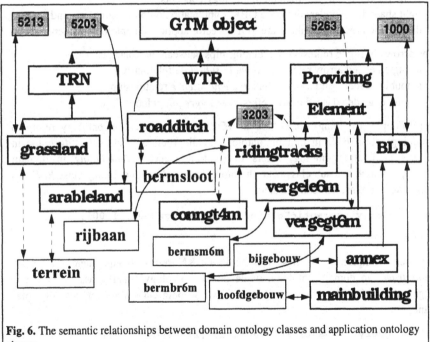

Fig. 6. The semantic relationships between domain ontology classes and application ontology classes.

Here also there is no 1-to-1 correspondence between building objects of the Real World and building objects represented in TOP10vector. The TOP10vector abstraction rules state that a building object is represented in TOP10vector if the building in the Real World:

- is situated in urban area, accessible, with area $> 9m^2$, or

- is situated in urban area, not accessible, with area > $50m^2$, or
- is situated in rural area, with area > $9m^2$.

If the last condition applies to the rightmost building in the Real World in Fig. 2 then it is represented in TOP10vector in Fig 5. Also, if *two (or more) buildings* in the terrain are *less than 2 meters* apart they are aggregated, as can be seen in Fig. 5. Furthermore, *ditches less than 6 meters wide* are represented as line objects in TOP10vector. So they do not appear in the partition of the TOP10vector map in Fig. 5. Note that *riding track between 4 and 7 meters wide* and *verge less than 6 meters wide* are aggregated to one road object (class *3203*).

4.2.5   Querying the Semantic Relationships

With the relationships defined and expressed between the classes of domain ontology and application ontologies we can ask questions about the semantic relationships between the object classes of the two application ontologies. See Fig. 6.

In Fig. 6 concepts are symbolized by:
- white rectangles: these are domain ontology concepts
- light shaded rectangles: these are GBKN application ontology concepts, and
- dark shaded rectangles: these are TOP10vector application ontology concepts.

The arrows in Fig. 6 represent the relationships between the concepts:
- a single headed arrow refers to a *domain sub-class* relationship
- a double headed solid arrow refers to a *equivalence* relationship
- a double headed dashed arrow refers to an *aggregate* relationship.

For example, (building) class *1000* in TOP10vector application ontology refers to (building) class *BLD* in domain ontology, while (building) class *hoofdgebouw* in GBKN application ontology refers to (building) class *mainbuilding* in domain ontology, which is a sub-class from the more general domain ontology class *BLD*. So both classes are semantically related:

In[ ]:=[2] `Query[ semanticRelatedClass[hoofdgebouw, 1000]]`

Out[ ]= `Yes`

Another example: (road) class *rijbaan* in GBKN refers to equivalent road class *ridingtracks* in domain ontology, while domain ontology (road) class *conngt4m* is aggregated in TOP10vector (road) class *3203*. So both classes are semantically relevant:

In[ ]:= `Query[ semanticRelevantClass[rijbaan, 3203]]`

Out[ ]:= `Yes`

---

[2] *In[ ]:=* and *Out[ ]=* are traditional *Mathematica* prompts.

4.2.6   Finding Corresponding Object Instances

The next task is how to find *corresponding object instances*, that means objects from semantically similar object classes from the different data sets involved, which in addition, share the same location (according to the definition in Section 2).

In order to determine if object instances share the same location we *overlay* both data sets (GBKN and TOP10vector) from our fictitious example, using their common spatial reference system, creating a new partition of faces. See Fig. 7.

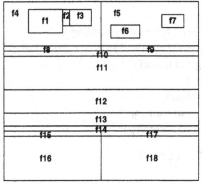

Every face refers to exactly one GBKN object instance and exactly one TOP10-vector object instance (and every object instance refers to exactly one object class).

The procedure for finding corresponding object instances takes as input the list of faces of this combination of GBKN data set and TOP10vector data set (as in Fig. 7) and proceeds with querying the semantic similarity of the object classes from every face, according to the previous subsection, which results in Table 1.

Fig. 7. The combination of GBKN (Fig. 4) and TOP10vector (Fig. 5).

Face-id	GBKN-oid	GBKN-class	TOP-oid	TOP-class	Semantic similarity
f1	gg1	hoofdgebouw	tt1	1000	related
f2	gg3	terrein	tt1	1000	incompatible
f3	gg2	bijgebouw	tt1	1000	related
f4	gg3	terrein	tt2	5213	relevant
f5	gg3	terrein	tt3	5203	relevant
f6	gg4	hoofdgebouw	tt4	1000	related
f7	gg3	terrein	tt5	1000	incompatible
f8	gg5	bermsloot	tt2	5213	incompatible
f9	gg5	bermsloot	tt3	5203	incompatible
f10	gg5	bermsloot	tt6	5263	incompatible
f11	gg6	bermbr6m	tt6	5263	relevant
f12	gg7	rijbaan	tt7	3203	relevant
f13	gg8	bermsm6m	tt7	3203	relevant
f14	gg9	bermsloot	tt7	3203	incompatible
f15	gg9	bermsloot	tt8	5213	incompatible
f16	gg10	terrein	tt8	5213	relevant
f17	gg9	bermsloot	tt9	5203	incompatible
f18	gg10	terrein	tt9	5203	relevant

Table 1. The faces from the example with the semantic similarity of their classes.

Semantically similar faces (equivalent, related, or relevant) are stored in a list; semantically incompatible faces in another. Faces in the first list are re-grouped using the object-id's from both GBKN object instances and TOP10vector object instances. The same happens to the second list after discarding object-id's that appear in the first list. What follows are two lists:

1. a list of corresponding object instances:

```
{
{{gg1, gg2}, {tt1}}, {{gg10}, {tt8, tt9}},
{{gg3}, {tt2, tt3}}, {{gg4}, {tt4}},
{{gg6}, {tt6}}, {{gg7, gg8}, {tt7}}
}
```

In this list:

- gg1 and gg2 are the buildings that is also represented by building tt1
- terrain object gg10 is similar to the aggregated terrain objects tt8 and tt9
- terrain object gg3 is similar to the aggregated terrain objects tt2 and tt3
- gg4 and tt4 represent the same building
- gg6 and tt6 represent the same terrain object
- riding track gg7 and verge gg8 are similar to road object tt7

2. a list of object instances in both maps that have no correspondences at all:

```
{
{{gg5}, {}}, {{gg9}, {}}, {{}, {tt5}}
}
```

In this list:

- road ditches gg5 and gg9 are not represented in TOP10vector
- building tt5 has no counter object in GBKN.

4.2.7   Consistency Checking

Now that the relationships between semantically similar object instances are established, it is possible (and necessary) to check correspondences for *consistency*. Consistency, in this context, means: *in accordance with the abstraction rules of both data sets*. For example, capture criteria for buildings (as part of the abstraction rules) were formulated in subsections 4.2.3 and 4.2.4, but these capture criteria do not appear as *restrictions* (or *constraints*) in the *refersToEquivalentClass* or *refersToAggregateClass* relationships. Take, for example, the corresponding building object instances:

$$\{\{gg4\}, \{tt4\}\}$$

If GBKN object instance gg4 has as attributes:

- address: True
- situated in: rural area
- accessible: True
- area category: $20m^2 - 50m^2$

and TOP10vector object instance tt4 has as attributes:

- situated in: rural area
- accessible: True
- area category: $20m^2 - 50m^2$

then according to the abstraction rules for buildings there must be a representation in *both* GBKN and TOP10vector. So we may conclude that

{{gg4}, {tt4}}

is a 1-to-1 correspondence that is semantically related *and* consistent with the abstraction rules. In a similar way other correspondences can be checked (using procedures for checking areas or distances).

5   A Practical Test

In this section we test our geographic data set integration framework in the test area Zevenaar.

5.1   The Test Area Zevenaar

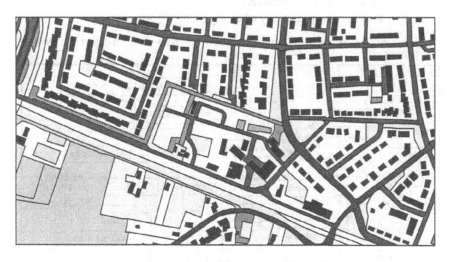

Fig. 8. The TOP10vector map of the test area Zevenaar.

The test area Zevenaar is a (mainly) built-up area (See Fig. 8). Its size is 0.3 km^2. The combination of GBKN and TOP10vector data sets is a partition of 1661 faces, with:

- 690 GBKN object instances, from nine object classes:
  - road ditches (labeled *bermsloot*: 6 instances)
  - large flowerbeds (*bloemenperk1*: 46 instances)
  - small flowerbeds (*bloemenperk2*: 24 instances)
  - buildings (*gebouw*: 450 instances)
  - parking strips (*parkeerstrook*: 27 instances)
  - road surfaces (*rijbaan*: 34 instances)
  - railways (*spoorbaan*: 1 instance)
  - side walks (*trottoir*: 71 instances)

  – terrain's, or anything that can not be classified according the classes
    mentioned before (*terrein*: 31 instances).
- 281 TOP10vector object instances, from twelve object classes:
  – buildings (labeled *1000*: 167 instances)
  – barns (*1050*: 2 instances)
  – green houses (*1073*: 3 instances)
  – roads with a paved surface less than 4 meters wide (*3103*: 4 instances)
  – roads with a paved surface 4 to 7 meters wide (*3203*: 1 instance)
  – roads with a paved surface more than 7 meters wide (*3303*: 1 instance)
  – streets (*3533*: 27 instances)
  – cycle tracks (*3603*: 3 instances)
  – leaf wood land (*5023*: 8 instances)
  – arable land (*5203*: 3 instances)
  – grass land (*5213*: 22 instances)
  – land not classified in any other way (*5263*: 40 instances).

The relationships between the object classes from both data sets, and the domain

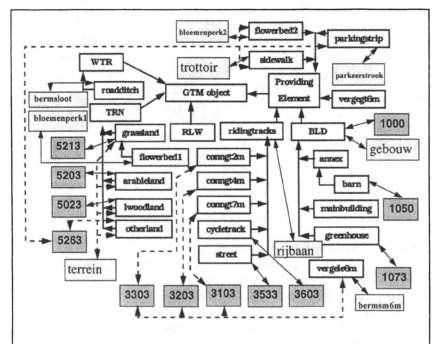

Fig. 9. The relationships between the object classes from GBKN and TOP10vector data sets, and the domain ontology. See text for explanation.

ontology are represented in Fig. 9.
Again, the rectangles represent the concepts:
- White rectangles: these are domain ontology concepts

- Light shaded rectangles: these are GBKN application ontology concepts, and
- Dark shaded rectangles: these are TOP10vector application ontology concepts.

The "tangle of lines" are the relationships between the concepts:
- a single headed arrow refers to a *domain sub-class* relationship, e.g. the Prolog fact
    `taxon[parkingstrip, providingelement].`
    expresses that domain ontology object class *parkingstrip* is a sub-class from
    domain ontology object class *providing element.*
- a double headed solid arrow refers to a *equivalence* relationship, e.g. the Prolog
    fact
    `refersToEquivalentClass[parkingstrip, parkeerstrook].`
    expresses that GBKN application ontology object class *parkeerstrook* is equivalent
    with the domain ontology object class *parkingstrip.*
- a double headed dashed arrow refers to an *aggregate* relationship, e.g. the four
    Prolog facts

    ```
    refersToAggregateClass[parkingstrip, 5263].
    refersToAggregateClass[sidewalk, 5263].
    refersToAggregateClass[flowerbed2, 5263].
    refersToAggregateClass[otherland, 5263].
    ```

    expresses that TOP10vector application ontology object class *5263* is aggregated
    from (= composed of) domain ontology object classes *parkingstrip, sidewalk,
    flowerbed2* and *otherland.*

If we query the classes of every face of the GBKN/TOP10vector partition for its
semantic similarity, and apply the procedure for finding corresponding object instances then we get the following result:
- 204 correspondences, involving 483 GBKN instances, and 268 TOP10vector
  instances
- 207 GBKN instances and 13 TOP0vector instances that have no corresponding
  instance at all.

6   Discussion and Conclusion

In the previous section we did an experiment on ontology-based geographic data set
integration with practical data from the test area Zevenaar (Fig. 8). In the next Section
the result of this experiment will be evaluated.

6.1   Types of Errors

There are two main sources for errors:

1. The abstraction rules are not applied correctly, including classification errors, and
   up-to-date-ness
2. The different accuracy's of the geographic data sets involved.

The last error will influence the result, because the mechanism for relating corresponding object instances, relies on the assumption that semantically similar object
instances do, at least partly, overlap.

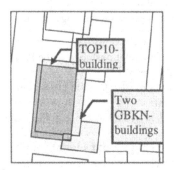

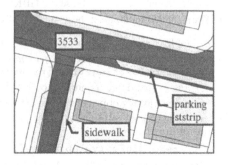

Fig. 9. A (wrong) correspondence between one TOP10vector building (gray) and two GBKN buildings (light gray).

Fig. 10. A *sidewalk* outside (street) *3533* (= correct) and a *parkingstrip* inside *3533* (= wrong).

In Fig. 9 is a (wrong) correspondence between one TOP10vector building instance and two GBKN building instances because there is also an overlap between the TOP10vector building and the small GBKN building. The overlapping face is not filtered out because it is just above some threshold. This example emphasizes the importance of checking all found correspondences for this kind of error before starting the consistency checking, as mentioned is Section 4.

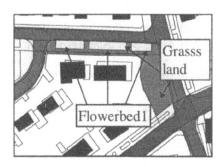

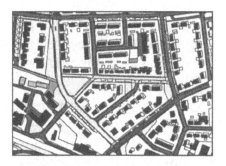

Fig. 11. Three GBKN flowerbed1 *(bloe-menperk1)* objects (gray) correspond correctly with a TOP10vector grass land *(5213)* object (darker gray), but differ greatly in extension.

Fig. 12. A *5-to-3* type correspondence of road objects (light color): five GBKN riding tracks *(rijbaan)* objects, with three TOP10vector road objects (one *3103*, two *3533* objects).

If we look at the 220 instances that have no corresponding object, then 12 (or 5.5%) of them should have a corresponding object. See Fig. 10, where GBKN class parking strip *(parkeerstrook)* is overlapped by TOP10vector road class *3533*, which is not in accordance with the TOP10vector abstraction rules (Fig. 9). The reason for this error maybe two-fold: the abstraction rules are not applied well for TOP10vector object class *3533* or it is due to a road reconstruction, that means up-to-date-ness. We repeat here that both data sets should have the same time stamp, that means should be synchronized.

Another source for errors is when after synchronization both maps represent scenes that match partly or not at all. See Fig. 11.

Here also some kind of error checking should signal these mismatches.

Finally, some of the correct correspondences are from a complex *n-to-m* type, that is not very useful in pinpointing updates. See Fig. 12. Here five GBKN road objects correspond to three TOP10vector road objects. A solution for, at least, road networks is to fragment them first to homologous parts, like road segments and road junctions, as explained in [23].

6.2 Conclusion

Ontology-based geographic data set integration is a formal, yet simple and efficient, approach. With only a small set of rules, relationships are defined between concepts from the domain ontology and concepts from the application ontologies. Introduction of the abstraction rules gives, in principle, the possibility of consistency checking of the corresponding object instances. Future research will concentrate on this issue.

References

1. H. T. Uitermark, "The integration of geographic databases. Realising geodata interoperability through the hypermap metaphor and a mediator architecture", presented at Second Joint European Conference & Exhibition on Geographical Information (JEC-GI'96), (M. Rumor, R. McMillan, and H. F. L. Ottens, eds.), Vol. I, pp. 92-95, Barcelona, Spain, IOS Press, March 27-29, 1996.
2. F. A. van Wijngaarden, J. D. van Putten, P. J. M. van Oosterom and H. T. Uitermark, "Map Integration. Update propagation in a multi-source environment", presented at 5th ACM Workshop on Advances in Geographic Information Systems ACM-GIS'97, (R. Laurini, ed.), pp. 71-76, Las Vegas, Nevada, USA, ACM, New York, November 13-14, 1997.
3. H. T. Uitermark, P. J. M. van Oosterom, N. J. I. Mars and M. Molenaar, "Propagating updates: finding corresponding objects in a multi-source environment", presented at 8th International Symposium on Spatial Data Handling (SDH98), (T. K. Poiker and N. Chrisman, eds.), pp. 580-591, Vancouver, Canada, International Geographical Union, July 11-15, 1998.
4. A. B. M. Vogels, Propagatie van GBKN-wegenmutaties naar de TOP10vector (in Dutch). Master Thesis, Geodesy Department, Technical University Delft, Delft, The Netherlands, 1999.
5. C.-J. Kim, Implementation of semantic translation for finding the corresponding geometric objects between topographic databases. Master Thesis, International Institute for Aerospace Survey and Earth Sciences (ITC), Enschede, The Netherlands, 1999.
6. S. Spaccapietra, C. Parent and Y. Dupont, "Model independent assertions for integration of heterogeneous schemas", VLDB Journal, Vol. 1, pp. 81-126, 1992.
7. T. Devogele, C. Parent and S. Spaccapietra, "On spatial database integration", Int. J. Geographical Information Science, Vol. 12, No. 4, pp. 335-352, 1998.
8. M. Sester, K.-H. Anders and V. Walter, "Linking objects of different spatial data sets by integration and aggregation", GeoInformatica, Vol. 2, No. 4, pp. 335-357, 1998.
9. P. E. van der Vet and N. J. I. Mars, "Bottom-up construction of ontologies", IEEE Transactions on knowledge and data engineering, Vol. 10, No. 4, pp. 513-526, 1998.

10. J. Malpas, PROLOG: a relational language and its applications. London: Prentice-Hall International, 465 pages, 1987.

11. P. J. M. van Oosterom, "Maintaining consistent topology including historical data in a large spatial database", presented at Auto-Carto 13, pp. 327-336, Seattle, Washington, USA, 1997.

12. W. Kuhn, Semantics of geographic information, Geoinfo-series, Vol.7. Vienna: Department of Geoinformation, Technical University pages, 1996.

13. F. Hernández Rodríguez, G. Bravo Aranda and A. Martín Navarro, "An ontology-based approach to spatial information modelling", presented at 7th International symposium on Spatial Data Handling (SDH'96), (M. J. Kraak and M. Molenaar, eds.), Vol. II, pp. 12B.17-12B.29, Delft, The Netherlands, International Geographical Union, August 12-16, 1996.

14. N. J. I. Mars, "What is an ontology?", in The impact of ontologies on reuse, interoperability, and distributed processing, (A. Goodall, ed.), pp. 9-19, Uxbridge, Middlesex, U.K.: Unicom, 1995.

15. Ravi, "Geo-information terrain model. A Dutch standard for: Terms, definitions and general rules for the classification and coding of objects related to the earth's surface (NEN3610)", Ravi Netherlands Council for Geographic Information, Amersfoort, The Netherlands, 1995.

16. Open GIS Consortium Inc., "The OpenGIS Abstract Specification Model", Open GIS Consortium, Wayland, Massachusetts, USA, 1998.

17. S. Wolfram, Mathematica. A system for doing mathematics by computer, 2nd ed. Reading, Massachusetts, USA: Addison-Wesley, 961 pages, 1991.

18. R. E. Maeder, "Logic Programming I: The interpreter", The Mathematica Journal, Vol. 4, No. 1, pp. 53-63, 1994.

19. A. Sheth and V. Kashyap, "So far (schematically) yet so near (semantically)", presented at IFIP, (D. K. Hsiao, E. J. Neuhold, and R. Sacks-Davis, eds.), pp. 283-312, Elsevier Science Publishers B.V. (North-Holland), 1993.

20. M. Molenaar, An introduction to the theory of spatial object modelling for GIS. London: Taylor and Francis, 246 pages, 1998.

21. M. A. Salzmann, "On the modeling of geometric quality for large-scale mapping products", Surveying and land information systems, Vol. 56, No. 3, pp. 149-155, 1996.

22. P. C. M. van Asperen, "Digital updates at the Dutch Topographic Service", presented at XVIII ISPRS-Congress, Vienna, Austria, July 9-19, 1996.

23. H. T. Uitermark, A. B. M. Vogels and P. J. M. van Oosterom, "Semantic and geometric aspects of integrating road networks", presented at Second International Conference on Interoperating Geographic Information Systems INTEROP'99, (A. Vckovski, K. E. Brassel, and H.-J. Schek, eds.), pp. 177-188, Zürich, Switzerland, Lecture Notes in Computer Science, Vol. 1580, Springer, March 10-12, 1999.

The Italian Cadastral Information System: a Real-Life Spatio-Temporal DBMS

(Extended Abstract)

Franco Arcieri[1], Carmine Cammino[2], Enrico Nardelli[3,4],
Maurizio Talamo[3,5], and Antonino Venza[2]

[1] Consultant to AIPA for the
SICC ("Sistema di Interscambio Catasto Comuni") project
[2] SOGEI - "Societa' Generale di Informatica" SpA, Roma, Italia
[3] "Coordinamento dei Progetti Intersettoriali" of AIPA
"Autorità per l'Informatica nella Pubblica Amministrazione", Roma, Italia [§]
[4] Univ. of L'Aquila, L'Aquila, Italia, nardelli@univaq.it
[5] Univ. of Roma "La Sapienza", Roma, Italia, talamo@dis.uniroma1.it

Abstract. In this paper we describe the technical and organizational solution that has been designed and implemented in Italy to deal with cadastral data management. The system, named "Sistema di Interscambio Catasto-Comuni" (SICC), allows to exchange cadastral data among the principal entities interested in Italy to the treatment of cadastral information, that are Ministry of Finance, Municipalities, Notaries, and Certified Land Surveyors. The system is accessible nation-wide through a WEB-based interface since September 1998 and the effectiveness of its use is demonstrated by the sharp increase in the number of requests managed during the first months: in January 1999 it has been used by more than 15.000 end-users.

Keywords: cadastral data, distributed systems, interoperability.

1 Introduction

Cadastral data are an important example of spatio-temporal data. They have three very peculiar characteristics.

Firstly, from the temporal point of view they have a particular nature, since their changes with time are always of punctual type. Changes to cadastral data in fact never happen in a continuous way, like it usually happens to navigation data for mobile objects (e.g. airplanes, cars, etc.) that are continuously monitored. Hence variation of cadastral spatial values with time are always of discrete nature.

Secondly, cadastral data have an official role in supporting certification of location, shape, and ownership of properties. On these basis, many countries

---

[§] M.Talamo is the CEO of the Initiative for the Development of an IT Infrastructure for Inter-Organization Cooperation (namely, "Coordinamento dei Progetti Intersettoriali") of AIPA - "Autorità per l'Informatica nella Pubblica Amministrazione".

determine taxation related to land properties and real estates. Hence it is clear that the utmost care should be put into the management of changes to them. Also, given this official role, all historical changes to cadastral data have to be maintained with the same level of care and are usually queried. Since discussions on legal and economic issues related to the use and/or ownership of land may go on for many years, queries about the past are as important as queries regarding current situation.

Finally, cadastral data are usually managed by many offices, that are geographically distributed and directly deals with data regarding the part of land assigned to them, even if in every country there is some form of centralized coordination and control.

In recent years, with the spread of low cost technologies for cadastral data acquisition, storing and processing, cadastral data are also being more and more used for general planning purpose related to land. The approach is to use cadastral data as a basic geographic information layer providing geo-referencing and descriptive data of objects existing over the land. On this layer more sophisticated and advanced land information systems are then built for the general planning and management needs of institutional decision makers.

In this paper we describe the technical and organizational solution that has been designed and implemented in Italy to deal with cadastral data management.

While working on this issue, we defined a new architectural approach, namely the **Access Keys Warehouse** approach, described more extensively elsewhere [10, 11]. This approach proposes a novel role for the concept of Data Warehouse, namely suggests that a (new kind of) warehouse can be set up to guide and control accesses to the underlying databases. This allows to solve coherence problems always rising up in such a framework with good overall performances and to provide a methodological guidance for the system development.

The SICC system has been implemented using the AKW approach and is being used nation-wide since September 1998. It currently deals each month with more than 100.000 end-user queries.

The structure of the paper is the following. In Section 2 we describe the italian situation in the sector of cadastral data, while we discuss official regulations regarding them in Section 3. The main technical problems are discussed in Section 4, while an overview of the Access Keys Warehouse approach is given in Section 5. Subsequently, Section 6 describes the organization of cadastral data within the system, while Section 7 discusses organizational aspects. Finally, Section 8 briefly discusses the current status of the system and shows examples of interactions with it, while Section 9 concludes the paper.

2   Cadastral Data in Italy

2.1   The Cadaster

The Cadaster, in the italian situation, has the role of being the public registry of real estates and land properties and it was established for fiscal purposes. As such, it has always been managed at the central administration level, namely by the italian Ministry of Finance. The access key in the Cadaster to data about real estates and land properties is expressed in terms of the unique code of municipality where they are located and of four cadastral codes referring to cadastral maps of increasing level of detail.

From a physical point of view, Cadaster data are managed by the Land Department of the Ministry of Finance through its Land Offices ("Uffici del Territorio") that are present at the level of the about 100 Provinces (one Office for each Province), which are a subdivision of the main administrative partition of Italy in Regions and an aggregation of Municipalities.

The Ministry of Finance, as required by the law, uses Cadaster data to keep record of and to certify location and planimetry of properties. Note that, according to italian law, taxes on real estates and land properties have to be based on their cadastral value ("rendita catastale"), that is strictly depending on location and planimetry of properties.

Furthermore, through its Estate Public Registry Offices ("Conservatorie Immobiliari"), the Land Department of the Ministry of Finance also keeps record of and certify ownership rights and mortgage rights relative to properties. These Offices have a slightly different, but comparable, distribution from the Land Offices' one. There about 120 Estate Public Registry Offices located according to the competence area of Legal Courts ("Tribunali"), approximately corresponding to a Province area but not exactly the same. This is mainly due to historical reasons and to the role played by such Offices in certifying property.

There are three principal kinds of spatio-temporal databases for the Cadaster:

- *geometric* data base ("Catasto Geometrico"), giving the geometric and spatial reference for all kinds of land parcels; it has about 300.000 maps (with scales 1:1000 or 1:2000 or 1:4000), of which approximately one third are in an electronic form, and about 130.000 trigonometric reference points, of which approximately 30% are in an electronic form;
- *land parcel* data base ("Catasto Terreni"): it records about 45 millions of distinct owners and about 90 millions of items of land parcels; records in this data base are directly correlated to records in the geometric data base.
- *real estates* data base ("Catasto Fabbricati"): it records about 40 millions of owners and about 47 millions of items of real estate; sometime the record of a real estate has a direct correlation to a current land parcel in the geometric data base and sometime only the reference to the original land parcel is found.
  In the latter case the geo-referencing of the real estate has to be obtained indirectly by navigating through the history of modifications to the original land parcel: more precisely, the history is found both in the geometric database (for the geo-referenced part) and in the land parcel database (for the descriptive part).

The latter two spatio-temporal databases, collectively known as *income* ("censuari") databases, have moreover a subdivision in *current* database and *suspended* database. The current database describes the current and past situation. The suspended database keeps record of changes that have not yet been executed to the current database, because some piece of information is missing or wrongly correlated to spatio-temporal data already stored in the current databases. The size of suspended databases, in percentage over the corresponding current database, is around 10% for the real estate data base and around 15% for the land parcel data base.

Note also that Cadaster databases are not managed at a single central location but at the more than 100 Land Offices of the Ministry of the Finance. This means that there is not a single centralized system, but more than 100 systems, geographically distributed over the whole italian territory.

Also databases storing information managed by the Estate Public Registry Offices are geographically distributed. These are temporal databases, since for legal reasons have to keep track of past owners, containing only non-spatial data. Reference to the spatial location of real estates and land properties, and hence to spatio-temporal databases for the Cadaster is made through a unique cadastral identification code, made up by Municipality code, map sheet number, parcel number and flat number.

The central offices of Land Department, in Rome, have then a role of defining technical and organizational rules for the management and the evolution of Cadaster and Estate Public Registry databases and of coordinating their implementation. From an operational point of view, they have moreover the possibility of cross-querying various databases and correlating them both for coherence enforcing objectives and for institutional purposes (e.g., checking tax declarations).

Typical queries on Cadaster databases are:

- *cadastral certification* query ("Visura Catastale"), requiring a certificate about the location and the cadastral value of a real estate/ land parcel; please note that such a certificate is needed by notaries in all sale acts and buyers pay a fee to obtain it from the Cadaster;
- *planimetry certification* query, requiring a certificate about planimetry of a real estate; such a certificate is often required during sale transactions to check if the current situation of the real estate is coherent with respect to the situation recorded in the cadastral databases;
- *update* query, submitting a request to change, for a given real estate/ land parcel, some piece of information of geometric nature or of descriptive nature.

Every year in Italy there are about 1.5 million certification queries and in on of the largest provinces there are about 100.000 yearly requests.

A typical query on Estate Public Registry databases is:

- *property certification* query ("Ispezione Ipotecaria"), requiring a certificate about the current and/or past owner(s) of a real estate/ land parcel; please note that also such a certificate is needed by notaries in all sale acts and buyers pay a fee to obtain it from the Estate Public Registry Office;

Remember that, given the existence of changes not yet executed on the current databases, suspended databases have also in many cases to be queried. This happens by means of non-standard queries, defined an a case-by-case basis by highly skilled Cadaster database technicians ("Visuristi") of the Land Department.

Also consider that, given that a direct correlation between a real estate and its current land parcel is many times missing, such a correlation has to be established each time this piece of information is needed. This is done as well by the "Visuristi" of the Land Department by means of non-standard spatio-temporal queries.

The number of yearly geometric updates to cadastral databases is about 250.000. These updates always triggers further spatio-temporal updates, since a geometric change affects one or more of the following aspects of a real estate or land property, and past values have to be maintained on-line for future queries:

- property rights and mortgage rights,
- fiscal nature,
- destination and allowable usage.

2.2 Municipalities

A Municipality uses cadastral data mainly for planning and managing land use. For this purpose it refers to cadastral information in terms of toponymy attributes of properties. Hence access key for Municipalities is street name, plus possibly house number on the street and flat number.

Municipalities therefore have their own spatio-temporal databases about real estates and land properties. These are used, as required by the law, to support and manage actions in the following main areas:

- *Toponymy*, giving names to public circulation areas and numbers to accesses from public circulation areas to the inner spaces of buildings and private areas;
- *Fiscal*, defining and collecting taxes for the permanent use of a public area and for the waste collection service;
- *Public Works*, dealing with all maintenance works and management of public buildings and monuments, with all private actions affecting the public land, with the management of public green and public lighting, and with the uses of drinkable water;
- *Land Management*, for environmental planning and control actions, for planning and management of the development of urban areas, for all major building actions affecting private buildings and private areas.

Size of spatio-temporal cadastral databases managed by Municipalities is largely variable, considering that about 6.000 of the 8.102 italian municipalities have less then 5.000 citizens, but 8 of the 20 Region chief towns have more than one million inhabitants.

2.3 Notaries and Certified Land Surveyors

Notaries have the responsibility of ensuring in all sale transactions relative to land parcel/ real estate the correct identification of items that are object of the transaction and of the relative property/ mortgage rights so that the transaction itself and the consequent obligations have full validity.

They use Cadaster and Estate Public Registry databases both in the preliminary phases, when the buyer is investigating the current status of cadastral objects, and in the final one, when the transaction actually happens and required certificates have to be attached to official acts.

Certified Land Surveyors have the responsibility of producing all technical documentation of geodetic or geometric nature required in transactions relative to partitioning or use change of land parcel/ real estate. They also are in charge of preparing the above kind of documents for Land Use Plans defined by a Municipality (for public terrains) or by a private. Finally, they are clearly involved in all local check actions on the actual situation of a land parcel/ real estate conducted by Municipality and local Land Offices to re-establish a correspondence between cadastral databases and reality.

2.4 Interactions

It is hence clear that there is a continuous exchange flow of cadastral data among Municipalities, Ministry of Finance, Notaries and Certified Land Surveyors. More details on their interactions and roles can be found in [9].

In 1995, when the SICC project was started by AIPA to support the implementation of new directions in cadastral data management set forth by new regulations (see Section 3), the situation was the following :

- cadastral data stored in Cadaster are not, in general, up to date with cadastral data stored in Municipalities, and both are not, in general, exactly describing the situation in reality. It has been estimated through a sample of 5% of the overall data, that about 40% of the whole set of data held in Cadaster data bases is not up to date with the reality. Please note that this refers to the *overall* set of data, including both data generated by the cadastral offices and data received from the outside. Data generated inside cadastral offices are usually up-to-date, hence the Cadaster is able to perform its main role. The greatest source of incoherence is in data received from the outside, and the consequence of this is a great difficulty to establish a reliable correlation between a situation represented in in Cadaster databases and a situation represented in databases of other organizations;
- the way cadastral data change as consequence of actions taken by Municipalities, on one side, and by the Ministry of Finance, on the other side, are usually different. This is the main reason for the lack of correlation between data held by Municipalities and data held by Ministry of Finance, notwithstanding the large efforts that are periodically taken to force the correlation. It has been estimated that about 10% of the overall data changes every year.

3   Italian Regulations Regarding Cadastral Data

In recent years a number of laws have defined new organizational approaches for the management of cadastral data. The Law Decree n.557 of 30/dec/93 and the Law n.133 of 26/feb/94 required to set up an information system for cadastral data exchange by means of telematics communication among Ministry of Finance, Municipalities, and Notaries.

They also required that in such a system it should have been possible for Municipalities and Notaries to access databases of the Cadaster and of the Estate Public Registry and for the Ministry of Finance to receive information from Municipalities about the situation regarding its territory.

These provisions were required to allow:

- a de-centralization of services regarding cadastral data and property/mortgage rights,
- the complete automation of update processes of Cadaster databases and of Estate Public Registry databases,
- the monitoring and checking of distributed transactions.

The above regulations were then made more precise by the Labor Decree n.112 of 31/mar/98 establishing that:

- the central government keeps the management of estate public registry databases recording ownership and mortgage rights,
- Municipalities store and manage cadastral data about land properties and real estates existing within their territory,
- the central government maintains addressing and coordination functions regarding cadastral data management; more specifically, functions remaining to the central government are:
  - the definition of classification methods for land properties and real estates,
  - the definition of procedures to compute cadastral values of land parcels and real estates,
  - managing and certifying data about mortgage rights,
  - ruling tax legislation related to cadastral properties,
  - the definition of methods for topographic data acquisition and cadastral map generation,
  - checking data quality during update processes,
  - coordinating distributed access to cadastral data through the unitary network of the Public Administration [2].

From the above description it is clear that in such a work organization the biggest technical problem from the data management point of view is how to ensure the *coherence of the overall (distributed) set of spatio-temporal data*. On one side, in fact, data are going to be independently and autonomously managed by the various organizations. On the other one, data are needed and used also outside the organization producing/managing them and controlling their changes. Hence the problem is that an organization needs to use some data but has not a full control over them and the way they change.

These clashing situations are likely to produce incoherence in the overall set of spatio-temporal data, sooner or later, with absolute certainty. Since the lack of coherence derives mainly from organizational aspects, then the technical solution has to be designed in a way to match needs and behaviour of the organizations involved. Moreover, the technical solution has to be designed so to ensure the overall system has good performances.

4   How Incoherence is Generated

We now describe a typical interaction among entities that interact in the case of cadastral data to show how incoherence of the overall set of spatio-temporal data may be generated.

A Certified Land Surveyor prepares for a client a request for a variation to an apartment (e.g., to divide a large apartment in two smaller ones). The request is composed by some descriptive data and some geometric data and is stored in a database in the Surveyor's office.

The Surveyor prints the request and send it by registered mail to the pertinent Cadaster office of the Ministry of Finance. The office, having checked that everything has been done according to current laws and that data are coherent with data stored in Cadaster databases executes the update.

The municipality the apartment is located in has an interest in knowing such a change for local tax reasons (e.g., the two smaller apartments are different subjects, from a fiscal point of view, than the previous one). The surveyor has on obligation to get an approval for the change from the Building Service of the municipality before submitting the request to the Cadaster. Of course, until the request is received from the Cadaster the change has not really happened.

But neither the Cadaster office nor the Surveyor have any legal obligation to inform the municipality when the change really happens, i.e. when the request has been accepted by the Cadaster. This is the duty of the owner of the apartment and if he/she forgets to comply with this obligation, the municipalities may never be aware of the change until an inspector is sent to the place to check the situation.

The above example illustrates a case of incoherence *directly* generated during interaction among various organizations. But there is also a more subtle incoherence that can be *indirectly* generated.

Assume that, in the division of the apartment in two smaller ones, one of the two has received a new apartment number which has been registered in Cadaster databases. Assume now the municipality is informed of the change, when it happens, but it discovers that the way the apartment has received the new number is incoherent with municipal regulations for numbering apartments (e.g., the new number is one plus the old highest number in the building while the current regulations require adding a letter to the old number). Note that such a mistake may have been unnoticed or unchecked in the prior request for approval submitted from the Surveyor to the municipality. In fact, the Building Service of the municipality is not the one in charge of such a check on apartment numbering (the Toponymy Service is in charge) and regulations require that the submission of the change request to the Cadaster only needs the approval of the Building Service.

When the municipality receives the communication of the change it will try to have the Surveyor and the Cadaster change their databases according to such a regulation. But since most probably Cadaster databases will already have been updated by then and since this issue of apartment numbering is not something the Cadaster has, by the law, to really care about, no action will be taken and the incoherence will remain.

5 An Overview of the Access Keys Warehouse Approach

To technical solution allowing to solve the coherence maintenance problem is provided the **Access Keys Warehouse** (AKW) approach. This is a novel architectural approach of general value, discussed in more detail elsewhere [10, 11], allowing to smoothly develop, in a cost-effective way, cooperative information systems supporting interaction among autonomous organizations.

This approach gives the possibility of taking into account the impact on performances during the rightsizing phase and to define the system according to these requirements. Other approaches based on principles and techniques from, e.g., classic distributed DBMSs [1], or object-oriented DBMS [3], or standard data warehouse techniques [4], could not provide adequate solutions to our requirements [10, 11].

We now informally describe, at a high abstraction level, the AKW approach.

The technical device allowing to control the evolution of the overall system so to ensure distributed databases are always up-to-date with the original sources of data is a mapping among the data items existing in the relevant distributed databases.

This mapping is created and maintained by the system services of the AKW approach, and is realized through an **exchange identifiers database**. This is a *data repository* containing, *from a virtual point of view only*, all data items that can be found in various databases of a distributed systems. From a physical point of view most of data items remains at their locations.

The consequence is that with the use of the exchange identifiers database one needs to propagate variations only for access keys and not for every data items changing its value.

The *exchange identifiers database* is physically built, but contains only *access keys* and *logical links* for data items in the various databases of the distributed system. The access keys are attribute names, selected from the existing attributes in the underlying databases: the main rule in order to select them is that their concatenation constitutes a unique identifier for the data item. Logical links provide the access paths to the physical (distributed) databases where further data elements about the identified data can be found. Hence attributes in the exchange identifiers database act towards distributed databases as access keys: their value is used to query distributed databases. Hence they are **not** physical pointers, and the distributed databases maintain their independence and transparency both with respect to location and to implementation.

A system implemented according to the AKW approach has therefore also an *access management* role, guiding accesses to the distributed databases referred by the logical links so that accesses are minimally intrusive, have a minimal impact on their performances and correlations required for coherence maintenance internally to the distributed databases can be efficiently executed.

In the design of the exchange identifiers database attribute names have to be selected for it with two criteria:

1. the set of selected attributes has to be small enough so that its materialization can be efficiently managed and queried;
2. the set of selected attributes has to be large enough so to be able to contain all access keys needed to deal with coherence maintenance issues internally to the distributed databases while keeping their performances at an acceptable level.

The exchange identifiers database is populated using data existing in the various distributed locations. Values of access keys are supplied by the organizations involved in the interaction while the correlation of these values is knowledge added during the design and materialization process of the exchange identifiers database.

A **Supplier** is any entity generating a data item and/or entitled to change it, while a **User** is any entity interested to use a data item for its own purposes. The exchange identifiers database keeps a record of which are Users and Suppliers for the various data items.

A given organization can be, of course, both a Supplier and a User, even for the same data item. The Supplier of an attribute name in the exchange identifiers database is the only that can insert, modify, or delete values for that attribute in the database itself.

The active part of a system based on the AKW approach features two main components, each of them providing a class of services:

- *application services*, allowing Users to access data items they need, and allowing Suppliers to change data items or to generate new ones, both in a punctual way (i.e., one at a time) and in a batch one (i.e., a set at a time);
- *system services*, to keep coherence among the various sources of data items and of changes to them, to avoid incoherence during updates from Suppliers and their dispatching to Users, to certify answers to Users queries, to implement security and access right controls.

6   Data Organization

Cadastral data managed by SICC can be accessed by means of four classes of keys, that are specific of Cadaster and Estate Public Registry databases:

- *identifier codes for cadastral objects*: these are expressed in terms of Municipality code, section code (within the Municipality), map sheet number, parcel number and flat number;
- *identifier codes for subjects having rights on cadastral objects*: these are given name, family name, and fiscal code for people, and company code ("Partita IVA") for organizations;
- *identifiers of cadastral documents*: in terms of kind of document, protocol number and date,
- *attributes of cadastral objects*: these concern toponymy and geometric or geographical location

Cadastral data have then to be correlated with data stored in other databases at the Municipalities, that normally use other classes of keys. The most relevant databases in Municipalities for dealing with cadastral data are:

- *resident people database*: using as access keys given name, family name and fiscal code;
- *building works license database*: using license identifiers;
- *street database*: using toponymy codes;
- *technical office database*: using map codes of the Municipality land usage plan.

We now discuss typical services that SICC is able to support regarding exchange of cadastral data among Land Department of Ministry of Finance and Municipalities. They are described from the Municipality side:

- communication of changes in the usage or in the composition of a real estate, obtained from the owner's declaration or from a Municipality direct inspection;
- communication regarding a change in the internal structure of a real estate, obtained from the owner's declaration or from a Municipality direct inspection;
- sending cartographic data acquired during field campaign executed for municipality purposes;
- sending toponymy variations;
- sending changes to street layout and their connection network;
- signaling errors found by Municipality in data stored in the Cadaster databases;
- sending list of resident people subject to house municipal tax and asking for correlation with income tax databases at the Ministry of Finance;
- sending request for changes submitted to the Municipalities by Notaries and Certified Land Surveyors;

- sending request for changes regarding cadastral objects managed directly by the Municipality;
- asking to the Land Department to approve changes in real estates classification for fiscal purposes;
- asking to the Land Department to issue certificates about descriptive and geometric attributes of cadastral objects;
- interacting with other Public Administration organizations in the view of a better coordination for land management and planning, also for local tax legislation purposes.

The technical device allowing to address the above requirements is the *exchange identifiers database* introduced in the previous section.

In the case of SICC such a database contains about thirty exchange identifiers, selected among the more than two hundred attributes relevant for cadastral information in the various organizations, during a refinement and prototyping phase that has involved all the main entities interested in Italy with the treatment of cadastral data.

The exchange identifier database for cadastral data is then organized in four layers, each containing access keys of different type for the elements in Cadaster, Estate Public Registry, and Municipality databases. Namely, the four layers are:

- *descriptive*, containing all descriptive attributes used as access keys for cadastral objects and subjects;
- *cartographic*, containing all cartographic attributes used as access keys for cadastral objects and toponymy objects;
- *localization*, containing access keys for trigonometric reference points (i.e., the "maglia dei punti fiduciali" = network of geodetic reference points) and topographic map sheets: it hence allows to access geo-referencing data for cadastral objects;
- *correlation*, keeping correlation among the access keys in previous three layers and other databases.

Each of the above layer establishes a correlation among access keys referring to different databases. Hence each of the above layer contributes to the process of maintaining the overall coherence. In particular, the correlation layer allows to check coherence among the other layers and among the corresponding databases referred by them.

Note also that each of the above layer is spatio-temporal, since in each of them is made reference to information changing with time (e.g., the owner of a parcel, the shape of a parcel, and so on).

Once that in the various layers the values of the various access keys for the same piece of cadastral information have been inserted and validated, it is relatively easy to transform accesses and updates to a given database in references for other databases.

This approach based on the exchange identifier database allows to satisfy two important and always conflicting requirements:

- to decouple information systems of the various organizations, so that the role of each organization in governing its own databases is fully respected;
- to allow the synchronization among changes to data in the various distributed databases, thus avoiding to lose coherence in the overall set of spatio-temporal data.

7   Organizational Aspects

There are three main entities interacting among themselves through the exchange identifiers database of SICC:

- *End-user Information System*: a person working in a Municipality or a Notary or a Certified Land Surveyor, who accesses SICC by means of his/her workstation at three different levels of interaction:
  - to *browse* through cadastral databases to get acquainted with what kind of information is available for his/her purposes and at which level of detail; for this kind of interaction the security subsystem only keeps a record of data exchanged;
  - to ask and to receive a *certificate* regarding the current or the past status of a cadastral objects, in itself and in relation with subjects and cadastral documents; this kind of interaction is certified, i.e. the written output of SICC has a full legal value;
  - to submit *update* proposals for changes to cadastral objects; on this kind of requests the system executes a number of checks, to verify all information submitted are coherent with the situation currently recorded in Cadaster databases and are compliant with regulations;

- *Technical Management Center*: this is the operational arm of the Land Department of Ministry of Finance managing the Cadaster; it is physically made up by the Data Processing Centers of the various Land Offices and Estate Public Registry Offices. It performs the following functions:
  - to manage all queries from the end-users, first accessing the exchange identifier database to get, depending on the end-user provided identifiers, the access keys for the relevant local cadastral databases, and then issuing the corresponding requests and activating the procedures (technical and/or organizational) corresponding to the kind of query (i.e., browsing, certification, updating) issued;
  - to act as technical reference point for all the end-users that are under its geographical area of competence, providing the necessary service certification levels (i.e., security, accounting, quality, and so on).

- *Land Department Information System*: this is the reference point for all Technical Management Centers, from which it receives update requests relative to end-users the Centers have the competence on. It executes the following actions:
  - to send back, after having executed checks required by laws and regulations, validation notes for the submitted update requests;

- to directly provide certification services, for which the Technical Management Center has acted as a collection and refinement point;
- to carry out the cross-checks with other Ministry of Finance offices and/or other organizations to guarantee the overall quality of update processes.

Clearly, remote access to official data is an issue requiring an adequate level of security. The Land Department, as an organizational structure, carries out the necessary security check activities, for both its Computerized Information System and the Technical Management Centers. It also ensures security and consistency of execution for the access procedures to Cadaster databases and the organizational procedures controlling their use.

For what regards external entities, that is Municipalities, Notaries and Certified Land Surveyors, security is currently only managed by means of a user-id/secret-password mechanism. It is currently being planned the introduction in the SICC system of public-key/ private-key mechanism to encrypt exchanged data together with an electronic signature procedure to ensure a certified identification of end-users. This is made possible by recently introduced italians laws and regulations regarding electronic document management and exchange[5].

8   The Current Status of SICC

8.1   Status

The first prototype of the SICC project was implemented in 1995 by AIPA and the italian National Research Council. This prototype proved the feasibility of the technical solution and of the organizational model proposed.

Then SOGEI, the italian company managing the computerized information system of the Ministry of Finances, developed a second prototype, with a better degree of integration among cadastral data and services. This prototype has been put into operations in peripheral offices of Neaples municipality in May 1997.

It was then subsequently validated, through the involvement of about 100 Municipalities ranging from Region chief towns to very small ones and a small sample of notaries and certified land surveyors, for about one year [6, 8].

Finally, in September 1998 the engineered system, named SISTER [7] and developed as well by SOGEI, has been put into nation-wide operation.

Access to the system is through a WEB-based interface and the effectiveness of its use is demonstrated by the sharp increase of requests managed by it during the first months. In the month of January 1999 there has been already more than 100.000 cadastral certification queries. Remember that such a query is usually paid by its final user.

The WEB server is a multi-processor machine: one processor is dedicated to the exchange identifier database management, a second processor manages Intranet services (i.e., communication among Technical Management Centers and between them and the Land Department Information System), while a third one takes care of Internet requests with the relative security level (HTTPS protocol). Applets, written in JAVA, interact through the TCP/IP communication layer with the transaction management subsystems in the Data Processing Centers of the various Land Offices and Estate Public Registry Offices to send user data for queries and to receive results.

The final phase of the whole project is running in 1999 and aims at extending the range of services provided to end users.

In the following pages you can see hardcopies of screens during a real interaction with SICC through the WEB. In some case values used in the queries have been partially hidden in respect for the privacy of subjects involved.

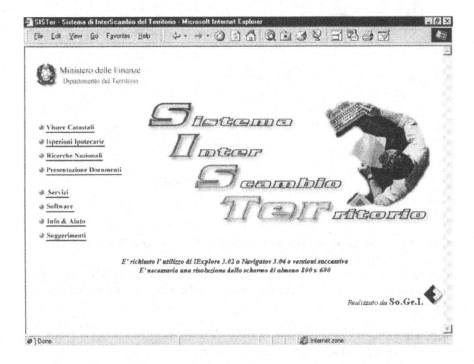

Fig. 1. The initial screen of the system.

8.2 Examples

We now present three examples of real-life situations where Cadaster data are involved and for each them we first present how the case is treated without SICC and then how it is now being managed using it and which is therefore the innovation in the provided service.

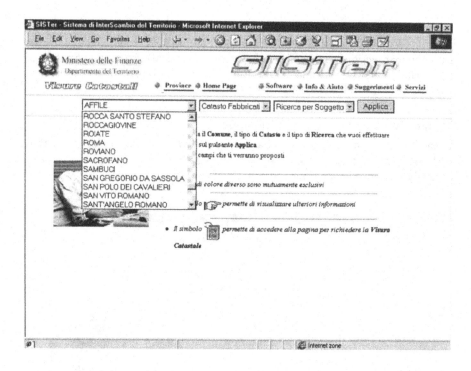

Fig. 2. Choosing the type of search.

Change in the Internal Structure or Usage of a Real Estate

Consider the case of a change in the internal structure or usage of a real estate, that is made known either from the owner's declaration or from a Municipality direct inspection.

without:
- no information is sent to the Cadaster;

with SICC:
- Municipality, after having inspected the place and having possibly noticed mismatches with request presented (by the owner or its delegate), sends through SICC an update advice to Cadaster, containing Cadaster identifiers of the real estate and of the subject(s) having rights on it, and a description of changes,
- Cadaster, when receives through SICC the update request from the owner or from the Municipality, executes on its databases the required changes (e.g., classification of the real estate), after having checked everything in the update request matches with the previous update advice and no incoherence is introduced in Cadaster databases;

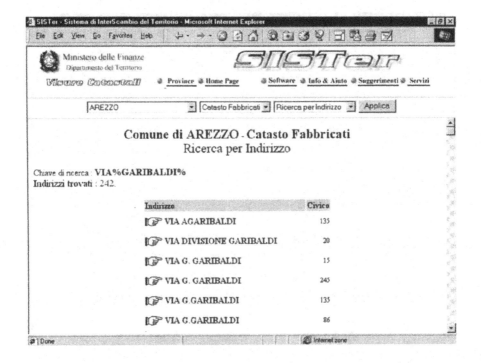

Fig. 3. Querying the real estate database with a partial address.

innovation:

- the owner can submit all documents required for the changes to the Municipality only,
- it is possible to cross-check coherence between changes to Cadaster databases and authorizations given by a Municipality to change internal structure or use of a real estate,
- it is possible to avoid fiscal evasion deriving from avoiding to submit the update request to the Cadaster.

Signaling Errors Found in Cadaster Databases

Consider the case of an error found in data stored in the Cadaster databases either by the person having rights on the cadastral object or by the Municipality during a direct inspection.

without:

- the person having rights or the Municipality presents an update request to the Cadaster, possibly attaching documents showing evidence of the found error and how it should be corrected,

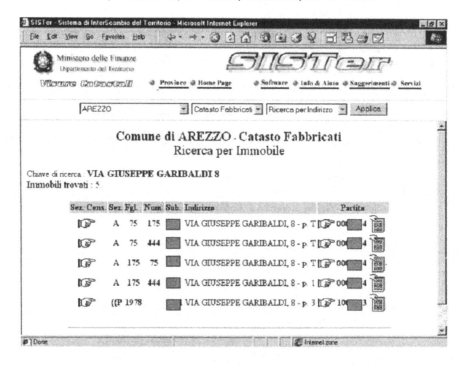

Fig. 4. Querying the real estate database with a property identifier.

- Cadaster, after having checked validity of the request and its attached documents (possibly using previous documents related to the same cadastral object) and having checked coherence of the changes implied by the request, updates its databases;

with SICC:

- the person having rights or the Municipality presents an update request directly to the Municipality offices, possibly attaching documents showing evidence of the found error and how it should be corrected,
- Municipality send an update request to Cadaster through SICC,
- Cadaster, after having executed its checks as described in the absence of SICC, updates its databases;

innovation:

- a change in Cadaster databases is activated by means of a request presented at Municipality offices.

Change Requests by Notaries and Certified Land Surveyors

Consider an update request submitted by a Notary or a Certified Land Surveyor to the Cadaster.

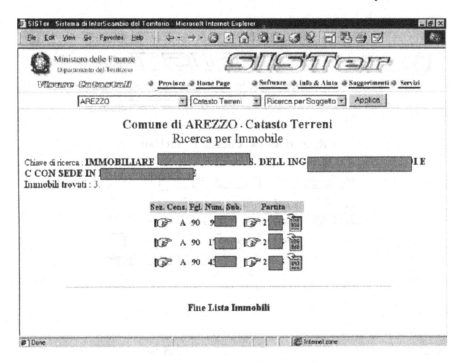

Fig. 5. Querying the land parcel database with a subject.

without:
- cadastral documents describing the current situation have to be obtained from Cadaster and Estate Public Registry, through of a direct request to them,
- cadastral documents with update annotations have to be presented at the offices of Cadaster and Estate Public Registry,

with SICC:
- Notaries and Certified Land Surveyors may ask cadastral documents describing the current situation through Municipality offices,
- Notaries and Certified Land Surveyors present update requests in electronic format at the Municipality offices only,
- Municipality send requests to Cadaster and Estate Public Registry through SICC,
- Cadaster and Estate Public Registry, after having executed their validity checks, update their databases;

innovation:
- a change in Cadaster databases is activated by means of an electronic request presented at Municipality offices.

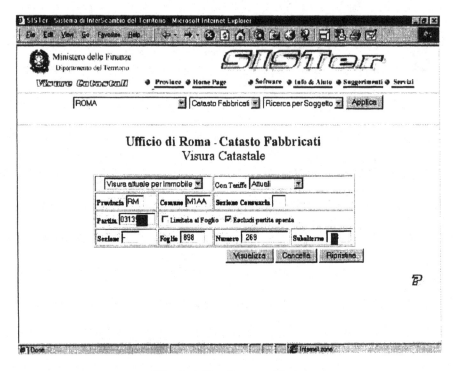

Fig. 6. Asking for a certificate.

9   Conclusions

In this paper we have discussed the spatio-temporal DBMS "Sistema di Inter-scambio Catasto-Comuni" (SICC), allowing to exchange cadastral data among the principal entities interested in Italy to the treatment of cadastral information, that are Ministry of Finance, Municipalities, Notaries, and Certified Land Surveyors.

Such a spatio-temporal DBMS allows a de-centralized management of cadastral data while allowing, at the same time, to keep the coherence among distributed databases during updates.

The system is accessible nation-wide by end-users through a WEB-based interface allowing them to query directly relevant databases. Through the use of a novel architectual approach, namely the **Access Keys Warehouse** approach [10] the system is able to check for validity all update requests and to accept only those matching with information currently stored in the (distributed) cadastral databases.

To the best of authors' knowledge this is the first time that a real-life working DBMS is able to guarantee this kind of performances in a scenario of such a complexity.

References

1. M.Tamer Ozsu, P.Valduriez, Principles of Distributed Database Systems, Prentice Hall Canada, 1999, 2nd edition.
2. AIPA, Feasibility Study of the Public Administration's Unified Network, January 1996, http://www.aipa.it/english/unifiednetwork[2/feasibilitystudy[1/index.asp.
3. A. Umar, Object Oriented Client/Server Internet Environments, Prentice Hall, 1997.
4. D.Calvanese, G.De Giacomo, M.Lenzerini, D.Nardi, R.Rosati, Source Integration in Data Warehousing, 9th International Workshop on Database and Expert Systems Applications (DEXA-98), pp.192–197, IEEE Computer Society Press, 1998.
5. Decree of the President of the Republic n.513 of 10/nov/97 and Decree of the President of the Council of Ministers of 8/feb/99, (in italian).
6. M.Talamo, F.Arcieri, G.Conia, Il Sistema di Interscambio Catasto-Comuni (parte I), *GEO Media*, vol.2, Jul-Aug 1998, (parte II), *GEO Media*, vol.2, Sep-Oct 1998, Maggioli Editore, Roma (in italian).
7. Il Catasto Telematico, *Notiziario Fiscale*, n.11-12, pp.19–22, Nov-Dec 1998, Ministry of Finance, Roma (in italian).
8. M.Talamo, F.Arcieri, G.Conia, E.Nardelli, SICC: An Exchange System for Cadastral Information, 6th Int. Symposium on Large Spatial Databases (SSD'99), Hong Kong, China, Jul.99, Lecture Notes in Computer Science, Springer-Verlag.
9. C.Cannafoglia, A.De Luca, F.Molinari, G.F.Novelli, Catasto e Pubblicita' Immobiliare, pp.406-420, Nov. 1998, Maggioli Editore, (in italian).
10. F.Arcieri, E.Cappadozzi, P.Naggar, E.Nardelli, M.Talamo, Access Keys Warehouse: a new approach to the development of cooperative information systems, 5th International Conference on Cooperative Information Systems (CoopIS'99), Edinburgh, Scotland, Sep.99, Lecture Notes in Computer Science, Springer-Verlag.
11. F.Arcieri, E.Cappadozzi, P.Naggar, E.Nardelli, M.Talamo, Specification and architecture of an Access Keys Warehouse, Tech.Rep.7/99, Univ. of L'Aquila, Mar.99.

Using Interactive, Temporal Visualizations for WWW-based Presentation and Exploration of Spatio-Temporal Data

Hartmut Luttermann and Manfred Grauer

University of Siegen, D-57068 Siegen, Germany
{hartmut,grauer}@fb5.uni-siegen.de
WWW home page: http://www-winfo.uni-siegen.de/winfo/english

Abstract. In recent years, spatio-temporal data are increasingly recorded in database-enabled information systems. To share the benefit, often, a public data access is provided utilizing WWW-based visual interfaces. If spatio-temporal data are queried, data visualization and exploration in a spatial and temporal context is needed to better present and analyze spatio-temporal behaviours and relationships. In existing WWW-based interfaces of temporal geographical information or scientific data visualization systems, only videos, static visualizations (images) or, recently, VRML-worlds (Virtual Reality Modeling Language) are applied which support neither 3D- nor temporal navigation, respectively. Additionally, these interfaces offer only small support for further exploratory tools according to the temporal domain and to conceptual database entities which users are often aware of. In this paper, we propose an extension to VRML which supports the description of spatio-temporal (temporal 3D-)graphics and entities by integrating the valid time dimension and the entity concept. This is realized by a set of new VRML-nodes representing temporal geometries, time references and database entities and a set of interactive visualization techniques extending standard VRML-browsers to perform temporal navigation and to further explore the visualization during presentation. One result of this proposal is that a new type of visualizations, i.e. interactive, temporal visualizations (animations), can be generated, stored in files, integrated in Web-pages and explored spatially and temporally by interaction or animation. This is demonstrated by two decision support applications from water management and urban planning.

1 Introduction

In recent years, the amount of spatio-temporal data stored in conventional file systems or in modern GIS- and data warehouse applications has increased dramatically. In many applications these data are displayed and analyzed to obtain knowledge on technical and environmental processes as well as to plan, simulate, explain and evaluate management decisions.

In order to analyze spatio-temporal data, data visualization techniques are used [3, 34]. This involves several steps: Querying and filtering the data set from the database or file system by applying a database query language (e.g. SQL) or a visual query tool, mapping the data into some graphics by applying specific data type- and task-dependent visualization methods, and then visually analyzing the graphics in relation to spatio-temporal behaviours and relationships of conceptual entities as well as certain inherent structures of linear or cyclic processes. These steps are done interactively and iteratively to extract new knowledge or to create visualizations for explanation and public presentation.

Often, public access to the data sets of spatio-temporal databases is provided to facilitate data commercialism or cooperative work. In this case, the main graphical user interface between the "everyone" user (e.g. practioneers, decision makers, researchers) and databases or database applications (e.g. data archives, e-commerce) is becoming WWW-pages. This is the platform most preferred because of its simplicity, ease of use, system-independency and the possibility to integrate and combine different data types in one interface.

In existing WWW-based visual interfaces of temporal geographic information systems and scientific data visualization servers only static time-referenced visualizations (images and, recently, static VRML-worlds) [11, 20, 38, 2] and, in order to keep the temporal nature of the data, videos [16, 20] or, recently, animated VRML-worlds [6, 38] are used to visualize spatio-temporal data. Although video-players offer controls for temporal navigation of the video (e.g. pause, backward), they do not support a 2D/3D-navigation in the video-content. On the other side, VRML itself permits 3D-navigation, but does not feature a technique which controls the time domain of 3D-animations during the presentation.

However, with data visualizations more simple and easy to use, exploratory tools are wanted by the end user to facilitate private analysis and learning [6, 26, 18]. These tools change the way the data are viewed and may help different features (information aspects) of the data to be made salient [41]. Besides exploring the spatial and temporal dimension of the data (with techniques like temporal navigation, spatial and temporal focusing and brushing, temporal comparing [16, 27]) the conceptual data structures (entity modeling) are becoming more important for the viewer working with data sets of databases. This makes exploratory tools available which link the entity description (i.e. the non-spatial attributes) with the graphic (e.g. linked brushing).

In this paper, we propose a seamless extension of VRML which supports the description of spatio-temporal graphical objects and entities by conceptually integrating a valid time dimension and an entity concept. VRML is a standardized file format and high-level description language for interactive 3D-graphics on the internet which is supported by many browsers. It integrates user interaction with, an event/message passing between the objects in the visualization and a prototoying and programming mechanism to extend the language with new object types and behaviour [42]. This proposal is realized by a set of new VRML-nodes expanding VRML to be a description language for temporal 3D-graphics with entity features, and by a set of interactive visualization techniques extending standard VRML-browsers to perform temporal navigation, object identification and the exploration of temporal data and entity characteristics. With this extension, visualizations of spatio-temporal data sets and entities can be described as *interactive (explorable), temporal visualizations (animations)*, stored in VRML-files on the internet, integrated in Web-pages, and explored in a spatial, temporal, and thematical context in standard VRML-browsers during presentation possibly being a part of a public WWW-based visual database interface.

The paper is organized as following: In section 2, we review existing visualization techniques for spatio-temporal data, and in section 3, we give a short overview on current graphic technologies competing with VRML. In section 4, we show which different features of spatio-temporal data exist possibly inherent in visualizations and in section 5 which types of exploratory tools are needed to reveal it. In section 6, we explain the newly designed VRML-nodes and their implications. In section 7, we present some example applications and conclude this paper with a discussion and the plans for future works in section 8.

2   Visualizing Spatio-Temporal Data

In cartographic applications (e.g. cadastral systems), the visualization of spatio-temporal data mainly comprises the mapping of states and changes on static maps [22]. Whereas time-referenced states are visualized in 2D or 3D applying traditional cartographic visualization methods (e.g. choropleth maps, isarithmic maps, dot maps, net maps), change is mapped on temporal maps classified in static and strip maps. Strip maps are multiple time-referenced snapshots ("small multiples", cartoon) where change is shown via the differences between the individual maps depicting subsequent snapshots. In static maps, time is mapped on a visual design variable [4] (i.e. shape, size, color, orientation, location, lightness or texture) resulting in e.g. space-time-objects or time series plots (time as a geometric dimension), particle trace maps (spatial behaviour of particles), super-imposed (overlayed) maps/spaces, arrow/flow maps (symbolized motion), isochrone diagrams, period-referenced difference maps/spaces.

However, with static maps it is difficult to view the data both in a spatial and temporal context facilitating an understanding of processes rather than states and the investigation of spatio-temporal relations and patterns. Generally, on dynamic presentation systems (and devices) time is used as a new visual design variable inducing not only one but six new dimensions [25]: duration, frequency, ordering, rate of change, synchronization and presentation time. However, presentation time is the most used dimension to present spatio-temporal data resulting in the generation of animations and videos.

Two different types of animations are distinguished [9, 31]: a) *temporal animations*: a change in the presented object's location, shape or attributes is based on temporal data, i.e. there is a direct relation between world time which is part of the data and presentation (system/real) time which is used to show the animation; and b) *cartographic animations*: the animation method is applied to non-temporal data, such as the camera position (viewing), light (rendering) or other animation variables and techniques [33], e.g. object change/motion (e.g. bubbles in water showing the stream), time-variant symbols for data values (e.g.

rain symbol), presentation change (e.g. highlighting). Also, user interaction may be a cause for cartographic animations [31], e.g. observer motion (e.g. zooming), change of visualization parameters (e.g. isolines, color-mapping), the visualization method (e.g. re-expression, sequencing), the scientific model (e.g. triangulation, classification) or the original data set (e.g. filtering). If temporal and cartographic animations are mixed, a temporal legend is needed to differentiate between world and presentation time [21].

Interactivity is becoming a main thread in exploring static and temporal visualizations (animations). It is ascertained that animations are more effective in information transmission if they can be temporally controlled by the viewer [16]. More interactive visualization methods (e.g. information hiding, linked brushing, data probing) do not increase effectivity but allow experienced users to enlarge their knowledge about the visualized data by exploring different features (information aspects). More complex and partial relationships or causal dependencies which are not so easily visible from analytical comparisons may be revealed. This forces the current development, evaluation and integration of many user-driven exploratory techniques into the presentation systems of animations and visualizations [6, 10, 1, 31].

3   Transmiting Interactive Animations on the Web

In the internet, the visualizations of the queried data set of Web-enabled databases as well as exploratory methods are required to be present at the client side. Therefore, some systems transmit the underlying spatio-temporal data set from the server to the client where specialized visualization and exploration software is used for presentation (*client-side data visualization*), like in [6] or MapObjects [13]. Although, this scenario allows many exploratory tools such as data manipulation or visualization parametrization, some drawbacks exist: on the client side, operational and scientific knowledge in visualizing data is needed if not the visualization is pre-defined or restricted; specialized software produces system-dependencies if not Java is used; no standard exists to transmit spatio-temporal data and entities on the internet (however, HDF exists for scientific data) causing software-dependencies; explorable visualizations can not be stored; and data distributors loose the control on the data set and its type of visualization.

A newly proposed approach is to attach the algorithm of a single visualization method as executable to the data set and send both to the user where this method is applied to the data [18]. But this requires special authoring systems, is limited to only one visualization method and depends on the operating system.

A better solution may be a graphical description of the visualized data which is generated on the server and sent to the client interface where simple interactive visualization tools may be hosted for presentation and exploration (*server-side data visualization*), like in [38, 2]. If this description is enhanced with information on time-references, change and database entities it allows more exploratory tools than in standard 3D-graphics (we assume spatio-temporal data as 3D+t-data).

Different graphical descriptions for interactive (explorable) animations and videos exist:

MPEG-4 is a recently standardized but not yet implemented video standard [28]. It supports the description of spatio-temporal objects via animated textures on animated 2D/3D-shapes in a synchronized spatio-temporal context and allows limited spatial and temporal navigation as well as further object interaction (e.g. hiding, moving). MPEG-4 is designed for storage and public presentation and needs the spatio-temporal graphics being encoded and then decoded for presentation which limits server-side data visualization on-demand.

Recently, new graphic file formats for (streamed) 3D-animations (e.g. Fluid3d [30], B3D [5], ScriptV [40]) were developed which are used only for presentation puposes with no or few features for user interaction. Also, new 3D-graphic libraries or programming languages (e.g. Java3D, Hypercosm with OMAR [17]) may be interesting for interactive WWW-based interfaces. But every automatically generated graphic need to be compiled on the server before transmitted to the client for execution because each graphic description is a program.

VRML is a standard graphic description format for object-oriented, interactive and animated 3D-graphics [42]. Visualizations of spatio-temporal data can be described as animated 3D-graphics but which until now can neither be interactively stopped nor run forwards nor backwards (possibly with different speeds) in the browser because the unique time concept inherent in VRML is a model of the "real time". This is also recognized in [29] where objects in VRML are extended with an additional time sensor to animate its time-variant behaviour on external events. But VRML offers the possibility to integrate new language concepts and to enhance the presentation systems with new interactive visualization methods, e.g. temporal navigation.

4   Analyzing Spatio-Temporal Data

Querying and interacting with databases means visualizing the data sets which are in the database and analyzing them by placing the data in different spatial, temporal or thematical context. This process stimulating mental cognition and understanding leads through several distinct levels which also characterizes the distinct functions of visualizations: ranging from exploration (discover unknown) and analysis (check, test and evaluate hypothesis) with more interactivity until synthesis (identify and combine different results) and presentation (convincingly communicate results to the public) [26]. On each level, the viewer follows different tasks to reach distinct interpretations of the data [19]: identify values, find values, compare values of one or multiple variables, recognize clusters and trends in one variable or correlation between multiple variables.

So, normally each specific user question requires a different visualization being the most efficient in transmiting the information or the features of the data to the viewer, i.e. being easily recognized and correctly interpreted [41]. This depends not only on the graphical design [4] but also on the user's knowledge, the visualization task and on the type of information being transferred [6]. In visual database interfaces providing access to the public, often, only basic background knowledge and a diffuse understanding of the data and visualization aims can be assumed. In this scenario, interactive visualization methods may help different features of the data to be made salient in *one* dynamic visualization which results in fewer server-client interactivity if server-side data visualization is used.

We first clarify which interpretations (information aspects) of the visualized spatio-temporal data may be revealed. This can be derived from the visualization tasks mentioned above. Then (in the next section), we examine possible exploratory tools which support the revelation of these data aspects.

The analysis of the spatial data component induces questions according to the spatial existence (if?), spatial location (where?) and spatial extend or distribution, i.e. shape (form?), size (how big?) and texture (variation) of objects and natural conditions. In relation to multiple objects spatial associations/dependencies (relationships?), spatial distance (how far?), spatial clustering (contiguity?) or spatial patterns (arrangements?) are of interest.

The analysis of the temporal data component may answer questions related to the existence and non-existence (if?), temporal location (when?), and duration (how long?) of single objects, facts and events. In relation to multiple objects temporal associations/dependencies (relationships?), temporal distance (how long?), temporal clustering (contiguity?), or temporal sequences/patterns (order?) may be investigated [21].

If both components are analyzed in combination other interpretations (information aspects) may be revealed [23, 7]. Commonlly, the user are interested in states and conditions anchored in the spatio-temporal context (what?, where? and when?) and in spatio-temporal change of objects or facts, especially in its existence (if?), location (when? and where?), type (how? about location: moving, rotating; about extend: growing, shrinking, deforming; about non-spatial: increasing, decreasing), pattern (how often?), rate (how fast?), sequence (which order?), trend, and in case of sets of changing objects in the associations/dependencies (about locations: approach, leave; about extend: merge, split, absorb, release), correlation or causal relationships.

5   Exploring Data with Interactive Visualizations

Interactive (exploratory) visualization techniques are implemented on different levels in visualization systems ranging from direct, easy to use techniques like changing 2D/3D-viewing parameters until indirect, algorithmic tools such as changing the parameters of data filters. The given information aspects may be revealed mostly by applying the exploratory tools distinguished in following categories [41]: viewing, encoding/filtering, reordering and algorithmic transformations. This categorization is motivated by the level of user knowledge and the data context needed to perform the tools.

For spatio-temporal data, first, interactive visualization methods which change the *viewing* of the visualization are required. This incorporates techniques for spatial navigation (zoom (with level of detail), pan, rotate), temporal navigation (start, direction, speed and resolution of animation) and presentation of a spatial and temporal overview with current position and current time, respectively. These techniques are wellknown, easy to use and exist in many presentation tools. Only the spatial 2D/3D and temporal context of the objects in the visualization are needed for execution.

For analyzing the existence of data in time and space as well as clusters and patterns, interactive tools for *encoding* and *filtering* different features of data are needed, e.g. linked brushing and focusing. They are performed on graphical objects or time-referenced states by selecting specific spatial, temporal or thematical values or value ranges. The operations are highlighting, colouring, hiding, filtering or aggregating the data. Additionally, tools which switch the visibility of graphical objects (visibility layers) or other data (e.g. transient labels, annotations, graphics, details) on some action (e.g. moving the mouse on an object) are useful. These tools need the structural information on objects and attributes.

In order to better compare multiple variables simultaneously in the spatial and temporal dimension, interactive tools for *reordering* the objects of the visualization are useful, such as spatial and temporal transformations (scale, move, rotate) or a change of the graphical design (colors, lights).

Other exploratory tools (*algorithmic transformations*) may also be of value, such as investigating the original data (e.g. data probing) or computing new data (e.g. height, distance, areas) through the graphics (*measuring*), changing the parameter of visualization methods (e.g. color-mapping) or the methods itself, e.g. re-expressions of time (linear vs. cyclic perspective) or space, or querying, filtering, transforming and manipulating the data from databases. But these tools are not considered for implementation because they need the underlying spatio-temporal data set to be performed and further knowledge in data visualization on the viewer side.

For better analysis of data sets of spatio-temporal databases exploratory tools of the first and second category are very important. However, in order to implement these tools in the client interface temporal and structural information of entity properties in the visualization description are needed.

6   Extension of VRML

In order to support the description of spatio-temporal entities and to implement many important exploratory tools for the analysis of spatio- temporal data, two new concepts are integrated in VRML: a) *valid time*, to permit the description of temporal behaviour and a temporal navigation functionality; and b) the *entity concept*, to leverage the abstraction level from single graphical object to conceptual entities known by the user from conceptual data modeling and querying databases. Both concepts are realized by creating new and redefining existing VRML-nodes via the PROTO-mechanism and implementing its behaviour in Java. After a short introduction to VRML, the concepts and the newly designed VRML-nodes are described. A subset is already proposed in VRML History [43] and deeply explained in [24]. All VRML-nodes are defined by their type and the list of attributes, each specified by the event type, data type, attribute name and default value.

6.1 Introduction to VRML

In VRML every visualization (3D-scene/world) is described by a set of objects (called nodes) which are instantiations of some pre-defined object types (e.g. geometries, materials, lights, sensors) and characterized by its attributes (called fields) and the graphical and logical behaviour. The objects are organized in a hierarchical scene graph via transformations (rotation, scale, translation) which determines the location and visibility of the objects. A special object type is the Viewpoint which specifies the position and viewing direction of the viewer in the world.

Utilizing an event mechanism, all object are able to send messages to other objects to modify their attributes. Sensor objects produce events on special system states (e.g. user interaction, clock) and are, therefore, the origin of action and animation in the world. An integrated interface to a programming language as well as a prototyping mechanism allow the definition of new object types with special behaviour.

6.2 Integrating Valid Time

The time concept already existing in VRML simulates approximately "real time" by generating unchangeably events as time passes. For a better distinction, it is called *system time* in this context.

In order to model temporal data in VRML-worlds, *valid time* is integrated as a new time dimension in VRML which specifies the time when a fact in the world was, is or will be valid. With valid time, each object in a VRML-world is transformed in a temporal object $o : (a_0, ..., a_n, vp)$ with the attributes a_i and the *valid period vp*. The valid period limits the *time of existence* or *validity* of the object to a specified time period $[t_0, t_n)$ where changes to object's characteristics may appear. Outside this period the object does not exist. By default, all objects are always valid, i.e. the valid period specifies $(-\infty, \infty)$.

Transaction time which is used in databases to model the time when a fact is recorded [35, 36] is not integrated in this proposal because this time concept is not relevant in data visualization, i.e. it has no special meaning in the visual understanding of processes and spatio-temporal data. However, visualization methods which show the difference between two versions of the same temporal data are possible.

The valid period as well as the times of change are defined by a list of consecutive times $(t_0, ..., t_n)$ via the *period* field of the newly designed *ValidPeriod* node. The n times $t_0, t_1, ..., t_n$ partition the time domain $(-\infty, +\infty)$ into $n+2$ subintervals called *version time periods* where each of them may be associated with an object or attribute *version*, except the first and last one.

```
ValidPeriod {
   exposedField  SFBool  isCyclic        FALSE
   exposedField  MFTime  period          []
   exposedField  SFTime  periodOffset    0.0
   exposedField  SFNode  reference       NULL
   exposedField  SFBool  fromStartOfRef  TRUE
}
```

All time values are specified as floating point numbers relative to a node-specific, local time origin which may be the global time origin or the starting/ending time of another already specified valid period (via field *reference*) (for temporal causal dependencies), moved by an offset (field *periodOffset*). This model gives much flexibility in defining absolute, relative and cyclic times where manipulations, e.g. moving an object in time, can easily be realized. Additionally, it avoids parsing different date formats and calendars and allows some kind of independence of the time unit (e.g years, days, seconds) and of the resolution of discrete time values.

6.3   Temporal Data Modeling Concepts

The research in spatio-temporal data modeling has identified different types of spatio-temporal data [32, 39, 12]: spatial objects a) without change (*time-invariant objects*), b) which only move, c) which only change its extent or d) both (*time-variant objects*) and e) changing spatial fields which despite the differences in database modelling may also be represented as time-variant objects in visualizations [39].

Time-invariant objects possess only one non-changeable representation valid during the given valid period. Any time-variant object possesses different time-referenced representations (*versions*) during its valid period which compose the *version history* of this object. The description of these representation is done with the known concepts of temporal data modeling [12, 35, 36], i.e. time-(in)variant attributes, discrete(event-oriented)/step-wise/linear versioning (how do attributes evolve over time?), and tuple-/attribute-timestamping. These results in the following newly designed nodes which may be used in connection with the existing graphical VRML-nodes (i.e. shape, appearance, lights, environment, sensors).

Limited Validity and Time-Referenced Object Versions

The new grouping node *History* is designed to limit the validity of its versions. Each version v_i specifies a local temporal VRML-world whose validity is given by the associated version time period $[t_i, t_{i+1})$ specified in the field *period* of the ValidPeriod node which is the value of the field *validPeriod* of this node type.

```
History {
   exposedField  SFNode  validPeriod  NULL
   exposedField  MFNode  version      []
}
```

This node may be used: a) to limit the validity of a time-invariant object defined as the first version; or b) to specify a time-variant object whose representation is changing in a step-wise mode, i.e. consists of a series of constant, time-referenced object versions.

Time-Variant Attributes

Attributes of time-variant objects may be time-invariant or time-variant. Time-variant nominal attributes (of textual, boolean, image or node type) have to be modelled via time-referenced object versions. Numerical time-variant attributes as well as attributes for coordinates and colors, no matter whether changing instantly or continuously, are modelled via time series decribed in the next subsection.

Attributes of VRML's graphical shapes for the geometry and texture object are handled separately because different types of these objects exist which may change in valid time (geometry: e.g. Box, Cone, IndexedFaceSet; texture: e.g. MovieTexture, PixelTexture). The *HistoryGeometry* and *HistoryTexture* nodes are designed to handle discrete or step-wise versioned geometry and texture types respectively.

```
HistoryGeometry/Texture {
  exposedField  SFNode  validPeriod        NULL
  exposedField  MFNode  geometry/texture   []
}
```

Both nodes allow a possible later implementation of interpolation (i.e. morphing) algorithms for geometry and texture types.

Time Series of Numerical Attributes

Time series conceptually describe a list of pairs of attribute and associated time values which are the base points of a somehow interpolated attribute function. For flexibility, this is divided into the definition of two nodes: the *time value* (ValidTimeSensor) and the *attribute value* definition (Interpolator). The times of the base points list are specified in the field *validPeriod* of the *ValidTime-Sensor* node, the attribute values in the different data type-dependent VRML-Interpolator (e.g. Normal, Coordinate, Scalar, Color) which uses linear interpolation to compute new values.

```
ValidTimeSensor {
  exposedField  SFBool   enabled            TRUE
  exposedField  SFNode   validPeriod        NULL
  eventOut      SFFloat  fraction_changed
  eventOut      SFBool   isActive
  eventOut      SFTime   validTime
}
```

Both nodes and the specific numerical attribute are linked by employing VRML's event/message routing technique. On every temporal navigation action, i.e. the viewer moves temporally in the given time periods of the time value definition, the ValidTimeSensor produces events which are sent to the Interpolator and then to the attribute to change its value. Quadratic, cubic or other functional descriptions may reduce the amount of base points needed to approximate a given time-variant behaviour in the interpolator, but linear interpolation is much easier to model, faster in execution and even used in databases [12].

6.4   Temporal Navigation

In order to investigate the temporal dimension of the visualization a specific navigation method is needed. Like in 3D-navigation, a "viewpoint" is integrated in the valid time dimension which is responsible for the current presentation of the temporal world. Only those objects and their representation are shown which are valid at the time given by the current viewpoint (like a time-slice or snapshot of the temporal world). The extended *Viewpoint* node specifies spatial and temporal key locations given by the fields *position*, *orientation*, and *valid time*.

```
Viewpoint {
   ...
   exposedField SFRotation orientation 0 0 1 0
   exposedField SFVec3f    position    0 0 10
   exposedField SFTime     validTime   0.0      # added
   ...
}
```

Changing the valid time allows the viewer to move through the temporal dimension of the world (i.e. doing a time journey), interactively via the new navigation paradigms or automatically by animating the field *validTime* of the Viewpoint node via the TimeInterpolator. The *TimeInterpolator* node interpolates linearly among a list of time values specified in the field *keyValue*.

```
TimeInterpolator {
   eventIn       SFFloat  set_fraction
   exposedField  MFFloat  key            []
   exposedField  MFTime   keyValue       []
   eventOut      SFTime   value_changed
}
```

The navigation paradigm describes the way the position, orientation *and* valid time of the current viewpoint may be changed. Two new navigation paradigms are introduced which can be set in the field *type* of the *NavigationInfo* node to explore the temporal domain of the visualization: TIME_WALK and TIME_STUDY. TIME_WALK allows walking with changing speed forward or backward in the temporal domain, TIME_STUDY allows to investigate the local surrounding of the current valid time.

The temporal navigation is performed in parallel to the spatial navigation and globally to the scene, i.e. synchronously to all objects defined in the temporal VRML-world. This is more intuitive for the viewer and the presented scene is easier to be understood and recognized than if the local valid time of each object is changed independently like in [14]. Instead, if some applications (e.g. scheduling, simulations) need to view simultaneously objects at different valid times, it is easier to temporally move the valid period of these objects along the valid time dimension.

6.5   Temporal Legend and Temporal Data Presentation

A temporal legend is developed to facilitate two main functions [21]: a) interacting with the temporal domain of the visualization and b) interpreting the shown graphics in the temporal sense, i.e. distinguishing between a cartographic and temporal animation. In order to perform these functions the legend consists of two components (Fig. 1):

- the *controls* allow to navigate interactively in the temporal domain according to the navigation paradigms, to jump to a newly set current time value, and 'to start an animation with user-defined speed and direction over a specified period;
- the *time display* shows textually the current valid time used for temporal presentation as, e.g. a date, numbers, or simulation ticks since a pre-defined time origin.

For temporal analysis, a presentation of the temporal data components may be valuable. This is done in a *temporal overview* which renders the times of existence (valid period) of the temporal graphical objects in relation to the current valid times over the current visible part of the time line. This is important for event-oriented graphical objects with a moment-like valid period which, generally, are hard to be discovered while navigating temporally because they often fall between two presented snapshots. The rendered valid periods are enhanced with symbolized information, such as the base points of change, the type of versions, and the information if the time definition is cyclic or linked to another valid period. Additionally, a standard or user-defined cyclic reference devision of the time line (e.g. in years, weeks) is displayed for a better orientation in time.

In this implementation the legend and temporal overview are integrated in the browser's display to facilitate a link to the currently presented VRML-world.

Two further exploratory methods are implemented: temporal focusing and temporal brushing. In *temporal focusing* all events and objects are shown which are valid at a user-defineable period. In *temporal brushing* several periods of the time line may be selected which then constitute the new temporal basis for temporal navigation. This technique filters certain periods in time and is often used with a cyclic perspective of time to analyse long-time trends of cyclic phenomena (e.g. wheather cycles) [16].

Navigation Controls   Time Display   Temporal Overview

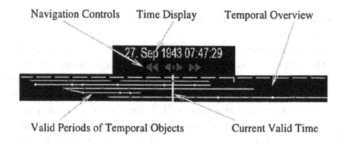

Valid Periods of Temporal Objects   Current Valid Time

Fig. 1. Appearance of the temporal legend and temporal overview

6.6   Exploring Spatial-Temporal Entities

The user's view on data stored in databases is heavily influenced by conceptual
data modeling whose main constructs are entities with its attributes and relationships. Even spatial data are modeled via the entity concept [39]. The new
node *Entity* (such as proposed in [8]) is designed to group a set of VRML-nodes
forming a spatio-temporal database entity. All entities created by this node type
are grouped in layers and listed in a "entity"-window which can additionally be
displayed in the user interface.

```
Entity {
    exposedField    SFString    id              ""
    exposedField    SFString    layer           ""
    evenOut         SFString    selectedId
    eventIn         SFBool      isSelected
    exposedField    SFBool      isVisible       TRUE
    exposedField    SFBool      isHighlighted   FALSE
    exposedField    MFNode      shape           []
    exposedField    MFNode      attribute       []
}
```

Program logic, located internally or externally of a VRML-world, can be
used to switch visibility (field *isVisible*), to highlight (field *isHighlighted*) or to
select (field *isSelected*) one entity. In the latter case it causes the entity to send
its id (via the field *selectedId*) back to the scene where this information may be
used to interact with a database [8]. The field *shape* contains the possibly time-
variant shape, the field *attribute* the possibly time-variant detail informations of
the entity which are displayed textually in an additional "entity details"-window
and which are also sensitive on temporal navigation. Detailed information may
be meta data or non-spatial entity characteristics. The following node types are
allowed in that field which have no graphical effect.

```
NumericalAttribute {
    exposedField SFString    name
    exposedField SFNode      validPeriod
```

```
    exposedField MFInt32     versionType
    exposedField MFFloat     value
    eventOut     SFFloat     value_changed
}
```

Similar node types exist for temporal textual (*TextAttribute*) and temporal time attributes (*TimeAttribute*). The field *value_changed* returns the currently valid value of the time-variant attribute back to the scene while navigating temporally.

Based on this entity concept, some of the exploratory tools mentioned in the preceding section are implemented to allow private investigation of spatio-temporal data. Layers of entities can be made interactively (un)visible to reduce the amount of displayed information and facilitate the concentration on certain features (*information hiding*). A *linked brushing* method is implemented between the "entity"-window, the presented scene and the temporal overview to locate and distinquish entities in different context. In *temporal comparison* the viewer apply a temporal transformation (move, scale) to the time definition of one single entity to simultaneously compare and find correlations in the spatio-temporal behaviour of entities which are normally temporally distanced.

7   Applications

Two example applications show how the proposed VRML-nodes are used to explore spatio-temporal data sets for decision support: visualizing temporal finite-element method (FEM) data in water management and temporal GIS-data in urban planning. Each visualization is published in the internet [43], stored as a normal VRML-file, and can be presented and explored with the described tools using a standard VRML-Browser and the implementation of the proposed node types [43].

7.1   Visualizing Temporal FEM-Data

In water management, FEM-simulation are often used to solve optimization problems in order to support the decision process [15]: In a high water region the ground water head has to be kept below a certain level utilizing several wells whose yearly pumping cost has to be minimized according to the temporal flow and rise of new ground water. In Fig. 2 (visualized with Netscape Navigator and Cosmo's CosmoPlayer), several snapshots of two ground water heads, i.e. the original, already practiced (black) and the optimized (dark grey) pumping rate, over 4 years are shown including the location of the well, some control points (dark grey bars), different depth levels (almost transparent grey rectangle) and the upper level (dark grey rectangle). Aspects of anlaysis are the spatio-temporal behaviour of the ground water head at times when the pumping rate changes, the well's spatial influence on the ground water flow process, and correlations and differences between the two ground water heads.

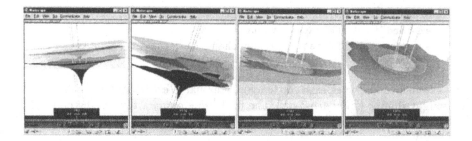

Fig. 2. Snapshots showing two temporal ground water heads

The VRML-file contains two resulting FEM-simulation data sets (106 FEs) mapped onto colored triangle irregular networks (TIN) at 160 different valid times. The time-referenced TINs are modelled as the base points of a geometrical time series which during presentation yields a continuously changing shape by linear interpolation. The VRML-file's size is about 10 MB, compressed 1.5 MB.

7.2 Visualizing Temporal GIS-Data

In this example the proposed VRML-nodes are used to visualize a set of synthetically produced temporal GIS-data representing the possible data of an urban planning application. i.e. constructions and natural objects (e.g. buildings, places, streets, parcs, trees) and events (e.g. reconstruction, demolition) of the historical development of a city (Fig. 3). Aspects of analysis are the visualization of historical maps and city views, the architectural and social development of certain city districts as well as periods of much construction activity.

Fig. 3. Snapshots showing historical views of a city

The data stored as the temporal visualization are sets of entities with time-variant geometries and appearances which exist at different periods in time. The time-variant sea level changes according to the tides. Note, that the waves are animated not by valid but by system time which can not be changed by the viewer. This time concept can be used for further cartographic techniques, such as object flashing for getting attention, time-variant symbols (e.g. rain symbol) or change in object's representation (e.g. re-expression). The VRML-file's size is about 38 kB.

8   Discussion and Future Work

One big advantage of our approach is that each interactive, temporal visualization can be stored in a file and integrated in a Web-page for later presentation or publication in the WWW, e.g. for knowledge transmission, cooperative work, marketing or documentation. The exploratory tools are kept with the new language constructs.

The document description language XML may be the new emerging standard for documents containing structured informations in the WWW. Because graphics are always a part of documents, their file formats should be integrated into this language to allow a tight interaction. X3D is the proposal of the VRML-community to reach this aim [44]. One future plan is the integration of the node types proposed in this paper in this process to feature interactive, temporal visualizations.

Many more exploratory tools are mentioned but not yet implemented, e.g. spatial focusing, spatial transformation, focusing and brushing based on the detail information, transient labels over visualized data with informations, such as names, detail informations, time series diagrams or non-spatial time-variant attributes.

In this implementation, temporal focusing involves a simple temporal aggregation technique which is adequate for events. For temporal graphical objects with longer valid periods only the first version is taken until now which is not adequate. Aggregation techniques which include the time-dependency of the spatial and non-spatial data are more appropriate.

Chaotic or non-linear behaviour of objects or object sets, especially, if the components start and cease to exist at different times (e.g. particles, smoke, explosion), is badly described by linear or step-wise functions. More special, i.e. functional, stochastic or evolutionary descriptions would better match these needs.

Contrary to this proposal, the user handles time information in form of readable dates and times based on specific calendars. For efficiency, it is assumed that authoring and presentation systems perform these transformations.

One inevitable disadvantage of spatio-temporal data is the size of the description. Generally, the size of each temporal object or attribute description is determined by the non-temporal description multiplied with the number of time-referenced changes. In relation to static worlds this increases the size of the VRML-file and download time multiple times. There are various approaches to reduce the file size: Authors can reduce the spatial and temporal description of less important objects by using linear interpolation or aggregation methods, i.e. reducing the number of polygons/vertices and times forming the base points of the temporal description. Content-independent approaches discussed by the

VRML-community are: object referencing, file compression, binary file formats or content streaming. Especially content streaming seems to be very useful for temporal data: the first snapshot can already be presented while the others are still be loaded.

The size of the spatio-temporal description leads also to a huge scene graph and object storage in the browser. If no temporal navigation is performed this has no effect on the processing time for each image (i.e. frame rate). However, on each temporal navigation action, performed interactively or via animation, the list of Validperiod nodes is parsed for validity at that specific time. If valid, the specific version of the object is determined which then changes the spatial appearance of the object in the scene graph. These steps increase processing time. So, reusing ValidPeriod and ValidTimeSensor nodes for multiple temporal attribute description and reducing the number of versions of each object is good practise in describing visualizations. Further techniques may be a level of detail for the spatial dimension of spatio-temporal objects and a level of interest for the temporal dimension to reduce the number of temporal objects parsed.

A browser-specific enhancement concerns the scene graph. Many objects do not need to be processed because they are not visible in the current view depending on the current viewpoint position, orientation and valid time. For static temporal scenes, a spatio-temporal access method may be very usable to reach the relevant set of objects in a short time [37].

9   Conclusion

This paper outlines our approach for a graphic description language for a new type of visualization, i.e. interactive, temporal visualizations (animations). Since 3D-graphics are not adequate for displaying data sets of spatio-temporal databases both in a spatial and temporal context, we propose to extend VRML with a new time dimension (valid time) for the description of temporal object informations, and an entity concept to organize graphical data in structures known from database modeling. With these constructs the WWW-based presentation systems or browsers (like WWW-based visual database interfaces) can offer a rich set of simple and easy to use exploratory tools during presentation to the public end user which can be applied for an improved, individual analysis of the distinct features (information aspects) of spatio-temporal data.

References

1. Andrienko, G.L., Andrienko, N.V.: Interactive Maps for Visual Data Exploration. On: ICA Commission on Visualization Meeting, Warshaw (1998)
2. Advanced Visual Systems Inc.: AVS/Express. At: http://www.avs.com
3. Bernard, L., Schmidt, B., Streit, U., Uhlenküken, C.: Managing, Modeling and Visualizing High-Dimensional Spatio-temporal Data in an Integrated System. In: GeoInformatica 2(1). Kluwer Academics Publishers (1998) 59-77
4. Bertin, J.: Semiology of Graphics: Diagrams, Networks, Maps. University of Wisconsin Press (1983)

5. Brilliant Digital Entertainment Inc.: B3D. At: http://www.bde3d.com (1999)
6. Buziek, G., Hatger, C.: Interactive animation and digital cartometry by VRML 2.0 and Java within a temporal environmental model on the basis of a DTM of the Elbe estuary and a 12 hour tide period. On: ICA Commission on Visualization Meeting, Warshaw (1998)
7. Claramunt, C., Thériault, M.: Managing Time in GIS: an Event-Oriented Approach. In: Clifford, J., Tuzhilin, A. (eds.): Recent Advances in Temporal Databases. Springer-Verlag (1995) 23-42
8. Coors, V., Jung, V.: Using VRML as an Interface to the 3D Data Warehouse. In: Proc. of 3. Symp. on VRML. ACM Press (1998)
9. Dransch, D.: Computer-Animationen in der Kartographie - Theorie und Praxis. Springer-Verlag (1997)
10. Dykes, J.A.: Exploring Spatial data Representation with Dynamic Graphics. In: Computer & Geosciences 23(4). Elsevier Science (1997) 345-370
11. Edsall, R., Peuquet, D.: A Graphical User Interface for the Integration of Time into GIS. Research Paper of The Apoala Project. Pennsylvania State University. Online Publication: http://www.geog.psu.edu/apoala/newPaper.html (1997)
12. Erwig, M., Güting, R.H., Schneider, M., Vazirgiannis, M.: Spatio-temporal Data Types: An Approach to Modeling and Querying Moving Objects in Databases. In: Proc. 1. CHOROCHRONOS Workshop on Spatio-Temporal Database Systems. ChoroChronos TR CH-97-02 (1997) 79-86
13. Esri Inc.: MapObjects. At: http://www.esri.com
14. GRAPE Manual. Inst. of Applied Mathematics. Univ. of Bonn and Univ. of Freiburg (1997)
15. Grauer, M., Barth, T., Kaden, S., Michels, I.: Decision Support and distributed Computing in Groundwater Management. In: Savic, D., Walters, G. (eds.): Water Industry Systems: Modelling and Optimization Applications. Research Studies Press Ltd. (1999)
16. Harrower, M., MacEachren, A.M.: Exploratory Data Analysis and map animation: Using temporal brushing and focusing to facilitate learning about global wheather. On: ICA Commission on Visualization Meeting, Warshaw (1998)
17. Hypercosm, Inc.: The Hypercosm 3D Graphics System. Rendering, Animation, Simulation, and VR System. At: http://www.hypercosm.com/ (1999)
18. Jern, M.: Information Visualization on the Web. On: CODATA Euro-American Workshop on Visualization of Information and Data (1997)
19. Jung, V.: Fuzzy effectiveness evaluation for intelligent user interfaces to GIS visualization. In: Proc. of 4th ACM Int. Workshop on Advances in GIS. ACM Press (1996) 157-164
20. Johnson, I.: Mapping the fourth dimension: the TimeMap project. In: Proc. of the 25th Conf. Computer Applications in Archaelogy (1997)
21. Kraak, M.-J., Edsall, R., MacEachren, A.M.: Cartographic Animation and Legends for Temporal Maps: Exploration and/or Interaction. In: Proc. of 18th Int. Cartographic Conf. in Stockholm (1997) 253-261
22. Kraak, M.-J., MacEachren, A.M.: Visualization of the Temporal Component of spatial Data. In: Waugh, T.C., Healey, R.G. (eds.): Proc. of 6. Int. Symp. on Spatial Data Handling. Taylor & Francis (1994) 391-409
23. Langran, G.: Analyzing and Generalizing Temporal Geographic Information. In: Proc. of GIS/LIS 1. ACSM-ASPRS-UIRSA-AM/FM (1993) 379-388
24. Luttermann, H., Grauer, M.: VRML History: Storing and Browsing Temporal 3D-Worlds. In: Proc. of 4. Symp. on VRML. ACM Press (1999) 153-160

25. MacEachren, A.M.: Time as a Cartographic Variable. In: Hearnshaw, K.M., Unwin, D.J. (eds.): Visualization in GIS. John Wiley & Sons (1994) 115-130
26. MacEachren, A.M., M.-J. Kraak, M.-J.: Exploratory Cartographic Visualization: Advancing the Agenda. In: Computers & Geosciences 23(4). Elsevier Science (1997) 335-343
27. MacEachren, A.M., Polsky, C., Haug, D., Brown, D., Boscoe, F., Beedasy, J., Pickle, L., Marrara, M.: Visualizing spatial Relationships among Health, Environmental, and Demographic Statistics: Interface Design Issues. In: Proc. of 18th Int. Cartographic Conf. in Stockholm (1997) 880-887
28. Moving Picture Experts Group. At: http://www.mpeg.org
29. Mirbel, I., Pernici, B., Vazirgiannis, M.: Modeling VRML Worlds with ECA Rules. Slides from the Dagstuhl Seminar: Integrating Spatial and Temporal Databases (1998)
30. Oz.com: Fluid3D. At: http://www.oz.com/fluid3d (1998)
31. Peterson, M.P.: Interactive and Animated Cartography. Prentice Hall (1995)
32. Pfoser, D., Tryfona, N.: Requirements, Definitions and Notations for Spatiotemporal Application Environments. ChoroChronos TR CH-98-09 (1998)
33. Shepherd, I.D.H.: Putting Time on the Map: Dynamic Display in Data Visualization and GIS. In: Fischer, P. (ed.): Innovation in GIS 2. Taylor & Francis (1995)
34. Schroeder, W.J., Martin, K.M., Lorensen, W.E.: The Visualization Toolkit: An object-Oriented Approach To 3D Graphics. Prentice Hall (1997)
35. Snodgras, R.T. (Ed.): The TSQL2 Temporal Query Language. Kluwer Academic Press (1995)
36. Tansel, A.U., Clifford, J., Gadia, S.K., Jajodia, S., Segev, A., Snodgras, R.T. (eds.): Temporal Databases: Theory, Design, and Implementation. Benjamin/Cummings (1993)
37. Theodoridis, Y.: Indexing Methods for Spatiotemporal Databases. In: Proc. 1. CHOROCHRONOS Workshop on Spatio-Temporal Database Systems. ChoroChronos TR CH-97-02 (1997) 37-42
38. Theodoulidis, B., Vakaloudis, A.: A Data Model and a Query Language for 3D Spatiotemporal Information. In: Proc. 1. CHOROCHRONOS Workshop on Spatio-Temporal Database Systems. ChoroChronos TR CH-97-02 (1997) 17-25
39. Tryfona, N., Jensen, C.S.: Conceptual Data Modeling for Spatiotemporal Applications. ChoroChronos TR CH-98-08 (1998)
40. Visviva Software Inc.: ScriptV. At: http://www.visviva.com (1998)
41. Tweedie, L.: Characterizing Interactive Externalizations. In: Proc. of CHI'97. ACM Press (1997)
42. VRML Architecture Group (VAG): The Virtual Reality Modeling Language Specifications ISO/IEC DIS 14772-1. At: http://www.web3d.org/Specifications/ VRML97/ (1997)
43. University of Siegen: The VRML History Homepage. At: http://www-winfo.uni-siegen.de/vrmlHistory/docs/index.html (1998)
44. Web3D Consortium: X3D. At: http://www.web3d.org (1999)

Nearest Neighbor Queries in a Mobile Environment

George Kollios[1], Dimitrios Gunopulos[2], and Vassilis J. Tsotras[2]

[1] Polytechnic University
Dept. of Computer and Information Science
Six MetroTech Center
Brooklyn, NY 11201-3840, USA
gkollios@db.poly.edu
[2] University of California, Riverside
Department of Computer Science and Engineering
Riverside, CA 92521, USA
dg@cs.ucr.edu, tsotras@cs.ucr.edu

Abstract. Nearest neighbor queries have received much interest in recent years due to their increased importance in advanced database applications. However, past work has addressed such queries in a static setting. In this paper we consider instead a dynamic setting where data objects move continuously. Such a mobile spatiotemporal environment is motivated by real life applications in traffic management, intelligent navigation and cellular communication systems. We consider two versions of nearest neighbor queries depending on whether the temporal predicate is a single time instant or an interval. For example: "find the closest object to a given object o after 10 minutes from now", or, "find the object that will be the closest to object o between 10 and 15 minutes from now". Since data objects move continuously it is inefficient to update the database about their position at each time instant. Instead our approach is to employ methods that store the motion function of each object and answer nearest neighbor queries by efficiently searching through these methods.

1 Introduction

A spatiotemporal database system manages data whose geometry changes over time. There are many applications that create such data, including global change (as in climate or land cover changes), transportation (traffic surveillance data, intelligent transportation systems), social (demographic, health, etc.), and multimedia (animated movies) applications. In general one could consider two spatial attributes of spatiotemporal objects which are time dependent, namely: position (i.e., the object's location inside some reference space) and extent (i.e., the area or volume the object occupies in the reference space)[8]. Depending on the application, one or both spatial attributes may change over time. Examples include: an airplane flying around the globe, a car traveling on a highway, the land covered by a forest as it grows/shrinks over time, or an object that concurrently moves and changes its size in an animated movie. For the purposes of this paper we concentrate on applications with objects which change position over time but whose extent remains unchanged. Hence for our purposes we represent such objects as points moving in some reference space ("mobile points").

The usual assumption in traditional database management systems is that data stored in the database remains constant until explicitly changed by an update. For example, if a price field is $5, it remains $5 until explicitly updated. This model is appropriate when data changes in discrete steps, but it is inefficient for applications with continuously changing data [20]. Consider for example a database keeping the position of mobile objects (like automobiles). The primary goal of this database is to correctly represent reality as objects move. Since objects move continuously updating the database about each object's position at each unit of time is clearly an inefficient and infeasible solution due to the prohibitively large update overhead. Updating the database only at few, representative time instants limits query accuracy.

A better approach is to abstract each object's position as a function of time $f(t)$, and update the database only when the parameters of f change (for example when the speed or the direction of a car changes). Using $f(t)$ the database can then compute the position of the mobile object at any time in the future (under the current knowledge about the motion characteristics of the database objects). Storing the motion function minimizes the update overhead, but it also introduces many novel problems since the database is not directly storing data values but functions to compute these values. Motion databases have recently attracted the interest of the database community. There is already a GIS system [2] that supports tracking and querying mobile objects. In the research front, [20–22, 8, 6] present Spatio-Temporal models and languages for querying the locations of such objects. Recently, [16] presents access methods for indexing mobile objects; the focus is on spatiotemporal range queries for objects moving in one and two dimensions. For example: "find the objects that will be inside a given query region P after 10 minutes from now".

In this paper we concentrate instead on answering nearest neighbor queries among the future locations of mobile objects. An example of such a spatiotemporal query is: "Report the object that will be the closest to an object o after 10 minutes from now". Since object o moves and it's motion information is known, the above query is equivalent to finding the object (except from object o) which will be the closest to position P after 10 minutes from now, where P is the position o will be in 10 minutes. Note that the answer to this query is tentative in the sense that it is computed based on the current knowledge stored in the database about the mobile objects' future motion functions. If this knowledge changes, the same query would produce a different answer.

We also examine nearest neighbor queries where instead of a time instant, an interval predicate in future is given as in: "Report the object that will be the closest to object o between 10 and 20 minutes from now". We will answer this query by reducing it to a combination of range queries and the above simple nearest neighbor queries.

We are not interested in providing new indices specifically designed for neighbor queries, as such would be of limited usefulness. In practice, neighbor queries are addressed by using traditional selection based indices (R-trees etc.) and modifying the search algorithm so that neighbor queries are also answered. We will follow the same approach here, thus utilizing the indexing techniques we have proposed in [16] and adapting them for neighbor searching.

As the number of mobile objects in the applications we consider (traffic monitoring, mobile communications, etc.) can be rather large we are interested in external memory solutions. While in general an object could move anywhere in the 3-dimensional space using some rather complex motion, we limit our treatment to objects moving in 1-dimensional space (a line) and whose location is described by a linear function of time. There is a strong motivation for such an approach based on the real-world applications we have in mind: straight lines are usually the faster way to get from one point to another; cars move in networks of highways which can be approximated by connected straight line segments on a plane; this is also true for routes taken by airplanes or ships. In addition, solving this simpler problem may provide intuition for addressing the more difficult nearest neighbor query among objects moving in 2- or 3-dimensional space.

2   Problem Description

We consider a database that keeps track of mobile objects moving on a finite line segment. We model the objects as points that move with a constant velocity starting from a specific location at a specific time instant. Using this information we can compute the location of an object at any time in the future for as long as its movement characteristics remain the same. Thus, an object started from location y_0 at time t_0 with velocity v (v can be positive or negative) will be in location $y_0 + v(t - t_0)$ at time $t > t_0$. Objects are responsible to update their motion information, every time when the speed or direction changes. When an object has reached the line segment limits, it has to issue an update. Such update can be either a deletion (the object is removed from the collection) or a reflection (direction and possibly speed change). Finally, we allow to insert a new object or to delete an existing one anywhere in the line segment, eg. the system is dynamic.

We first examine nearest neighbor queries described by a tuple (y_q, t_q) as in: "Report the object that will be closer to the point y_q at the time instant t_q (where $t_{now} \leq t_q$)". Section 3 describes two geometric representations of the problem, the primal plane (where object trajectories are represented as long lines in the time-position plane) and the dual plane (where a trajectory becomes a point). Two dual plane transformations are examined (Hough-X and Hough-Y). We present efficient algorithms for answering near neighbor queries in the primal and dual planes in section 4. A performance study appears in section 5. In section 6 we examine the nearest neighbor query with a time interval predicate ("Report the object that will be closer to the point y_q during the time interval $[t_{1q}, t_{2q}]$ (where $t_{now} \leq t_{1q}$)". We also discuss how our 1-dimensional results can be extended to apply on a limited 2-dimensional case, where the objects are restricted to moving in a given collection of line segments (like roads comprising a highway system). We call this the 1.5 dimensional case and discuss it in section 7. Finally, related work appears in section 8, while section 9 summarizes our findings and presents problems for future research.

3   Geometric representations

First, we partition the mobile objects into two categories, the objects with low speed $v \approx 0$ and the objects with speed between a minimum v_{min} and maximum speed v_{max}. We consider here the "moving" objects, eg. the objects with speed greater than v_{min}. The case of static or almost static objects can be solved using traditional approaches and we don't discuss this issue further.

The problem is to index the mobile objects in order to efficiently answer nearest neighbor queries over their locations into the future. The location of each object is described as a linear function of time, namely the location $y_i(t)$ of the object o_i at time t is equal to $v_i(t - t_{i_0}) + y_{i_0}$, where v_i is the velocity of the object and y_{i_0} is its location at t_{i_0}. We assume that the objects move on the $y-$axis between 0 and y_{max} and that an object can update its motion information whenever it changes. We treat an update as a deletion of the old information and an insertion of the new one. As in [16] we describe two geometric representations of the problem.

3.1   Space-time representation

In this representation we plot the trajectories of the mobile objects as lines in the time-location (t, y) plane. The equation of each line is $y(t) = vt + a$ where v is the slope (the velocity in our case) and a is the intercept, that can be computed by the motion information. In fact a trajectory is not a line but a semi-line starting from the point (y_i, t_i). However since we ask queries for the present or for the future, assuming that the trajectory is a line does not affect the correctness of the answer. Figure 1 shows a number of trajectories in the plane.

The query is expressed as a point (y_q, t_q) in the 2-dimensional space. The answer is the object that corresponds to the line that is closer to this point at the time t_q. So we have to consider the distance of the trajectories to the query point along the line $t = t_q$. For example in Figure 1 the answer to the nearest neighbor query is the object o_6.

3.2   The dual space-time representation

Duality is a transform frequently used in the computational geometry literature; in general it maps a hyper-plane h from R^d to a point in R^d and vice-versa. The duality transform is useful because it allows to formulate a problem in a more intuitive manner.

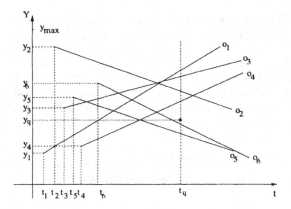

Fig. 1. Trajectories and query in (t, y) plane.

In our case we can map a line from the *primal* plane (t, y) to a point in the *dual* plane. In Figure 2, line l and point p are transformed to point l^* and line p^*. There is no unique duality transform, but a class of transforms with similar properties. Sometimes one transform is more convenient than another.

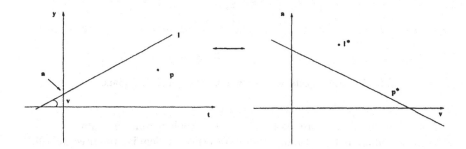

Fig. 2. Duality transform of a line and a point.

Consider a dual plane where one axis represents the slope of an object's trajectory and the other axis its y-intercept[1]. Thus the line with equation $y(t) = vt + a$ is represented by the point (v, a) in the dual space (this is called the Hough-X transform in [14]). While the values of v are between $-v_{max}$ and v_{max}, the values of the intercept are depended on the current time. If the current time is t_{now} then the range for a is $[-v_{max} \times t_{now}, y_{max} + v_{max} \times t_{now}]$.

The query is transformed to a line in the dual space. This line is the dual of the query point (t_q, y_q), thus it has the equation: $Q_l: a = -vt_q + y_q$ (Figure 3). Next we show the following lemma:

---

[1] The y-intercept is defined as the point where a given line intersects the y-axis. Similarly t-intercept is the point where a line intersect the t-axis.

Lemma 1. *The nearest neighbor to the query point (t_q, y_q), is the object whose dual point is closest to the line that is the dual of the query point.*

Proof. Assume a query point (s_1, t_1) and an object with trajectory $y = v_1 x + a_1$. The distance of this object to the query point at the time t_1 is $D = |v_1 t_1 + a_1 - s_1|$, and it is computed along the line $t = t_1$. In the dual plane the same distance has to be computed along the line $v = v_1$. If the Euclidean distance of the object to the query line in the dual space is d, then it is easy to show that $D = d\cos(\theta)$, where θ is the slope of the query line.   □

Thus we can use the Euclidean distance to compute the nearest neighbor in the dual space, although this is not true for the primal space.

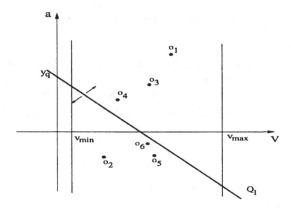

Fig. 3. Data objects and query in the Hough-X dual plane.

Note that the dual representation has the problem that the values of the intercept are unbounded. A simple solution to this problem is presented in [16].

To solve the problem we use our assumption that when an object crosses a border it issues an update (i.e. it is deleted or reflected). Combining this assumption with the minimal speed, we can assure that all objects have updated their motion information at least once during the last T_{period} time instants, where $T_{period} = \frac{v_{max}}{v_{min}}$. We can then use two distinct index structures. The first index stores all objects that have issued their last update in the period $[0, T_{period}]$. The second index stores objects that have issued their last update in the interval $[T_{period}, 2T_{period}]$. Each object is stored only once, either in the first or in the second index. Before time T_{period}, all objects are stored in the first index. However, every object that issues an update after T_{period} is deleted from the first index and it is inserted in the second index. The intercept of the first index is computed by using the line $t = 0$ and for the second index using the line $t = T_{period}$. Thus we are sure that the intercept will always have values between 0 and $v_{max} \times T_{period}$. To query the database we use both indices. After time $2T_{period}$ we know that the first index is empty and all objects are stored in the second index, since every object have issued at least one update from T_{period} to $2T_{period}$. At that time we remove the empty index and we initiate a new one with time period $[2T_{period}, 3T_{period}]$. We continue in the same way and every T_{period} time instants we initiate a new index and we remove an empty one. Using this method the intercept is bounded while the performance of the index structures remain asymptotically the same as if we had only one structure.

Another way to represent a line $y = vt + a$, is to write the equation as $t = \frac{1}{v}y - \frac{a}{v}$. Then we can map this line to a point in the dual plane with coordinates $n = \frac{1}{v}$ and $b = -\frac{a}{v}$ (Hough-Y in [14]).

4   Algorithms to answer nearest neighbor queries

An obvious approach would be to check all the objects and return the closest to the query point. However this method is inefficient since the number of mobile objects can be large. Hence, we discuss methods that avoid a linear scan on the data set by using index structures. For each representation we present possible indices and methods to use these indices for nearest neighbor search.

4.1   Using traditional methods

In the space-time representation we can use a Spatial Access Method (SAM) to index the lines or line segments. Possible methods include R-tree and Quadtree based indices. Then we can use the algorithms proposed by Hjaltason and Samet [12] or by Roussopoulos at. al. [17] to find the lines that are closer to the query point. These algorithms work for any hierarchical index structure which uses recursive partitioning. Note that in [5] it was shown that the algorithm in [12] is the optimal algorithm for nearest neighbor search, in the sense that we access the smallest number of pages to answer a nearest neighbor query, given an underlying index structure. The main idea of these algorithms is to traverse the hierarchical structure in a top-down fashion and keep for every visited partition a list of subpartitions ordered by their distance to the query point. We then visit the subpartitions in sorted order. We can prune some subpartitions, when the minimum distance of these partitions to the query point is larger than the distance of an already found object. In [12], a global priority queue is used to keep both the subpartitions and the objects found up to know in a sorted order. It is obvious that we can use the above algorithms to process our query, since these algorithms work for any type of objects. The only difference is the way we compute the distance of the objects to query point. We don't use the Euclidean distance but the distance along the line $t = t_q$.

The main problem of this approach is that there are no efficient index structures for indexing lines or very large line segments. In case of hierarchical methods with overlapping partitions, like R-tree[11] or R*-tree[4], the overlapping is extensive, resulting in a very poor query performance. On the other hand, methods that partition the data space into disjoin cells and use clipping(like PMR-quadtree[18] or R+-tree[19]), will have a very high space consumption (in our case probably superlinear).

4.2   Using *kd*-tree methods in the dual

There is a large number of access methods that have been proposed to index
point data[10]. All these structures were designed to address *orthogonal* range
queries, eg. queries expressed as multidimensional hyper-rectangles. However,
most of them can be used to answer nearest neighbor queries as well.

We use this approach to answer the nearest neighbor query in the dual Hough-
X space (Figure 3). An index structure based on *kd*-trees is used to store the dual
points. In our experiments we used the hB^{Π}-tree [9]. Next a traversal algorithm
similar to the algorithm presented in [12] is used to find the answer. The only
difference here is that we compute the distance of the regions or the data points
to the line that represents the query in the dual space and not to a point.

4.3   Using *B*+-trees in the dual

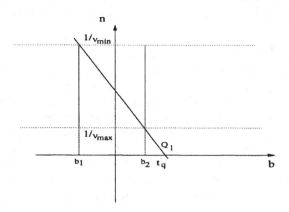

Fig. 4. Query in the Hough-Y dual plane.

A different approach is based on the *query approximation* method presented
in [16]. Consider the Hough-Y dual plane and a query line in that plane with
equation: $b = -y_q n + t_q$. We assume that the b coordinate is computed using a
general horizontal line with equation $y = y_r$, where y_r is a value between 0 and
y_{max} (note that the t-axis is the line $y = 0$). We can use an one dimensional data
structure (B+-tree) to index the dual points using only the b coordinate. The
query line is mapped to an 1-dimensional range on this structure, for example in
the Figure 4 the range is (b_1, b_2) where $b_1 = t_q - \frac{y_q - y_r}{v_{min}}$ and $b_2 = t_q - \frac{y_q - y_r}{v_{max}}$. Now
we can use this structure to answer the nearest neighbor query. Note however
that the size of the range query is proportional to $|y_q - y_r|$. So, we can decrease
the size of this range if we keep c index structures at equidistant y_r's (see Figure
5). While we can still get the correct answer with $c = 1$ using some limited
replication (small $c > 1$) we get better performance.

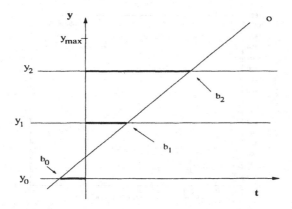

Fig. 5. Using three indices to store a moving object.

All c indices contain the same information about the objects, but use different y_r's. The i-th index stores the b coordinates of the data points using $y = \frac{y_{max}}{c} \times i$, $i = 0, .., c - 1$. However the index that is closer to the query point has a smaller range to search, and therefore we expect that the query time to process the nearest neighbor query will be smaller. In Figure 6 we describe an algorithm that is used to answer the nearest neighbor query using the above one dimensional structures.

1. Choose the structure that is the closest to the query point.
2. Find the range (b_1, b_2) where the query is mapped. Find the closest object to the query point y_q inside this range. This is the nearest neighbor (NN) so far.
3. Start visiting the previous and the next pages and update the NN if necessary. Stop condition: check if it is possible to find a nearest point than the current NN in the next pages using v_{min} and in the previous pages using the v_{max}. Stop when this is not possible.

Fig. 6. Algorithm to compute the nearest neighbor for mobile objects

5   A Performance Study

We present initial results for the nearest neighbor query, comparing the 1-dimensional structures, the kd-tree method and a traditional R-tree based approach. First we describe the way experimental data is generated. At time $t = 0$ we generated the initial locations of N mobile points uniformly distributed on the terrain $[0, 1000]$. We varied N from $100k$ to $500k$. The speeds were generated uniformly from $v_{min} = 0.16$ to $v_{max} = 1.66$ and the direction randomly positive or negative.[2] Then all points start moving. When a point reaches a border simply

---

[2] Note that 0.16 miles/min is equal to 10 miles/hour and 1.66 miles/min is equal to 100 miles/hour.

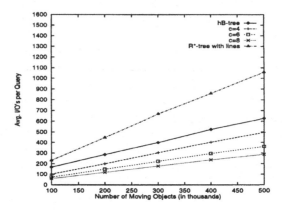

Fig. 7. Query Performance for Nearest Neighbor Queries.

it changes its direction. At each time instant we choose 200 objects randomly and we randomly change their speed and/or direction. We generate 10 different time instants that represent the times when queries are executed. At each such time instant we execute 200 nearest neighbor queries, where the y-coordinate is chosen uniformly between 0 and 1000 and the time instant between t_{now} and $t_{now} + 60$. We run the above scenario using a particular access method for 2000 time instants.

To verify that indexing mobile objects as line segments is not efficient, we stored the trajectories in an R*-tree. We fixed the page size to 4096 bytes. All methods had page capacity equal to 340 except the R-tree where the page capacity was 204. We consider a simple buffering scheme for the results we present here. For each tree we buffer the path from the root to a leaf node, thus the buffer size is only 3 or 4 pages. For the queries we always clear the buffer pool before we run a query. An update is performed when the motion information of an object changes.

In Figure 7 we present the results for the average number of I/O's per nearest neighbor query. The approximation method used $c = 4, 6$ and 8 B+-trees. As anticipated, the line segments method with R*-trees has the worst performance. Also, the approximation method outperforms the hB^{Π}-tree.

In Figures 8 and 9 we plot the space consumption and the average number of I/O's per update respectively. We did not report the update performance for the R*-tree method because it was very high (more than 90 I/O's per update). The update and space performance of the hB^{Π}-tree is better than the other methods since its objects are stored only once and better clustered than the R*-tree. The update performance of the hB^{Π}-tree and the approximation approach remain constant for different number of mobile objects. The space of all methods is linear to the number of objects. The approximation approach uses more space

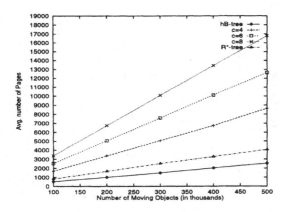

Fig. 8. Space Consumption.

due to the use of c observation indices. There is a tradeoff between c and the query/update performance.

6   Nearest Neighbor Queries with time interval predicate

Another interesting nearest neighbor query is a query where a time interval is given instead of a time point. This time interval and the trajectory of the query object create a line segment in the space-time plane. The answer to the query is the object that comes closest to the query object during this time interval, or equivalently to the query line segment. Note that this problem is important only in a spatiotemporal environment. For example in Figure 10, o_4 is the query object and $[t_{1q}, t_{2q}]$ the time interval. The answer to this query are the objects o_5 and o_6, since at some point during the time interval, these objects have zero distance from the query object. However if we ask for the three nearest neighbors, then the objects o_7 belongs also to the result. A method to answer the query is to find first the lines that intersect the query line segment. If there is no such line, then we run two nearest neighbor queries, one on each of the two ends of the line segment and keep the best answer. This is correct because the trajectories of the mobile objects are straight lines. In particular we can show that the time where an object is closer to the query object, has to be one of the time instants t_{1q} or t_{2q}, if the trajectories of the mobile objects have no common point during the query interval $[t_{1q}, t_{2q}]$.

In the primal plane we can modify the existing algorithms for query points and find the lines closest to the line segment. However the performance of these methods will be at least as bad as the case for query point.

In the dual plane we can use the method described above. The query to find the lines that intersect the query line segment is a non-orthogonal range query. To answer this query we can use the methods proposed in [16]. If no answer is

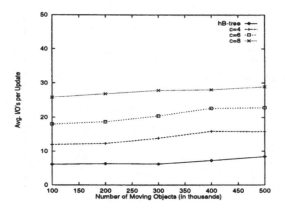

Fig. 9. Update Performance.

found, the we run two nearest neighbor queries for the time instants t_1 and t_2 and keep the closest object.

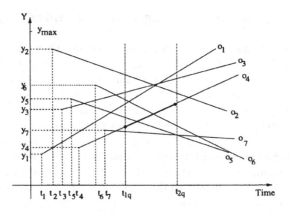

Fig. 10. Data objects and query with time interval predicate.

7   The 1.5-dimensional case

There is an interesting restricted version of the general 2-dimensional problem where our 1-dimensional algorithms can be easily extended. We consider objects moving in the plane but their movement is restricted on using a given collection of line segments (routes, roads) on the finite terrain. Due to its restriction, we call this case the 1.5-dimensional problem. There is a strong motivation for such an environment: in many applications objects (cars, airplanes etc.) move on a network of specific routes (highways, airways).

The 1.5-dimensional problem can be reduced to a number of 1-dimensional problems. In particular, we propose representing each predefined route as a sequence of connected (straight) line segments. The positions of these line segments on the terrain are indexed by a standard spatial access method (SAM). Given that the number of routes is usually much smaller than the number of objects moving on them, and that each route can be approximated by a small number of straight lines, maintaining such an index is straightforward (in addition, new routes are added rather infrequently.)

Indexing the objects moving on a given route is an 1-dimensional model and will use techniques from the previous section. Given a Nearest Neighbor query for a given two-dimensional point, we identify first the route that passes closest to the point. We could use the spatial access method and traditional NN techniques [12,17] for finding this route (line segment) as the collection of routes is rather static. Once the route that passes closest to the query point is identified, we find the Nearest Neighbor of the query point among the objects on that route. This object must also be the nearest point to the orthogonal projection of the query point on the route line. To find it, we take the orthogonal projection of the query point onto the route, and solve the one dimensional problem of finding the Nearest Neighbor of the projection among the points on the route. Let d be the distance of the nearest neighbor on the closest route and the query point.

Thus we obtain an upper bound, d, on the distance of the true nearest neighbor point to the query. Clearly we have to consider only the points that are on routes that are closer than d to the query time. To find those routes we perform a range query on the SAM data structure we use to keep all routes. This will return all routes with L_{inf} distance from the query point less than d. We sort the routes according to distance from the query point and find the nearest neighbor to the query point on each route, updating the global nearest point when a closer point is found. We terminate this process if the distance of the next route to be considered is larger than the nearest point found so far.

8 Related Work

There is a lot of work on the Nearest Neighbor problem in spatial domains. However this work has concentrated on the static case, where points or objects remain in a fixed location.

Roussopoulos et al [17] give an R-tree based algorithm to find the point closest to the query point. Hjaltason and Samet [12] give a different algorithm based on Quadtrees. These algorithms can be extended to handle moving points, where the trajectory of a point is modeled by a line, but this straightforward modification does not work very well, as our experimental results show.

In both of the previous approaches the points are stored in external memory. Recent work on the Nearest Neighbor problem is mainly on main memory algorithms and for the high-dimensional setting. Both the exact nearest neighbor problem [15] and the approximate nearest neighbor problem [13] [3] have been considered. These algorithms however have either query times that are exponential to the dimensionality of the space, or require more than linear space. In addition these approaches cannot be easily modified to find the closest point to a line (instead of a point).

We also note that computational geometry work on arrangements is very relevant in our setting. The trajectories of the n points in the time-space plane define an arrangement, that is a partition of the plane into convex regions. A point y_q at time t_q will be in the interior of one of these regions. To find the line that is closest to it, we have to find the lines that form the boundary of the convex region the point is in, and examine them only. It can be shown that this can be done in $O(\log n)$ time. However the arrangement of the lines takes $O(n^2)$ time to compute, in the main memory model, and also requires $O(n^2)$ space to keep [1].

9   Summary and Future Work

In this paper we present efficient external memory data structures to solve the nearest neighbor problem in the setting of points that move with constant velocity. The queries we want to answer are of the form: given a point y_q and a time instant t_q, find the point that is closest to y_q at the time t_q, or, given a (moving) point y_q, and a time interval, find the point that come closest to y_q during this time interval. We consider mainly the one dimensional case, and extend out results to the 1.5-dimensional case.

We plan to work on the nearest neighbor problem when the points move in two dimensional space. The main problem in two dimensions is that the trajectories of the points are lines in three-dimensional space, and therefore taking the duality transformation does not help. Since we are using the Euclidean norm, we cannot solve the problem separately in the x-axis and y-axis and combine the results either. Many points may be closer to the query point in the x-coordinate or the y-coordinate than the the nearest point, and yet have larger Euclidean distances.

Another area for future work is giving an algorithm for the join operation, that is, find for all points the nearest neighbor at a query time.

10   Acknowledgement

We were introduced to the problems of indexing moving points by Ouri Wolfson at the 1997 Dagstuhl Seminar on Temporal Databases. The authors would like to thank O. Wolfson, C. Faloutsos and V.S. Subrahmanian for many helpful discussions. We would also like to thank G. Evangelidis for the hB-tree code.

References

1. P. Agarwal and M. Sharir. Arrangements and their applications. in *Handbook of Computational Geometry*, (J. Sack, ed.), North Holand, Amsterdam.

2. ArcView GIS. ArcView Tracking Analyst. 1998.

3. S. Arya, D. M. Mount, N. S. Netanyahu, R. Silverman and A. Wu. An optimal algorithm for approximate nearest neighbor searching. Journal of the ACM, to appear.

4. N. Beckmann, H.-P. Kriegel, R. Schneider, and B. Seeger. The R*-tree: An Efficient and Robust Access Method For Points and Rectangles. In *Proc. ACM-SIGMOD International Conference on Management of Data*, pages 322–331, Atlantic City, May 1990.

5. S. Berchtold, C. Bohm, D. Keim, H.-P. Kriegel. A Cost Model For Nearest Neighbor Search in High-Dimensional Data Space. In *Proc. 16th ACM-PODS*, pp. 78-86, 1997.

6. J. Chomicki and P. Revesz. A Geometric Framework for Specifying Spatiotemporal Objects. *Proc. 6th International Workshop on Time Representation and Reasoning*, May 1999.

7. D. Comer. The Ubiquitous B-Tree. *Computing Surveys*, 11(2):121–137, June 1979.

8. M. Erwig, R.H. Guting, M. Schneider and M. Vazirgianis. Spatio-temporal Data Types: An Approach to Modeling and Querying Moving Objects in Databases. In *Proc. of ACM GIS Symposium '98*.

9. G. Evangelidis, D. Lomet, and B. Salzberg. The hB$^{\Pi}$-tree: A Modified hB-tree Supporting Concurrency, Recovery and Node Consolidation. In *Proc. 21st International Conference on Very Large Data Bases*, Zurich, September 1995, pages 551–561.

10. V. Gaede and O. Gunther. Multidimensional Access Methods. *ACM Computing Surveys*, 30(2):170-231, 1998.

11. A. Guttman. R-Trees: A Dynamic Index Structure For Spatial Searching. In *Proc. ACM-SIGMOD International Conference on Management of Data*, pages 47–57, Boston, June 1984.

12. G. R. Hjaltason and H. Samet. Ranking in Spatial Databases. In *Proc. 4th Int. Symp. on Spatial Databases*, pp. 83-95, 1995.

13. P. Indyk and R. Motwani. Approximate Nearest Neighbors: Towards Removing the Curse of Dimensionality. In *Proc.30th ACM-STOC*, pp. 604-613, 1998.

14. H. V. Jagadish. On Indexing Line Segments. In *Proc. 16th International Conference on Very Large Data Bases*, pages 614–625, Brisbane, Queensland, Australia, August 1990.

15. J. Kleinberg. Two Algorithms for Nearest-Neighbor Search in High Dimensions. In *Proc. 29th ACM-STOC*, pp. 599-608, 1997.

16. G. Kollios, D. Gunopulos and V.J. Tsotras. On Indexing Mobile Objects. In *Proc. 18th ACM-PODS*, 1999.

17. N. Roussopoulos, S. Kelley, F. Vincent. Nearest Neighbor Queries. In *Proc. ACM-SIGMOD Int. Conf. on Management of Data*, pages 71-79, June 1992.

18. H. Samet. *The Design and Analysis of Spatial Data Structures.*, Addison-Wesley, Reading, MA, 1990.

19. T. Sellis, N. Roussopoulos and C. Faloutsos. The R+-Tree: A Dynamic Index for Multi-Dimensional Objects. In *Proc. 13rd International Conference on Very Large Data Bases*, pages 507-518, Brighton, England, September 1987.

20. A. P. Sistla, O. Wolfson, S. Chamberlain, S. Dao. Modeling and Querying Moving Objects. In *Proc. 13th IEEE International Conference on Data Engineering*, pages 422-432, Birmingham, U.K, April 1997.

21. O. Wolfson, S. Chamberlain, S. Dao, L. Jiang, G. Mendez. Cost and Imprecision in Modeling the Position of Moving Objects. In *Proc. 14th IEEE International Conference on Data Engineering*, pages 588-596, Orlando, Florida, February 1998.
22. O. Wolfson, B. Xu, S. Chamberlain, L. Jiang. Moving Objects Databases: Issues and Solutions In *Proceedings of the 10th International Conference on Scientific and Statistical Database Management*. Capri, Italy, July 1998.

A Framework of a Generic Index for Spatio-Temporal Data in CONCERT

Lukas Relly[1,2], Alexander Kuckelberg[1], and Hans-Jörg Schek[1]

[1] Database Research Group
Institute of Information Systems, ETH Zürich
CH-8092 Zürich, Switzerland
{relly, kuckelbe, schek}@inf.ethz.ch
WWW home page: http://www-dbs.ethz.ch
[2] Current address: UBS AG
Postfach, 8098 Zürich
lukas.relly@ubs.com

Abstract. In this paper we present the prototype database system CON-CERT and the incorporation of a framework of a generic index tree for spatio-temporal data. We show the ideas behind the CONCERT architecture as far as they are important to understand the framework approach presented. We show how the index is based on the conceptual behaviour of data in contrast to generalized algorithms or methods. Because of the simplicity of R-trees we take an R-tree like structure to explain our generic spatio-temporal index. It is remarkable that in CONCERT a generic index can be defined without any predefined "hard-wired" spatial or temporal data types such as intervals or rectangles. As it turns out the only important properties needed are an OVERLAP and a SPLIT function, the first one checking for spatial or temporal overlap of objects, the second one providing a hierarchical decomposition of the data space into subspaces. If, in addition, splitting of data objects is allowed we are able to define manageable node sizes, leading to an improved generic index similar to R+-trees or other derivations.

1 Introduction

Spatio-temporal database systems have obtained increasingly high attention due to the fact of more spatial and temporal data being available and complex application requirements demanding an integrated view of space and time in large data collections. Traditional database systems and database technology is inadequate to fulfill these requests. Spatio-temporal applications have many special requirements. They deal with very complex objects, for example objects with complex boundaries such as clouds and moving points through 3D space, large objects such as remote sensing data, or large time series data. These complex objects are manipulated in even more complex ways. Analysis and evaluation programs draw conclusions combining many different data source. Therefore new techniques have to be found and well-established techniques from spatial only and temporal only databases have to be integrated. This integration relies upon a flexible and open system architecture allowing the combination of different — and so far studied isolated from each other — techniques of query processing, query optimization, indexing, and transaction management.

In order to better support advanced applications, the standardization effort of SQL3 specifies, among others, new data types and new type constructors. Most recently, SQL3 and object-orientation have fostered the development of generic extensions called datablades [13], cartridges [14], or extenders [11]. They are based on the concept of abstract data types and often come with specialized indexing. The important idea behind is to provide a generic system capable of being extended internally by application-specific modules integrating the functionality required for specialized applications as close as possible into the DBMS taking advantage of the monolithic architecture while avoiding its deficiencies. Figure 1 illustrates the general system architecture of extensible systems.

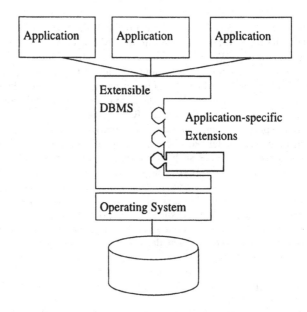

Fig. 1. The extensible system architecture

In this paper we will present the architecture of the database prototype system CONCERT, that follows the extensible system architecture. We show the ideas behind CONCERT and how this approach, which is based on the characterization of the behaviour of data and not on a type system, can be used to incorporate generic spatio-temporal indexes into the kernel system. The index together with the CONCERT kernel system forms a framework (in the sense of [6] or [12]) for spatio-temporal data management systems in which each limitation to "hard-wired" data types is avoided. We see this as the main contribution of the paper. The advantage of such an approach is that a generic R-tree like structure can be adapted to many variants of actual implementations of trees indexing spatio or temporal data or both just differing the functions OVERLAP and SPLIT.

1.1 Related Work

In [22], Stonebraker introduced the idea of a generic B-tree that depends only on the existence of an ordering operation to index arbitrary data objects. This idea is consequently extended in the CONCERT kernel system which identifies data by its behaviour and not by its type. In our own previous work [3, 18, 19] we presented algorithms for generic inverted file indexes, generic vertical partitioning, and simple generic spatial partitioning useful for raster data organization. The generic index presented here is closely related to generic search tree approaches such as GiST [10] with one main difference: GiST expects the implementation of certain generic methods for different key values data types (e.g. $\mathbb{Z}$ for B-trees or $\mathbb{R} \times \mathbb{R}$ for R-trees). In contrast CONCERT and our generic index is based on the classification of data behavior. The concrete data type is only published to the CONCERT system and all other extensions just use its classification but no knowledge about the data itself. However, the ideas in [10] are complementary and can easily be integrated into the generic index we present in this paper.

In the following Section 2 we first repeat some basic notions, ideas and architectural issues of the CONCERT system which are necessary to understand the generic index tree for spatio-temporal data which is presented in Section 3. We also discuss the generic algorithms for the construction and usage of the generic indexing structure in Section 3 before we conclude in Section 4.

2 The Concert Architecture

The CONCERT prototype database system's primary focus is to provide a platform for investigation of physical database design in an extensible kernel system as well as for generic query processing over heterogeneous distributed repositories [2, 18]. The CONCERT general architecture is similar to other extensible DBMS such as Postgres [17, 21], DASDBS [20], or Starburst [9]. It consists of a kernel system for low-level data management and query processing as well as an object manager providing advanced query functionality. The kernel is responsible for the management of individual objects within collections, resource and storage management and low-level transaction management. CONCERT provides a generic framework ([6]) for physical database design for external objects. The object manager combines different collections adding join capability to the kernel collections. Figure 2 shows an overview of the CONCERT architecture.

One of the important issues of the CONCERT architecture is it's built-in support for interoperability. Todays DBMS make the implicit assumption that their services are provided only to data stored inside the database. All data has to be imported into and being "owned" by the DBMS in a format determined by

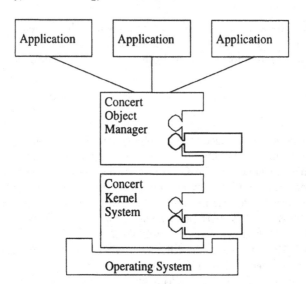

Fig. 2. Overview of the CONCERT system architecture

the DBMS. Traditional database applications such as banking usually meet this assumption. These applications are well supported by the DBMS data model, its query and data manipulation language and its transaction management. Advanced applications such as spatio-temporal applications however differ in many aspects from traditional database applications. Individual operations in these applications are much more complex and not easily expressible in existing query languages. Powerful specialized systems, tools and algorithms exist for a large variety of tasks requiring a spatio-temporal database system to interoperate with other systems. CONCERT's mechanism of providing the necessary infrastructure for application extensions can be used to interoperate with other systems. According to its system architecture consisting of a kernel system and an object manager layer, application extensions and interoperability can take place on both levels. The kernel is responsible for managing and performing physical database design for individual objects and allows access to individual remote data objects. The object manager handles collections of objects and combine them using a query language. In the same way as it combines *internal* collections, it can combine *external* collections made accessible through application-specific wrappers being plugged into the object manager. Details can be found in [16].

Throughout the rest of the paper, we illustrate how the CONCERT extensible architecture can be exploited for a flexible spatio-temporal DBMS. We particularly focus on a generic R-tree-like indexing mechanism but other indexing structures than trees might also be possible.

2.1   The Concert Kernel System

The CONCERT kernel system consists of two components, the Storage Object Manager (SOM) and the Abstract Object Manager (AOM). The SOM provides standard DBMS base services such as segment management, buffer management, and management of objects on database pages. It is tightly integrated into the underlying operating system exploiting multi-threading and multiprocessing. It uses a hardware-supported buffer management exploiting the operating systems virtual memory management by implementing a memory-mapped buffer [1]. Details of the CONCERT SOM can be found in [15].

The Abstract Object Manager provides the core functionality for extending the kernel with application-specific code. It implements a fundamental framework for the management of collections. It uses the individual objects handled internally by the SOM or, through its interoperability capability, by an external storage system, combining them into collections. The AOM collection interface defines operations to insert, delete and update individual objects. Retrieval of objects is performed through direct object access or through collection scans. Scans are initiated using an optional predicate filtering the qualifying objects. Figure 3 shows the (simplified) collection interface definition.

```
createInstance (coll_description) :- coll_handle
deleteInstance (coll_handle)

insertObject    (coll_handle, object) :- object_key
deleteObject    (coll_handle, object_key)
updateObject    (coll_handle, old_key, object) :- new_key
getObject       (coll_handle, object_key) :- object

scanStart       (coll_handle, predicate) :- scan_handle
scanGet         (scan_handle) :- object
scanNext        (scan_handle)
scanClose       (scan_handle)
```

Fig. 3. AOM collection interface (simplified)

Indexes are treated similar to base collections. From the AOM's perspective, they are collections of objects containing the index entry (the attribute to be indexed on) and the object key of the base collection. Accessing data using an index is performed by an index scan identifying all qualifying object keys that are subsequently used to retrieve the objects themselves. Depending on the kind of the index and the query, the objects retrieved might have to be filtered further performing a false drops elimination.

On object insertion, the object is inserted into the base collection first. The insertion operation of the base collection returns an object key that can be used for the index entry. Because the index uses the same interface as the base collection, hierarchies of indexes can easily be built. This allows for example an inverted file index to be indexed itself by a B-tree index. The conceptual equality of base collections of objects and the index collections of their keys enables the components to be combined in many different ways providing a powerful tool that goes fare beyond simple indexing and includes things such as constraint validation and trigger mechanisms.

A special aspect of the CONCERT approach is the fact, that indexing in particular and physical database design in general is performed for abstract data types. Obviously it is not possible to index completely unknown objects. Some knowledge of the user-defined objects has to be available to the storage system. In the following section, we address this issue identifying a small set of physical design concepts sufficient to allow most physical design decisions, specially R-tree like generic index frameworks with minimal restrictions to the flexibility of external objects.

2.2   Extensible Physical Database Design in the Concert Kernel

To explain the CONCERT physical database design extensibility idea, let us first look at a standard B-tree index [5], as it is implemented in most database systems. A B-tree stores keys of objects ordered by their values. The ordering operation is chosen depending on the data type of the key value: for data type "NUMBER", standard ordering over numbers is used whereas "STRING" data types are lexicographical ordered. Another ordering operation is used for "DATE" data types. Much more data types can be possible but the central aspect when data is indexed by an B-tree is that there is an attribute which can be ordered (see [22]). On the other hand data types which can't be ordered can't be indexed by a B-tree.

The generalization of this observation is the basis of the *abstract object storage type* concept in CONCERT: The knowledge of the type of data is not needed to manage it but its conceptual behaviour and the operations associated with these concepts, called *concept typical operations*[1]. Four concepts data type might follow can be identified:

- SCALAR: A data type belongs to the SCALAR concept, if there is an ordering operation. All data types behaving *like* a SCALAR can be indexed e.g. by a B-tree.
- LIST: A data type belongs to the LIST concept, if it consists of a set of components over which an iterator is defined. A data type behaving like a LIST might be a list of keywords, forming the inverted index of a text document. The concept typical operations are FIRST and NEXT.
- RECORD: A data type belongs to the RECORD concept if it is a ordered concatenation of components which themselves are arbitrary concepts. The concept

---

[1] By concept typical operations, we mean the methods the user must provide to allow CONCERT to interpret a given abstract object storage type. Concept typical operations are the means of extensibility of the CONCERT kernel.

typical operation is the SUB_OBJECT operation returning a component of the RECORD. A RECORD is the realization of object partitioning.

- SPATIAL: A data type belongs to the SPATIAL concept if it is extended in an arbitrary data space and can be indexed with respect to its spatial properties. This is the most important concept in the context of spatio-temporal data and will be explained in detail in the next subsection. Note that this concept is not limited to geometric space or time resp. the corresponding data types. The concept typical operations are OVERLAPS, SPLIT, COMPOSE and APPROX which are also explained in the following.

Spatial Indexes and the SPATIAL-Concept: Even if the SPATIAL-concept is not limited to geometric space or time data, these are the most common data spaces of this concept.

There exists a multitude of spatial and temporal index structures in the literature. Gaede and Günther give an overview of important multidimensional access methods in [7] and a comparison of access methods for temporal data can be found in [23].

In order to come up with a generic spatial-temporal index we observe that most spatial, temporal and spatio-temporal indexes are similar in the following way: they organize the objects according to their space-subspace-relationships. Typical queries that are well supported with spatial and temporal indexes include the search for objects in certain regions using spatial predicates (overlaps, intersects, covers) or objects concerning certain time intervals. In order to support such queries, most spatial indexes decompose the data space into — possibly overlapping — subspaces assigning these subspaces to subtrees of the index structure. Queries are well supported, if only a few subtrees have to be searched. Therefore, physical clustering of spatially and temporally neighboured objects is essential. Indexing structures other than trees are possible but are not discussed in this paper. The important point here is that indexing structures can be implemented and plugged into CONCERT independent of the data type indexed by just using the concept typical operations of data objects following the SPATIAL concept.

We found that there are three important spatial classes of objects involved in spatial indexing. These classes are closely related to each other:

- Application objects: In the context of extensible systems, these objects are abstract and might vary from one application area to the other.
- Query objects: These objects are used to formulate queries. Depending on the application, the type of these objects might be the same as for application objects. However, usually, only a small set of different object types are used for querying, the most important being the rectangular query window.
- Space covering objects: These spatial objects represent the space covered by a node or a subtree in the index structure. Typical index structures use rectangles for their subspace describing objects. Other more complex objects such as convex polygons are possible, but in order to keep index traversing operations efficient, simple geometric objects usually are preferred.

Note that at this point we are much more general and flexible that given implementations of trees: We only determine the concept of the node objects, not their structure or type.

In traditional systems, the third class of spatial objects is predefined by the index method provided and therefore "hard-wired" in the system, e.g. a space covering rectangle in the R-tree. Therefore, also the first two classes have to be predefined by the DBMS requiring the user to convert his or her data into the DBMS format. This clearly is not desirable in the context of extensible systems. CONCERT follows a different paradigm. Rather than predefining spatial index objects and thereby forcing the data structure of user objects and user queries, it allows the user to implement not only the application and query objects, but also corresponding index objects. The spatial index algorithm is written in a generic way only exploiting the spatial space-subspace relationships through method invocation.

These spatial[2] relationships define the concept typical operations of the SPATIAL concept as follows:

- The operation OVERLAPS checks for spatial overlap of two objects or data spaces. It is used by index tree navigation to prune the search space. It also helps finding the appropriate leaf node on index insertion, as we will explain in more detail in Section 3. It therefore is not defined as a simple predicate operation, but rather as an operation returning an integer value indicating the degree of overlap, while negative values are used as a measure for indicating the distance between two objects[3]. Finally, the OVERLAPS operation is used to approximate spatial and temporal overlaps, intersects and covers predicates.

- The SPLIT operation divides a spatial object into several (smaller) spatial objects. This operation can be used to a priori divide large user objects into smaller ones before inserting them or while reorganizing the search tree. It is also used to split index nodes when they become too large. The question when nodes are splitted and which concrete spatial object is returned is determined by the implementation of the SPLIT-operation of the associated data type following the SPATIAL concept. In this way, a split-operation can return a simple set of rectangles resulting from splitting a "large" rectangle (like in R+-trees) but also a set of complex polygons or spheres.

  Here the terms small and large are used in two contexts. Large objects can be objects occupying a lot of storage space, as well as objects covering a large data space. In both cases, it might be beneficial to divide a large object into several smaller ones. In the first case, memory allocation and

---

[2] Note, that with spatial, we do not restrict the objects to geometric space. The statements made are valid also for temporal space and other data spaces.

[3] Note, that there is no restriction about the implementation of these operations. Programmers might decide to only distinguish two values — overlapping and non-overlapping — for the OVERLAPS operation. The concepts described here will work in the same way, however, the optimizations described are not possible.

buffering is easier, in the second case, the data space in index nodes is smaller allowing a better pruning in the index structure. The behaviour depends on the implementation of the SPLIT-operation.

- The COMPOSE operation recombines spatial objects that have previously been splitted to an "overall" spatial object. This operation is used for the reconstruction of large data objects which have been splitted on insertion, as well as for index node description objects when index nodes are merged. Note that we make no assumption about the implementation of the operations for a given data type but only the conceptual behaviour of the data is important. The COMPOSE-operation is the inverse of the SPLIT-operation, which mean that if O is an object of concept SPATIAL then $O=\text{COMPOSE}(\text{SPLIT}(O))$ holds.

- Finally, the APPROX operation approximates a spatial object or a set of spatial objects with a new spatial object. This new spatial object is a representative of the data space covered by the objects to be approximated. The typical and most common approximation is the n-dimensional bounding rectangle. However, the approx operation is not restricted to the bounding rectangle — arbitrary operations can be used as long as they satisfy the condition of dominating predicates [24]. In our context this means that e.g. if the approximations of two objects do not overlap, the two original object must not overlap.

CONCEPT SPATIAL		
operation	*parameter*	*result*
OVERLAPS	spatial_object1, spatial_object2	→ INT
SPLIT	spatial_object	→ { spatial_object }
COMPOSE	{ spatial_object }	→ spatial_object
APPROX	{ spatial_object }	→ spatial_object

Table 1. The four concept typical operations of the SPATIAL concept.

Table 1 summarizes these four concept typical operation of the SPATIAL concept. The user implements these four operations for his application, query and index objects and registers them to the CONCERT kernel system.

In addition to the concept typical operations, a few basic object management operations such as a copy operation are needed. Using the management operations and the concept typical operations of the four concepts, CONCERT implements generic methods of physical database design and can deal each data type belonging to one of the concepts for which the necessary management and concept typical operations are implemented, independent of the concrete implementation of the data types. Indexing and query processing in the DBMS kernel is performed based only on these operations. For more information about the concepts, the operations and the CONCERT system in general see [15, 19, 18, 2].

In the next section we use this basic approach to data management to construct a generic spatio-temporal index based on a R-tree like structure which can be used as a framework for spatial indexing.

3   A Framework for Generic Spatio-Temporal Data Indexing

In order to keep the explanation of the generic spatio-temporal index and its integration into the CONCERT kernel system simple and understandable, we explain, how the well-known R-tree [8] could be implemented and generalized in this context. The R-tree certainly may not be optimal for indexing spatio-temporal objects, especially for temporal indexes (see [23] for more information), however, due to its simple and well-understood structure, it is useful to explain the extensibility aspects. We will abstract the R-tree approach to deal with concepts. In this way we get an index structure which is

- generic in the sense of data being used, because it is based only on the "behaviour" of it (the concept it belongs to) and
- generic in the sense of algorithms, because we use a generic heuristic functions which determine the tree-internal processes (varying the heuristics can change the R-tree like behaviour into an R+-tree or an other derivation), and
- generic in the sense of nodes covering search spaces, because we use spatio objects to approximate the space of subtrees and no fixed spatial shapes and which
- uses the features of the underlying CONCERT kernel system like abstract data type, arbitrary object size and management of distributed and external repositories.

3.1   From R-trees to Generic Trees

The traditional R-tree basically works as described in the following: It is a height-balanced tree with nodes of equal size storing pointers to data objects in its leaf nodes. Each data object to be indexed in the R-tree is represented by a minimal bounding rectangle. Associated with each leaf node is a rectangle defined as the minimal bounding rectangle of all object rectangles contained in the node. Inner nodes contain pointers to subtrees and have a rectangle associated defined as the minimal bounding rectangle of all objects in the subtree. Therefore the R-tree hierarchy corresponds to hierarchies of rectangular subspaces.

Bounding Boxes vs. SPATIAL Objects: We generalize the R-tree in the following aspects: While the R-tree is restricted to store rectangular data objects, we allow any objects conforming to the SPATIAL concept to be stored in the generic spatio-temporal tree. We exploit the CONCERT low-level storage capabilities providing an efficient multi-page storage system. Therefore, we do not restrict the generic spatio-temporal tree to have fixed node size. Nodes can be enlarged dynamically to virtually unlimited[4] size using a multi-page secondary storage allocation scheme [1]. The R-tree nodes have minimal bounding rectangles associated with them, while the generic spatio-temporal tree uses abstract spatial objects instead (e.g. spheres, convex polygons or just rectangles). These spatial objects are usually computed using the APPROX operation.

The only assumption we make here, which is implicit given by the SPATIAL-concept, is the existence of an APPROX-operation evaluable on node objects.

Object Lookup: The usual way of accessing spatial data in an R-tree is to start with a rectangular query window. At each level of the tree, all subtrees with non-empty overlap of the query window and the bounding rectangle of the subtree are recursively searched for matching objects.

The generic spatio-temporal tree uses a SPATIAL object to describe the data space of the query window, or more generally, the arbitrary query space.

With this knowledge the R-Tree algorithms as given in [8] can be extended to a a generic algorithm using the SPATIAL concept and its concept typical operation OVERLAP, as shown in Algorithm 1. Such algorithms can easily incorporated into the CONCERT system.

```
 1: find (query, node)
 2: for all e ∈ { node.entries } do
 3:    if leafnode(node) then
 4:       if OVERLAPS (query, e.object) then
 5:          report e.object
 6:       end if
 7:    else
 8:       if OVERLAPS (query, e.region) then
 9:          find (query, e)
10:       end if
11:    end if
12: end for
```

Algorithm 1: Lookup in a generic spatial index.

The concept typical operation used for spatial index lookup is the OVERLAPS operation. Note that the CONCERT spatial index is much more flexible than any given tree variant. If the abstract objects stored in the nodes are minimum bounding rectangles, and query objects are rectangles as well, Algorithm 1 behaves exactly as the R-tree lookup. Because CONCERT makes almost no assumption about the objects in the tree, Algorithm 1 works the same way also

---

[4] There is a hard limit of 4 GByte per node. However, in order to be efficient, inner nodes should not become larger than about 1 MByte.

for arbitrary n-dimensional spatial objects, as long as the subtrees form hierarchies of data spaces. Certain applications might prefer to e.g. use overlapping convex polygons to partition the data space or a sphere, if Euclidean distance is important in queries like nearest neighbor queries for point data.

If the objects contain, beside the spatial, a temporal dimension, Algorithm 1 can be used directly for spatio-temporal objects. Note, that it is the responsibility of the user implementing the OVERLAP operation to distinguish between the spatial and the temporal dimension.

Splitting a Node - The Dead Space Revival: One of the important issues often discussed for R-trees in the context of spatio-temporal applications is the problem of dead space in the rectangles. The larger the rectangles are compared to the data space covered by the objects contained in the node, the less efficient the R-tree becomes. Our generic tree provides an easy and flexible solution to this problem.

Index nodes as well as data objects stored in the index are spatially extended objects implementing the operations of the SPATIAL concept. Therefore, large objects can be split into several (smaller) ones by using the concept typical operation SPLIT. This operation can be called multiple times until the resulting objects have — from an application point of view — a good size. It is not the database system and its index structure that determines neither the split granularity nor the split boundaries. If from an application point of view, there is no point in splitting an object further, the SPLIT operation just returns the unchanged object.

Note that the SPLIT operation is much more powerful than just splitting an rectangle in multiple ones. The SPLIT operation needs an object of an arbitrary data type following the SPATIAL concept and returns a set of object. The only requirement is, that the resulting objects follow the SPATIAL concept. Such objects might be e.g. rectangles as in R-trees or spheres as in M-trees. The exact behaviour of a SPLIT operation is determined by its implementation.

As discussed earlier, CONCERT has virtually no size restriction for its index nodes. Using the OVERLAPS operation, the spatial index code therefore can handle arbitrary large objects — it just might not be very efficient, if the SPLIT operation is not actually splitting the objects. In any case, splitting is done exploiting application semantics rather than following a node-space constraint.

Splitting is possible in different situations. An important one is the a priori splitting of objects at insertion or update time. Such approaches are included in R-tree derived trees. By using the concept typical SPLIT operation we generalize these well studied split procedure. The concrete implementation of the operation can determine different application dependent heuristics adapted to the requirements.

One main reason for splitting objects is to avoid dead space in the tree nodes decreasing the efficiency of the index, This is done e.g. in R+-trees. Especially in spatio-temporal applications, objects might change their spatial extension with respect to the time dimension and therefore increase the dead space of their spatio-temporal approximation. Finally, splitting also can occur when performing a node split in the index tree during inserting or in case of reorganization of the tree.

Insertion of Objects: In principle, the insertion of objects into our generic spatial tree index follows the same steps as inserting them into any other tree like indexing structure. We generalize this approach – similar to the GiST approach in [10] – by encapsulating the tree strategies like e.g. "When should a node/object be splitted?" in single methods implementing the best heuristic for an application. In contrast to [10] we develop our algorithm based on the concept typical operations and the tree typical operations adapt to the concept driven approach whereas GiST follows a tree structure driven approach, generalizing operations in the context of tree management. Algorithm 2 shows the generic insertion procedure for our index.

```
 1: insert (object, node)
 2: if leafnode(node) then
 3:    Consider Split    /* Heuristics for splitting or enlarging leaf node */
 4:    Insert Object
 5: else
 6:    Choose Subtree    /* Heuristics for choice of best subtree */
 7:    insert (object, subtree)
 8:    Consider Subtree-Split    /* Heuristics for splitting or enlarging inner node */
 9: end if
10: Adjust Node
```

Algorithm 2: Insert into a generic spatial index.

Although similar from its outline, the generic spatial index has some important differences to the R-tree. While in the R-tree, nodes are of fixed size and therefore, a node has to be split according to application requirements, the generic index is more flexible. The operation `Consider Split` can implement a flexible splitting heuristics considering not only the size of the node, but also the spatial extension of the objects and the amount of dead space in the node. In this way the concrete choice of a heuristic determines the behaviour of the tree, let him behave like a R-, a R+- or any other indexing tree for spatial data.

The splitting itself is also more flexible. It can be performed not only by distributing the entries among the nodes (using an arbitrary splitting strategy such as one of the strategies discussed in [8]), but also by splitting large objects using the concept typical operation `SPLIT` reducing the dead space further. In this way, the implementation of `SPLIT` controls a part of the behaviour of our indexing framework.

Even the insertion of an object in a subtree is more flexible than in a concrete tree implementation: The insertion is handled by recursively passing the object down the tree. At each non-leaf node, an appropriate subtree has to be chosen for the recursion. This is done by the operation Choose Subtree. In the standard R-tree algorithm, the subtree is chosen based on the least enlargement of the bounding rectangle necessary. In the generic spatial index, the concept typical operation OVERLAPS is used. In order to optimize the choice for a subtree, OVERLAPS is not defined as a simple predicate but rather returns an integer value indicating the amount of overlap. In addition to the amount of overlap, the current size of the subtree and the amount of free space in the subtree can also be considered.

The additional flexibility over fixed multidimensional indexing tree gained with the operations Choose Subtree, Consider Split and Consider Subtree--Split together with the mechanism avoiding dead space using the concept typical operation SPLIT makes our approach to a useful framework of an R-tree like index for spatio-temporal applications.

The heuristics used in the algorithms are application and environment dependent and an important topic in ongoing research activities, e.g. in the CHOROCHRONOS[4] project. Some popular heuristics like these in R- or R+-trees are well known but not always the best choice in case of complex spatio-temporal data.

```
1: adjust node (node)
2: Consider Reorganization    /* Heuristics for reorganization with sibling nodes */
3: Adjust covering subspace    /* using the APPROX operation */
4: if node has been split then
5:    Create covering subspace of new node
6:    Propagate Split    /* to parent node */
7: end if
```

Algorithm 3: Adjust an index node.

Reorganizing the Tree: After insertion, nodes have to be adjusted using the Adjust Node operation as shown in Algorithm 3. Insertion into the generic spatial tree can bring the tree out of balance. This can be avoided by reorganizing the node moving some of its entries to sibling nodes. However, this operation might become very expensive and is therefore usually omitted. Rather from time to time, when the tree gets too much out of balance, a complete reorganization is performed.

Remembering that each node has a covering subspace object associated with it which follows the SPATIAL concept (e.g. a bounding rectangle in R-trees), this object has to be adjusted on insertion using the concept typical operation APPROX if reorganisation is necessary. Whether a node has to be adjusted is determined by the Concider Reorganization operation which implements the desired heuristic.

If the node has been split, the APPROX operation has to be calculated for both nodes and the split has to be propagated to the parent node. If the root node is split, the tree grows by one level.

Deletion of Objects: For object deletion, two strategies can be followed. It is possible always to recompute the spatial extent of each node using the APPROX concept typical operation. This keeps the space covered by each node minimal, but it requires substantial overhead each time, an object is deleted.

Alternatively, the spatial extent of the nodes is left unchanged. Deletion is more efficient and no deletion or adjustment of inner nodes will be necessary. If a node becomes too small, it can be merged with one of it's siblings. This keeps small the overhead for reorganizing the tree but decreases the efficiency of the index due to possible dead space in the covering objects of an node.

It is important to notice, that throughout the whole code of our generic spatio-temporal index, no explicit assumption is made about the data types and storage formats of the spatio-temporal data. Only the concept typical operations are used as an interface. The objects themselves are simply treated as abstract objects, i.e. uninterpreted byte sequences with a few operations defined on them. Therefore, it is irrelevant to the kernel system, where the real data objects reside — as long as they can be accessed via the concept typical operations. Instead of objects themselves, it is possible to store only place holders (e.g. a URL or any sort of a pointer to the actual object) and access the real objects only when processing the concept typical operations, for example via remote procedure call. This fact allows the kernel system to cope with the interoperability issue. The actual data can reside in heterogeneous, distributed repositories. The kernel only needs to know the operations and handles to access it and provide physical design and query capabilities over the (external) data. With this in mind we presented a framework of a generic tree index in the last section. It is

- generic in the sense of data type – it is valid and useable for all data type following the SPATIAL concept of CONCERT independent from their location or size – and
- generic in the sense of tree behaviour – changing the tree heuristics leads to different tree derivations – and it is
- derived from the main issue of each data management system – the data – in contrast to approaches which derive their genericity by generalizing algorithms or methods.

4   Conclusions

Advanced applications require the DBMS to be extended with additional application-specific functionality. We presented the CONCERT extensible architecture that provides a flexible base for spatio-temporal and advanced data handling.

We have introduced the CONCERT kernel system, it's mechanism of physical database design for external objects, and a generic indexing framework as an example for how to exploit extensibility in order to better support advanced indexing for query processing of abstract objects.

Using the well-known R-tree as an example, we have shown how such a generic tree index can be implemented and adapted to spatio-temporal application needs. The investigations the generic approach presented here is not complete yet and has to be evaluated and compared with "hard-wired" indexes. The potential for improvements particularly with respect to the heuristics must be explored and is subject of further research activity. We expect the framework presented to be flexible enough and expect acceptable overhead to be traded for increased flexibility.

4.1   Acknowledgement

We thank the reviewers for their detailled comments that have helped us to revise and to focus the paper.

References

1. Stephen Blott, Helmut Kaufmann, Lukas Relly, and Hans-Jörg Schek, *Buffering long externally-defined objects*, Proceedings of the Sixth International Workshop on Persistent Object Systems (POS6) (Tarascon, France) (M.P. Atkinson, V. Benzaken, and D. Maier, eds.), British Computer Society, Springer Verlag Berlin Heidelberg New York, September 1994, pp. 40–53 (english).
2. Stephen Blott, Lukas Relly, and Hans-Jörg Schek, *An open abstract-object storage system*, Proceedings of the 1996 ACM SIGMOD Conference on Management of Data, June 1996 (english).
3. Stephen Blott, Lukas Relly, and Hans-Jörg Schek, *An open abstract-object storage system and its application to geospatial metadata management*, EDBT'96 Exhibitions Program, Avignon, France, 25-29th March 1996.
4. *Chorochronos: A research network for spatiotemporal database systems*, http://www.dbnet.ece.ntua.gr/ choros/.
5. Douglas Comer, *The ubiquitous B-Tree*, ACM Computing Surveys 11 (1979), no. 2, 121–137 (english).
6. James O. Coplien and Douglas C. Schmidt (eds.), *Pattern Languages of Program Design*, Addison-Wesley, 1995, ISBN 0-201-60734-4.
7. Volker Gaede and Oliver Günther, *Multidimensional access methods*, ACM Computing Surveys 30 (3), 170–231 (Sept. 1, 1998).
8. Antonin Guttman, *R-Trees: A dynamic index structure for spatial searching*, ACM SIGMOD International Conference on Management of Data (1984), 47–57 (english).
9. L. M. Haas, W. Chang, G. M. Lohman, J. McPherson, P. F. Wilms, G. Lapis, B. Lindsay, H. Pirahesh, M. Carey, and E. Shekita, *Starburst mid-flight: As the dust clears*, IEEE Transactions on Knowledge and Data Engineering 2 (1990), no. 1, 143–160 (english).

10. Joseph M. Hellerstein, Jeffrey F. Naughton, and Avi Pfeffer, *Generalized search trees for database systems*, Proceedings of the 21st International Conference on Very Large Databases (Umeshwar Dayal, Peter M. D. Gray, and Shojiro Nishio, eds.), September 1995, pp. 562–573 (english).
11. *IBM corporation*, http://eyp.stllab.ibm.com/t3/.
12. *IBM* white paper, *Building Object-Oriented Frameworks*, http://www.ibm.com/java/education/oobuilding/buildingoo.pdf.
13. *Informix corporation*, http://www.informix.com/informix/products/options/udo/datablade/dbmodule/index.html.
14. *Oracle corporation*, http://www.oracle.com/st/cartridges/.
15. Lukas Relly, *Offene speichersysteme: Physischer datenbankentwurf für externe objekte*, Ph.D. thesis, Eidgenössisch Technische Hochschule (ETH), Zürich, CH-8092 Zürich, Switzerland, 1999.
16. Lukas Relly and Uwe Röhm, *Plug and play: Interoperability in CONCERT*, The 2nd International Conference on Interoperating Geographic Information Systems (Interop99), Lecture Notes in Computer Science, Springer Verlag Berlin Heidelberg New York, March 1999.
17. L. Rowe and M. Stonebraker, *The POSTGRES data model*, Proceedings of the Thirteenth International Conference on Very Large Databases (Brighton, England), 1987 (english).
18. Lukas Relly, Hans-J. Schek, Olof Henricsson, and Stephan Nebiker, *Physical database design for raster images in Concert*, 5th International Symposium on Spatial Databases (SSD'97) (Berlin, Germany), July 1997 (english).
19. Lukas Relly, Heiko Schuldt, and Hans-J. Schek, *Exporting database functionality — the Concert way*, Data Engineering Bulletin **21** (1998), no. 3, 43–51 (english).
20. Hans-Jörg Schek, H.-B. Paul, M.H. Scholl, and G. Weikum, *The DASDBS project: Objectives, experiences, and future prospects*, IEEE Transactions on Knowledge and Data Engineering **2** (1990), no. 1, 25–43 (english).
21. M. Stonebraker, L. Rowe, and M. Hirohama, *The implementation of POSTGRES*, IEEE Transactions on Knowledge and Data Engineering **2** (1990), no. 1 (english).
22. Michael Stonebraker, *Inclusion of new types in relational database systems*, Proceedings of the International Conference on Data Engineering (Los Angeles, CA), IEEE Computer Society Press, February 1986, pp. 262–269 (english).
23. Betty Salzberg and Vassilis J. Tsotras, *A comparison of access methods for temporal data*, TimeCenter Technical Report **TR-18** (1997).
24. P.F. Wilms, P.M. Schwarz, H.-J. Schek, and L.M. Haas, *Incorporating data types in an extensible database architecture*, Proceedings of the 3rd International Conference on Data and Knowledge Bases, Jerusalem, June 1988 (english).

The BASIS System: A Benchmarking Approach for Spatial Index Structures*

Christophe Gurret[2], Yannis Manolopoulos[1],
Apostolos N. Papadopoulos[1], and Philippe Rigaux[2]

[1] Data Engineering Lab., Aristotle Univ., 54006 Thessaloniki, GREECE,
[2] Cedric/CNAM, 292 rue St Martin, F-75141, Paris Cedex 03, FRANCE

Abstract. This paper describes the design of the BASIS prototype system. BASIS stands for Benchmarking Approach for Spatial Index Structures. It is a prototype system aiming at performance evaluation of spatial access methods and query processing strategies, under different data sets, various query types, and different workloads. BASIS is based on a modular architecture, composed of a simple storage manager, a query processor, and a set of algorithmic techniques to facilitate benchmarking. The main objective of BASIS is twofold: (i) to provide a benchmarking environment for spatial access methods and related query evaluation techniques, and (ii) to allow comparative studies of spatial access methods in different cases but under a common framework. We currently extend it to support the fundamental features of spatiotemporal data management and access methods.

Keywords: benchmarking, spatial access methods, spatiotemporal data management, performance evaluation

1 Introduction

Spatial data management has been an active area of research over the past ten years [LT92,G94]. A major component of such research efforts has been, and continues to be, concerned with the design of efficient spatial data indexing methods which reduce query response time during spatial query processing [Gut84,SRF87,HSW89,BKS90,KF94]. Some promising proposals have been reported in the literature aimed at enhancing these indices with additional, specific query handling capabilities [Are93,BKS93,RKV95]; a spatial data index may be specifically redesigned to support region queries, nearest-neighbor queries or spatial join queries. Another direction is the establishment of robust cost models for specific indices and query processing algorithms, i.e functions which estimate the cost of processing spatial queries [TS96,TSS98]. As spatial data management develops, particularly in spatiotemporal applications, we expect further proposals for indexing methods to appear.

---

* Work supported by the European Union's TMR program ("CHOROCHRONOS" project, contract number ERBFMRX-CT96-0056) and by the 1998-1999 French-Greek bilateral protocol.

The various index methods, then, behave differently according to certain settings, such as the buffering strategies and query profiles. Therefore, for any comparative performance test, the tester must be careful when declaring a clear winner. Moreover, all these methods have been proposed independently and, consequently, there is a lack of a general framework under which an extensive comparative study can be performed. Although several comparative studies have been performed, there is a lack of a spatial benchmark that could be used as a yardstick towards spatial indexing method design, implementation and performance evaluation.

As a solution to this problem, we are constructing an integrated benchmark development and execution environment: **B**enchmarking **A**pproach for **S**patial **I**ndex **S**tructures (BASIS). This is a platform which facilitates the incremental integration of multiple indexing methods, query algorithms, and data sets for use in benchmark runs. So far, the type of benchmarks supported are those designed to test only indexing methods and query processing algorithms.

Related work can be divided in three categories: (i) benchmarking for DBMS, (ii) generic index support environments, and (iii) recent benchmarking platforms. The first one has the longer history. To test relative performance of different DBMS, the research and industry community has sought a standard benchmark for all systems. Early benchmarks for DBMS, such as the Wisconsin benchmark [BDT83], measures the number of transactions per second (TPS) and produces price/performance ratings for systems in $/TPS. Later, the Transaction Processing Performance Council (TPC) published a number of benchmarks for specific application domains such as OLAP [TPCC97] and decision support systems [TPCD95]. With the emergence of object data bases a number of new benchmarks appeared; see [Cha95] for an annotated bibliography. This type of benchmark differs from the type supported by BASIS in that they attempt to test entire systems. More specifically, BASIS supports researchers working on particular modules of a complete system: index and query processor.

Generic index support environments include the DEVISE environment [LRB+97]. This is a visualization tool for index structures. The GiST project [HNP95] has produced a generic software package which can be used to generate different tree index structures based on the B-tree paradigm.

A benchmarking platform with a similar scope to that of BASIS is "A La Carte" [GOP+98] which is a benchmarking environment for testing spatial query processing algorithms. BASIS generalizes this objective by allowing the performance evaluation of other query types as well as of index structures.

The rest of the paper is organized as follows. The next section lists and discusses requirements for a benchmarking environment. Section 3 illustrates the architecture of BASIS. Section 4 discusses issues for spatial and spatiotemporal data management. An example benchmark is explained in Section 5. Finally, Section 6 concludes the paper.

2   Requirements for a Benchmarking Environment

The general requirement for a benchmarking environment is to aid a user to set up, run, and analyze the results of a benchmark. This process is decomposed into the following more specific requirements:

1. provide a rich variety of data sets of different data object types,
2. integrate different index structures,
3. integrate different query processing algorithms,
4. facilitate the analysis of benchmark results,
5. provide visualization methods for viewing data sets, index structures, and benchmark results

In the sequel, we discuss each topic in detail.

2.1   Datasets

The first fundamental requirement for a database benchmark is data. A benchmarking environment must provide the benchmark designer with as much data from the appropriate application domain as he may need. The nature of the data used in a benchmark run can greatly influence results. In the spatial application domain, some index structures are specifically designed for point data. Other index structures outperform the previous set of indexes when the data represent objects with extension, such as lines and regions. The benchmarking environment must therefore provide a variety of data to accommodate this aspect of benchmarking. At least part of the data must be real-life data. However, with the current poverty of large scale public real-life data, artificial data may also be provided.

2.2   Index structures

The environment should contain a number of different index structures. They might be provided as part of the platform (for instance, we already implemented several variants of the R-trees) or be added by some user to perform new experiments and comparisons. This involves some design issues. First, one must be able to use an existing structure without requiring a detailed knowledge of its internal implementation. From a practical point of view, this means that all structures should share a common design for the essential operations: data loading, scan, point and window queries, etc.

Second, at a lower level, the platform must provide the building blocks to create a new structure with minimal effort. This is necessary because, one the one hand, we want to save the tedious task of programming the memory management and I/O functionalities, whereas, on the other hand, a strong integration of the new structure in the platform implies first that the design is made according to some generic "pattern", and second that the implementation takes advantage as much as possible of low-level existing functionalities.

2.3   Query processing

As with indices, the environment should contain a number of different query processing algorithms. Again, these should accumulate within the environment without penalty to the implementation effort. Moreover, the techniques and algorithms already integrated should help any researcher who wants to extend the platform.

A significant ambition of the current work is to provide an open query processor which proposes a set of commonly used operators (such as external sorting for instance) and simultaneously allows to integrate the existing operators with new algorithms. We consider this requirement as very important because it does not limit the benchmarking work to the comparison of some isolated structures or algorithms, but permits to build arbitrarily complex algorithms by "assembling" together some operators extracted from the available library.

As a simple illustration, imagine that we want to compare to algorithms, A_1 and A_2, but the result of A_1 consists of records sorted on some attribute, while the result of A_2 consists of record ids (i.e, the address of each record on the disk). Clearly, a performance comparison of both algorithms is not fair: we must complete A_2 with two operators, namely a first one which fetches the records on the disk, and a second one which sorts the set of records.

More generally, in a context of spatiotemporal databases, one must be ready to mix several structures and algorithms on spatial, temporal and spatiotemporal data. The design of a benchmarking environment should allow such a merge of techniques issued from different fields, hopefully in a clean and elegant setting which permits an accurate reporting of results. We propose in BASIS a query execution model which is general enough to encompass relational and spatial data and makes easy the integration of new methods.

2.4   Analysis of benchmark results

A benchmark may be intended to show the consumption of various system resources, such as disk accesses, as a function of some variable, e.g. data set size. The environment should allow a benchmark to produce statistics covering various variables in the benchmark and a variety of resources. It may also provide statistics on the performance of individual index functions, such as building, update, insertion, and search times.

The conventional representation of benchmark results is to plot a graph on the use of one resource against some varying parameter. Typically, such a graph shows that one index progressively outperforms the other as the size of the data set increases. Thus the investigator can justify claims about such relative performance. However, it is becoming increasingly important to be able to explain the reasons of differing performance. For instance, which factors cause the inferior index to eventually require almost double the number of disk accesses?

The authors in [KS97] considered this question. Their response is an example of the form of results analysis that BASIS is designed to support. They compared the performance of two spatial index structures, R*-tree and SR-tree, with a large number of nearest-neighbor queries. The main difference between the two methods is that R*-tree groups objects into minimum bounding rectangles while SR-tree groups them into minimum bounding circles. They found that SR-trees outperform the former structure. The authors then investigated this difference by re-analyzing the benchmark data and calculating the average volume and diameter of the bounding shapes in the leaf nodes of the structure. Here the diameter of a rectangle is its diagonal. This produced two further graphs of volume against data size and diameter against data size. These graphs showed that the average volume of the rectangles was smaller than the circles but that the average diameter of the rectangles was larger. Put another way, R*-tree groups the points into small volume regions while SR-tree groups them into small diameter regions. All the queries of the benchmark were nearest-neighbor queries. Since short diameter is more significant than small volume, SR-tree is superior for such queries.

This work can be considered to be an ad hoc data mining process on benchmark results. A benchmarking environment should support such analysis as well as the simple conventional performance graphs.

2.5   Visualization

Visualization is a requirement in three areas: data sets, index structures, and results data. A user chooses data sets for a benchmark run that are appropriate for the specific benchmark. In particular, if artificial data are used, it is very difficult to verify that these data are appropriate. Some tool to give a visual representation of the data space distribution can aid the user greatly. Also, it can be of benefit to be able to view the index structure, for example tree fanout or height, when analyzing results. Finally, clear visual presentation of complex results is a key factor in their understanding and acceptance.

This is the set of requirements which have influenced the design of the BASIS system. So far the emphasis has been targeted to the first four requirements which are considered fundamental. The fulfillment of the last one is considered as future work. In the next sections we explain the way our system attempts to satisfy the fundamental requirements by illustrating the architecture and describing the internal components.

3   The BASIS Architecture

This section describes the fundamental components of the BASIS architecture. An outline of the architecture is depicted in Fig. 1. The platform has been implemented in C++ and runs on top of UNIX or Windows NT.

The platform is organized in three modules (Fig. 1), namely (1) the *storage manager* provides I/Os and caching services, (2) the *SAM toolkit* is a set of commonly used SAMs (Spatial Access Methods) and defines some design patterns which support an easy development of new structures, and finally (3) the *query*

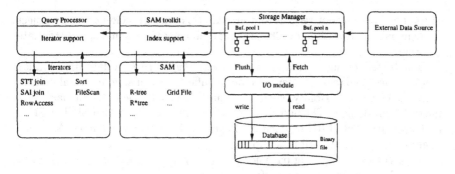

Fig. 1. The BASIS architecture

processor is a library of algorithms whose design follows the general framework of the *iterator model*, to be described below.

Each module defines a level in the architecture: this design allows an easy customization and extension. Depending on the query processing experiment, each level is easily extendible: the designer may add a new SAM, add a new spatial operator or algorithm at the query processor level, or decide to implement its own query processing module on top of the buffer management (I/O) module.

3.1   The storage manager

The storage manager is essentially in charge of managing a database. A database is a set of binary files which store either datasets (i.e., sequential collection of records) or SAMs. A SAM or index refers to records in an indexed data file through *record identifiers*.

Any binary file is divided into *pages* with size chosen at database creation. A page can be viewed (and accessed) as an array of bytes, but we provide a more structured and easy-to-use page representation. According to our alternative, a page is structured as a *header* followed by an array of fixed-size *records*. Therefore, a page is formatted and this allows for an easy access to any record by its rank. In addition, the interface to a formatted page is safer because invalid operations (such as an access beyond the limits of the pages) can be prevented.

Any information to be put in page is a CStorable object. The CStorable class defines the minimal behavior expected from such objects: essentially they must be able to dump/load their content to/from a given location. The storage manager provides a predefined list of such storables, including the atomic types CString, CInt, CDouble, the class CRecordRef which holds the address of a record, and the CRect class representing a bounding-box. By sub-typing the class CStorable, one can easily extend the storable types.

A *record* can now be built as a tuple of CStorable objects. Records are the main objects that BASIS deals with: as described above, a query execution plan can essentially be seen as a tree of operators which consume and produce records. BASIS also provides a dynamic type management: any operators knows the type of its input and output records and delivers this type as a `CRecordType` object on demand. Conversely, any `CRecordType` object can dynamically instantiate records.

The buffer manager handles one or several *buffer pools*: a data file or index (SAM) is assigned to one buffer pool, but a buffer pool can handle several indices. This allows much flexibility when assigning memory to the different parts of a query execution plan. The buffer pool is a constant-size cache with LRU or FIFO replacement policy (LRU by default). Pages can be *pinned* in memory. A pinned page is never flushed until it is unpinned.

All algorithms requiring page accesses uniformly access these pages through the interface provided by the buffer manager.

3.2   The SAM toolkit

Here are now the two main types of files which are handled by the storage manager:

1. *Data files* are sequential collections of formatted pages storing *records* of a same type. Records in a data file can either be accessed sequentially (with a `DataScan` iterator, described below), or by their address (`RowAccess` iterator in the sequel).

2. *SAMs* are structured collections of `IndexEntry`. An index entry is a built-in record type with two attributes: the key and a record address. The key is the geometric key, usually the MBR. The currently implemented SAMs are a grid file, an R-tree, an R*-tree and several packed R-trees. Fig. 2 shows some of these variants, built on the hydrography dataset of the Connecticut State (Tiger Data)

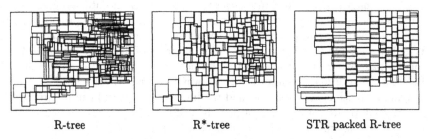

R-tree   R*-tree   STR packed R-tree

Fig. 2. R-tree variants (MBRs of leaf nodes) in BASIS

3.3   The query processor

One of the important design choices for the platform is to allow for any experimental evaluation of *query execution plans* (QEP) as generated by database query optimizers with an algebraic view of query languages. During optimization, a query is transformed into a QEP represented as a binary tree which captures the order in which a sequence of *physical* algebraic operations are going to be executed. The leaves represent data files or indices, internal nodes represent algebraic operations and edges represent dataflows between operations. Examples of algebraic operations include data access (`DataScan` or `RowAccess`), spatial selections, spatial joins, etc.

As a common framework for query execution, we use a demand-driven process with iterator functions [Gra93]. Each node (operation) is an iterator. This allows for a pipelined execution of multiple operations, thereby minimizing the system resources (memory space) required for intermediate results: data consumed by an iterator, say I, is generated by its son(s) iterator(s), say J. Records are produced and consumed one-at-a-time. Iterator I asks iterator J for a record. Therefore the intermediate result of an operation is not stored in such pipelined operations except for some specific iterators called *blocking iterators*, such as sorting.

Each iterator comes with three functions: `open`, `next` and `close`: `open` prepares each input source and allocates the necessary system resources, `next` runs one iteration step of the algorithm and produces a new record and `close` ends up the iteration and frees resources. This design offers two major advantages:

1. First it allows for simple QEP creation by "assembling" iterators together.
2. Second it is fairly easy to extend BASIS by adding a new iterator: providing that it defines the convenient interface as `open`, `next` and `close` (we provide the necessary C++ support for that), its integration in the BASIS iterator library is trivial.

We illustrate this feature with two examples of QEP on a same spatial join query $R \bowtie S$ (Fig. 3). We assume the existence of a spatial index I_S.

First (left of the figure), the QEP follows a the simple scan-and-index (SAI) strategy: relation R is scanned with a `DataScan` iterator, and for each tuple r in R, the `SAIjoin` iterator executes a window query on index I_S with key $r.MBR$. This gives a record ID *RecordID2*. Finally the record with id *RecordID2* in the datafile S is accessed with the `RowAccess` iterator.

Creating a QEP with BASIS in fairly simple. We give below the C++ code for evaluating the SAI join query (we omit the `RowAccess` iterators for simplicity):

```
...
CIterator *join, *scan;
CDataBase *db = new CDataBase (''tst'', 500)          (1)
...
CDataFile *df = db->getData ('R');                     (2)
CRtree *rtree = db->getIndex ('Is');                   (3)
...
scan = new CDataScan (df, READ_ONLY);                  (5)
join = new CSAIJoin (scan, 'MBB', rtree);              (6)
...
```

```
db->execQuery (join, stdout);                              (7)
...
```

Line (1) instantiates a storage manager on the database tst with a 500 pages buffer. Line (2) gets a handle on the datafile R and line (3) a handle on the R-tree Is.

Then the two following lines create the QEP: it consists of a sequential scan of the datafile, followed by window queries on the R-tree, using the MBB attribute as an argument. Note that scan is defined as the data source for join.

It remains to execute the query. This is done in that case with the execQuery method of CDataBase. The code is simple and is worth looking at:

```
execQuery (CIterator *root, FILE *cout)
{
  CRecord *record = root->getType()->newInstance();
  root->open();
  while (root->next(record)) record->print(stdout);
  root->close();
  delete record;
}
```

At this point we do not care at all about the structure of the QEP which can be arbitrarily complex. We just need to access the root which propagates the query operations down the tree to the leaves. An interesting property of each iterator is the getType method which delivers the type of the records which are output by the iterator. Knowing the types of the records in the datafile R and the index Is, respectively, a simple bottom-up type inference allows to know the type of the records manipulated by each iterator, including the intermediate ones. Given a type, we can instantiate a record with the newInstance method. Incidently, this shows that we only need one record in main memory for the whole query execution.

Now, assume that a new join algorithm is proposed, which constructs some structure and matches it with the existing index. Then it suffices to reuse all the iterators, save the SAIjoin one, which is to be replaced by NEWJoin (Fig. 3, right part).

The platform also provides some basic modules such as sorting: the Sort iterator takes any flow of record, a comparison function, and performs an external sort/merge. For example, one can introduce a Sort iterator[1] in the QEP of Fig. 3 to sort the data flow output by the SAI join on the *PageID* of the *RecordID2* component. This allows to access only once the pages of S instead of issuing random reads to get the S records, which might lead to several accesses to the same page.

In summary, this query execution model permits the construction of an extendible library which defines a physical algebra for query evaluation. The modular design and the support for type inference and iterator development allows for

---

[1] This iterator is *blocking*: almost all the job is done during the open operation. See the Appendix for a short description.

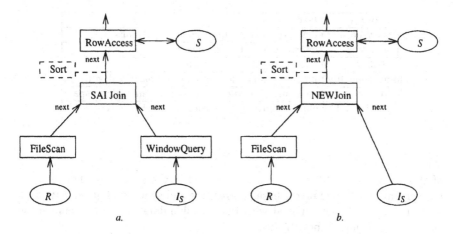

Fig. 3. Query execution plans

an easy integration of new components and provides a convenient framework for new experiments. We currently enrich the platform with temporal (cooperation with the MUST group [DFS98]) and spatiotemporal structures and algorithms.

4   Spatial and Spatiotemporal Data Handling

Access method performance varies considerably by modifying the characteristics of the data. For example, highly clustered data usually degrades performance as opposed to uniformly distributed data. In the BASIS project we support two fundamental types of data:

- real-life data (e.g. Sequoia 2000 [SFGM93], TIGER/Line [Tiger94], etc),
- synthetic data, obeying various distributions (e.g. uniform, normal, exponential, etc).

From one point of view, real-life data captures the characteristics of the data that real-life applications manipulate. However, to be able to change the data properties (population, distribution, coverage, etc.) synthetic data must be supported as well. Table 1 summarizes the most important properties of synthetic data.

Generally speaking, it is required to make the generated data seem less artificial than a simple uniformly distributed random placement of rectangles. Statistical properties of the generated data should be under the control of the user. In particular the user should exercise some control over the distribution of the objects in space and the size and shape of the objects. The data generator described in [GOP+98] meets these requirements. The data are generated by controlling the fundamental parameters, and a large number of different data sets can be generated. These data are ported into BASIS internal representation to be part

Property	Description
data type	points, rectangles, line segments, polygons
population	how many objects are generated
distribution	uniform, normal, exponential, fractal
dimensionality	number of dimensions of address space (2-d, n-d)
coverage	how many objects cover a point of the address space

Table 1. The most important properties of a synthetic data set.

of the database. Real-life datasets can be used in the same way. This enables the generation of benchmarks based on real-life and synthetic but realistic data sets. If the user is not satisfied with the available data, new data sets can be generated and ported into BASIS.

Spatial or spatiotemporal index structures can be build to support the underlying data sets. Currently, BASIS supports Grid-Files, R-trees and R*-trees in 1-D, 2-D or N-D spaces. Supporting multidimensional spaces is considered very important, since some applications require data manipulation in more than 2 or 3 dimensions. For example, some proposed spatiotemporal index mechanisms can be evaluated. The exploitation of 3-D R-trees is a straightforward solution to index multimedia objects, where the third dimension is time [TVS96]. BASIS supports such an index directly, by instantiating an R-tree or R*-tree in 3-D and passing as an input parameter the filename which contains the spatiotemporal data (x, y, $time$). Alternatively, a 2-D R-tree can be constructed to index the spatial attributes of the data and a 1-D R-tree can be utilized to index time intervals. Moreover, overlapping R-trees and RT-trees [XHL90] can be implemented very easily by performing modifications to the R-tree implementation.

Fig. 4. Primitive data types supported.

Some primitive data types have been defined to enable indexing and query processing (see Fig. 4). The fundamental data types currently supported are *points, rectangles, line segments* and *point trajectories*. The point trajectory can be viewed as a collection of consecutive positions in the space. The main purpose of this type is to support spatiotemporal benchmarking for moving point databases. For example, a database of moving points can be generated by instantiating a number of point trajectories. Each trajectory corresponds to a collection of records. The user can use these predefined types to generate new ones. For example, rotated MBRs can be generated by inheriting from the CRect class and adding some new member variables (e.g. rotational angle). During instantiation of an object the dimensionality must be specified.

Each spatial or spatiotemporal data type integrates some useful methods that enable processing. For example, the *intersects* method can be invoked between two rectangles or point trajectories to determine if they intersect or not; *inclusion* can be invoked to test if a point is enclosed by a rectangle. Since it is impossible to include every method that one may need, new methods can be defined using appropriate inheritance from the corresponding base classes.

So far the majority of benchmarks performed by several research efforts focus on spatial data only. We are currently working on performance evaluation of spatiotemporal access methods, and more specifically we focus on the case of moving point databases. In a moving point database each object is characterized by a point trajectory. The challenge is to index these trajectories to efficiently support *spatial-only*, *time-only*, and *spatiotemporal queries*. The first raised issue is if the index should be *sparse* or *dense*. If a separate index entry is created for each object position then a dense index is created. On the other hand, if several consecutive trajectory positions are grouped together a sparse index is created. Evidently, a dense index occupies more space than a sparse index which is very critical when the database need to be updated frequently, and the number of moving objects is relatively large. On the other hand, the fact that a dense index holds every position of the trajectory, eliminates the need to search the trajectory itself during query processing, because all information is maintained in the index. It is not evident which strategy is best suited for the three aforementioned query types.

The second interesting issue that needs investigation is the index type. There are several side effects if a 3-D dense R-tree is used to index a moving point database. Treating time as another dimension in such an index has the following consequences:

- MBRs are continuing to grow larger even if the data do not change their position from one time slot to the next one.
- The MBR enlargement is critical with respect to the index performance, due to more node overlaps.
- The index grows rapidly, independently of the object mobility.

We are studying these issues with respect to some important system and database parameters like the database size, the mobility of the objects, the number of moving objects, the size of the available buffer space, the complexity of the query execution plan.

5   An Example Benchmark

In this section we present some results with respect to the proposed benchmarking environment. The aim is to give some hints about how a benchmark can be generated and how the various iterators are combined together to produce a query execution plan. We illustrate how a two-way join can be modeled and executed in BASIS and give some experimental results regarding the performance evaluation of the various approaches. See [PRS99] for a more detailed treatment of spatial join processing.

5.1   Benchmarking Spatial Join Processing

Fig. 5 illustrates two possible QEPs for processing a two-way join $R_1 \bowtie R_2 \bowtie R_3$, using R*-trees I_1, I_2 and I_3. For the sake of illustration, we assume that (i) the optimizer tries to use as much as possible existing spatial indices when generating QEPs and (ii) that the 2-way join is first evaluated on the MBRs (filter step) and then on the exact geometry (refinement step, requiring 3 row accesses). Both QEPs are left-deep trees [Gra93]. In such trees the right operand of a join is always an index, as well as the left operand for the left-most node. Another approach, not investigated here, would consists in an n-way STT, i.e., a synchronized traversal of n R-trees down to the leaves.

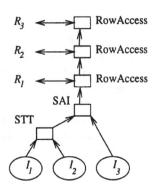
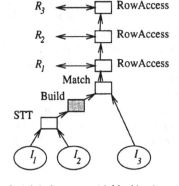

a. A left-deep tree with pipelined iterators   *b. A left-deep tree with blocking iterators*

Fig. 5. Two basic strategies for left-deep QEPs

The first strategy (Fig. 5.a) is fully pipelined: an STT (Synchronized Tree Traversal) join is performed as the left-most node, involving I_1 and I_2. Then an SAI (Scan-and-Index) join is executed for the following join: it takes a pair of `IndexEntry` from the STT iterator, and uses one of the MBR as an argument of a window query on I_3. The result is a 3-tuple record id: the records are then retrieved with `RowAccess` iterators, one for each relation, to perform the refinement step.

The second strategy (Fig. 5.b) uses instead of SAI a Build-and-Match strategy: since the repeated execution of window queries can be expected to be slow, one can imagine to organize first the result of the STT join (for instance by constructing an index) before performing the second join. Of course the building phase is implemented by a blocking iterator and requires memory space.

These two strategies fit easily in the query execution model of BASIS. Moreover, by considering the whole QEP, one gets an accurate view of the possible shortcomings of each method. For instance, the first strategy is fully pipelined and enjoys minimal memory requirements while the second one is memory consuming and enforces to wait for the completion of the STT join before proceeding with the second one.

Also, the refinement step could be done prior to the second join if it is expected that the candidate set contains a large number of false hits. By computing the refinement step in lazy mode, as suggested in Fig. 5, the cardinality of intermediate results is larger (because of false hits) but the size of records is smaller. All these "implementation details" are quite useful to determine whether an approach is realistic or not.

The benchmark outlined above allows to compare the relative efficiency of several solutions for the build-and-match strategy. We briefly describe three variants and report the experimental result.

STJ (Seeded-Tree Join)

The first one is the Seeded Tree Join (STJ) [LR98]. This technique builds from an existing R-tree, used as a *seed*, a second R-tree called *seeded R-tree* (i.e, the seeded-tree is built on the result of the STT join (Fig. 5) using I_3 as the seeding tree).

The construction of the tree is top-down: during the *seeding phase*, the top k levels of the seed are copied to become the top k levels of the seeded tree. Then records are inserted in the structure. We do not detail the whole algorithm: see [LR98].

STR (Sort-Tile-Recursive)

The second variant of Build-And-Match algorithm implemented, called Sort-Tile-Recursive (STR) and proposed in [LEL96], constructs on the fly a packed R-tree. Here the construction is bottom-up and aims at filling completely the nodes of the tree. It relies on a sorting phase which constitutes the most costly part of the algorithm.

SaM (Sort-and-Match)

The third Build-And-Match variant called Sort-and-Match (SaM) was proposed in [PRS99]. It uses the STR algorithm but the construction is stopped at the leaf level, and the pages are not written onto disk. As soon as a leaf l has been produced, it is joined to the existing R-tree I_R.

5.2   Two way joins

We now outline the results of a performance evaluation with BASIS on the two-way join benchmark previously described. In the sequel, the name of the algorithm denotes the second join algorithm, which takes the result of STT, builds a structure and performs the join with I_3.

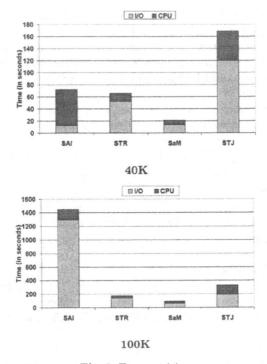

Fig. 6. Two way joins

We use three datasets which simulate respectively *Counties, Cities* and *Roads* [GOP+98]. The experiments are performed for the medium dataset size of 40K records and the larger size of 100K. The latter 2 way-join yields 865,473 records, whereas the former produces 314,617 records. A fixed buffer of 500 pages has been chosen.

Fig. 6 gives the response time for SAI and the three variants of Build-And-Match algorithms. Let us look first at SAI performance. For a small dataset size (40K), the index fits in memory, and only few I/Os are generated by the algorithm. However the CPU cost[2] is high because of the large number of intersection tests. For large dataset sizes, the number of I/Os is huge, rendering this algorithm definitely not the right candidate.

The results illustrated for STJ are not encouraging. STJ outperforms SAI for large datasets, but its performance is always much below that of SaM and STR. The explanation is mainly the very high CPU cost due to the quadratic split algorithm involved in the R-tree construction. Also, the resulting tree is often unbalanced and suffers from a bad space utilization. This leads sometimes to high I/O costs.

---

[2] For a detailed description of the cost calculation and the datasets used see [PRS99].

We found that the solutions based on sorting behaved better. SaM significantly outperforms STR, mostly because it saves the construction of the R-tree structure, and also because the join phase is very efficient. It is worth noting, finally, that SAI is a good candidate for small datasets sizes, although its CPU cost is still larger. One should not forget that SAI is, in that case, the only fully pipelined QEP. Therefore the response time is very short, a parameter which can be essential when the regularity of the data output is more important than the overall resource consumption.

6   Concluding Remarks and Future Work

BASIS is a prototype system aiming at performance evaluation of spatial access methods and spatial queries under a common framework. In the previous sections we discussed the fundamental issues behind the design and implementation of the BASIS system.

Currently we proceed with the extension and improvement of the core BASIS components, as well as with the design and implementation of new ones. We deliver a public release of BASIS to get some feedback from researchers working in spatial and spatiotemporal databases. The code and some documentation can be found at:

http://sikkim.cnam.fr/basis.html

Our second target is to study the performance of proposed spatiotemporal access methods, using BASIS as the benchmarking platform. Recall that although spatiotemporal access methods have been proposed, there is a lack of a thorough performance evaluation of these methods. Finally, we aim at providing flexibility in query evaluation plans, by incorporating dynamic plans and integrating the modules by means of a friendly user interface.

Acknowledgments

The authors are very grateful to Prof. Michel Scholl for his helpful comments and suggestions that improved this paper considerably.

References

[Are93]   W. Aref: "Query Processing and Optimization in Spatial Databases" Technical Report CS-TR-3097, University of Maryland at College Park, 1993.

[BDT83]   D. Bitton, D. DeWitt and C. Turbyfill: "Benchmarking Database Systems: a Systematic Approach", *Proceedings 9th VLDB Conference*, pp.8-19, Florence, Italy, 1983.

[BKS90]   N. Beckmann, H. P. Kriegel and B. Seeger: "The R*-tree: an Efficient and Robust Method for Points and Rectangles", *Proceedings 1990 ACM SIGMOD Conference*, pp.322-331, Atlantic City, NJ, 1990.

[BKS93]   T. Brinkhoff, H-P. Kriegel and B. Seeger: "Efficient Processing of Spatial Joins using R-trees", *Proceedings 1993 ACM SIGMOD Conference*, pp.237-246, Washington DC, 1993.

[BKV98]   L. Bouganim, O. Kapitskaia and P. Valduriez: "Memory Adaptive Scheduling for Large Query Execution", *Proceedings 7th CIKM Conference*, 1998.

[Cha95]   A. B. Chaudhri: "An Annotated Bibliography of Benchmarks for Object Databases", *ACM SIGMOD Record*, Vol.24, No.1, pp.50-57, 1995.

[DFS98]   M. Dumas, M.-C. Fauvet and P.-C. Scholl: "Handling Temporal Grouping and Pattern-Matching Queries in a Temporal Object Model", *Proceedings 7th CIKM Conference*, 1998.

[G94]   R. H. Güting: "An Introduction to Spatial Database Systems", *The VLDB Journal*, Vol.3, No.4, pp,357-399, 1994.

[GOP+98] O. Günther, V. Oria, P. Picouet, J-M. Saglio and M. Scholl: "Benchmarking Spatial Joins A la Carte", *Proceedings International Conference on Scientific and Statistical Databases (SSDBM '98)*, 1998.

[Gut84]   A. Guttman: "R-trees: a Dynamic Index Structure for Spatial Searching", *Proceedings 1984 ACM SIGMOD Conference*, pp.47-57, Boston, MA, 1984.

[Gra93]   G. Graefe: "Query Evaluation Techniques for Large Databases", *ACM Computing Surveys*, Vol.25, No.2, pp.73-170, 1993.

[HNP95]   J. M. Helerstein, J. F. Naughton and A. Pfeffer: "Generalized Search Trees for Database Systems", *Proceedings 21st VLDB Conference*, pp.562-573, Zurich, Switzerland, 1995.

[HSW89]   A. Henrich, H. W. Six and P. Widmayer: "The LSD-tree: Spatial Access to Multidimensional Point and Non-Point Objects", *Proceedings 15th VLDB Conference*, pp.45-53, Amsterdam, Netherlands, 1989.

[KF93]   I. Kamel and C. Faloutsos: "On Packing R-trees", *Proceedings 2nd CIKM Conference*, 1993.

[KF94]   I. Kamel and C. Faloutsos: "Hilbert R-tree: an Improved R-tree Using Fractals", *Proceedings 20th VLDB Conference*, pp.500-509, Santiago, Chile, 1994.

[KS97]   N. Katayama and S. Satoh: "The SR-tree: an Index Structure for High-Dimensional Nearest Neighbor Queries", *Proceedings 1997 ACM SIGMOD Conference*, pp.369-380, May 1997.

[LEL96]   S. Leutenegger, J. Edgington and M. Lopez: "STR: a Simple and Efficient Algorithm for R-tree Packing", *Proceedings 12th IEEE ICDE Conference*, 1996.

[LRB+97] M. Livny, R. Ramakrishnan, K. Beyer, G. Chen, D. Donjerkovic, S. Lawande, J. Myllymaki and K. Wenger: "DEVISE: Integrated Querying and Visual Exploration of Large Datasets", *Proceedings 1997 ACM SIGMOD Conference*, 1997.

[LT92]   R. Laurini and D. Thomson: *"Fundamentals of Spatial Information Systems"*, Academic Press, London, 1992.

[LR98]   M.-L. Lo and C.V. Ravishankar: "The Design and Implementation of Seeded Trees: An Efficient Method for Spatial Joins", *IEEE Transactions on Knowledge and Data Engineering*, Vol.10, No.1, 1998.

[ND98]   B. Nag and D. DeWitt: "Memory Allocation Strategies for Complex Decision Support Queries", *Proceedings 7th CIKM Conference*, 1998.

[PRS99]   A.N. Papadopoulos, P. Rigaux and M. Scholl: "A Performance Evaluation of Spatial Join Processing Strategies", *Proceedings International Conference on Large Spatial Databases (SSD'99)*, Honk-Kong, China, 1999.

[RKV95]   N. Roussopoulos, S. Kelley and F. Vincent: "Nearest Neighbor Queries", *Proceedings 1995 ACM SIGMOD Conference*, pp.71-79, San Jose, CA, 1995.

[SFGM93] M. Stonebraker, J. Frew, K. Gardels, and J. Meredith: "The Sequoia 2000 Storage Benchmark", *Proceedings 1993 ACM SIGMOD Conference*, pp.2-11, Washington DC, 1993.

[SRF87]   T. Sellis, N. Roussopoulos and C. Faloutsos: "The R$^+$-tree: a Dynamic Index for Multidimensional Objects", *Proceedings 13th VLDB Conference*, pp.507-518, Brighton, UK, 1987.

[Tiger94] Bureau of the Census: "Tiger/line files", Washington DC, 1994.

[TPCD95] Transaction Processing Performance Council TPC. *TPC Benchmark D Specification*, version 1.1 edition, December 1995.

[TPCC97] Transaction Processing Performance Council TPC. *TPC Benchmark C Specification*, revision 3.3.2 edition, June 1997.

[TS96]   Y. Theodoridis and T. Sellis: "A Model for the Prediction of R-tree Performance", *Proceedings of the 15th ACM SIGACT-SIGMOD-SIGART Symposium on Principles of Database Systems (PODS'96)*, Montreal, Canada, 1996.

[TSS98]   Y. Theodoridis, E. Stefanakis and T. Sellis: "Cost Models for Join Queries in Spatial Databases", *Proceedings Intl. Conf. on Data Engineering (ICDE'98)*, 1998.

[TVS96]   Y. Theodoridis, E. Stefanakis, and T. Sellis: "Spatio-Temporal Indexing for Large Multimedia Applications", *Proceedings of the IEEE International Conference on Multimedia Systems*, Hiroshima, Japan, 1996.

[Val87]   P. Valduriez: "Join Indices", *ACM Transactions on Database Systems*, Vol.12, No.2, pp.218-246, 1987.

[XHL90]   X. Xu, J. Han and W. Lu: "RT-Tree: an Improved R-tree Index Structure for Spatiotemporal Databases", Proceedings 4th Symposium on Spatial Data Handling (SDH'90), pp.1040-1049, 1990.

Appendix - Iterators

We give in this appendix a description of the iterators. Each iterator comes with three functions: open, next and close: open prepares each input source and allocates the necessary system resources, next runs one iteration step of the algorithm and produces a new record and close ends up the iteration and relaxes resources.

To illustrate this, consider the trivial example of the DataScan iterator which sequentially accesses a data file. It is implemented as follows: (i) Open opens the data file, and sets a cursor to the beginning of the file, (ii) Next reads the file page addressed by the cursor, returns the current record to the father node iterator, and sets the cursor to the next record, (iii) Close closes the file. The following table summarizes the iterators used in this study.

	open	next	close
DataScan		Retrieve the record; Advance the cursor;	Close the file
RowAccess	Open input; Open the file;	Call **next** on input; Read the record;	Close input Close file
Project	Open input;	Call **next** on input; Project out attributes	Close input Close input
Sort	Open input *Repeat*: fill the buffer from input; sort the buffer; flush in runs. Merge until only one step is left. Close input.	Process one merge step	Release the buffer and tmp files
SegSort	Open input. *Prepare*: put records in the buffer from input; sort on R record ids; read records from R; sort on S record ids.	Take the next pair in the buffer; read the record from S Buffer empty? Then execute *Prepare*	Close input
STT	Init. the paths in each R-tree; Pin and sort pages as required.	Get next pair of entries; When a page is scanned: unpin, get the next one, sort and pin.	Close both inputs
STJ	Open input; Build the seeded tree from input. Close left input Init. as in STT.	Same as STT	Close right input
STR	Open input; Build the STR from input; close left input; Init. as in STT	Same as STT	Close right input
SaM	Open input; Sort on x. Sort the first slice on y. Get the first matching leaf in the R-tree; sort it (on y)	Get next pair of entries. *Event.*: get the next leaf in the R-tree; sort it *Event.*: get the next slice on y	Close both inputs

Table 2. Description of iterators.

Evaluation of Access Structures for Discretely Moving Points

Mario A. Nascimento[1], Jefferson R. O. Silva[2], and Yannis Theodoridis[3]

[1] Institute of Computing, State Univ. of Campinas, Brazil
`nascimento@computer.org`
[2] Telecommunications R&D Center, Brazil
`jeff@cpqd.com.br`
[3] Computer Technology Institute, Greece
`yannis.theodoridis@cti.gr`

Abstract. Several applications require management of data which is spatially dynamic, e.g., tracking of battle ships or moving cells in a blood sample. The capability of handling the temporal aspect, i.e., the history of such type of data, is also important. This paper presents and evaluates three temporal extensions of the R-tree, the 3D R-tree, the 2+3 R-tree and the HR-tree, which are capable of indexing spatiotemporal data. Our experiments focus on discretely moving points (i.e., points standing at a specific location for a time period and then moving "instantaneously", and so on and so forth). We explore several parameters, e.g., initial spatial distribution, spatial query area and temporal query length. We found out that the HR-tree usually outperforms the other candidates, in terms of query processing cost, specially when querying time points and small time intervals. However, the main side effect of the HR-tree is its storage requirement, which is much larger than that of the other approaches. To reduce that, we explore a batch oriented updating approach, at the cost of some overhead during query processing time. To our knowledge, this study constitutes the first extensive, though not exhaustive, experimental comparison of access structures for spatiotemporal data.

1 Introduction

The primary goal of a spatiotemporal database is the accurate modeling of the real world; that is a dynamic world, which involves objects whose position, shape and size change over time [19]. Real life examples that need to handle spatiotemporal data include storage and manipulation of ship and plane trajectories, fire or hurricane front monitor and weather forecast. Geographical information systems are also a source for spatiotemporal data [5]. As another example domain, consider the problem of video (or multimedia in general) database management. Objects that appear in each frame can be considered two-dimensional moving objects, upon which one may want to keep track over time or exploit relationships among them. Indeed, a "database application must capture the time-varying nature of the phenomena they model" [26, Ch. 5]. Spatial phenomena are no exception to this observation. Therefore, spatiotemporal databases should florish as current technology makes it more feasible to obtain and manage such type of data ([4] is a good example of that trend).

Among the many research issues related to spatiotemporal data, e.g., query languages and management of uncertainty [24], we focus on the issue of optimizing access structures, hence speeding up query processing. Despite the fact that there is much work done on surveying and evaluating access structures for temporal [15] and spatial data [6], not much has been done regarding spatiotemporal data. This paper deals with this very point.

In particular, we focus on benchmarking access structures that maintain the whole "history" of each moving object and which are able to answer queries of the type "which objects were located within a specific area at a specific time instance (or during a specific time interval)". This class of access structures currently includes a very limited number of proposals; to our knowledge, there exist only five, namely MR-trees and RT-trees [25], 3D R-trees [22], and more recently, HR-trees [13] and Overlapping Linear Quadtrees [23], based on the popular R-trees [7, 17, 1, 8] and Quadtrees [16].

There also exist a small number of proposals aiming at supporting queries that deal with the future, i.e., "which objects will (certainly or probably) be located within a specific area after (or within) a certain time". This class of access structures usually store current location and some extra information (such as speed and direction) to make safe predictions for the future locations of objects [9, 24].

Although we admit that both applications are of equal importance, in this paper we only consider the former class. Indeed, in many real life examples, it is discrete locations rather than continuous motion that is detected by, e.g., a global positioning system (GPS) and stored in a database. Thus point trajectories are actually "simulated" either by storing discrete locations and valid time or by linearly interpolating consecutive points (the so-called projection versus interpolation-based approaches in [20]) and this simulation could be enriched by adding tolerance due to imprecision [14]. In the rest of the paper, we evaluate the first approach, i.e., discuss indexing of discretely moving points.

In [19], a set of seven criteria were proposed to characterize spatiotemporal data and access structures in the class of interest:

1. *Data types supported*: whether it supports points and/or regions;
2. *Temporal support*: whether the supported temporal dimension is that of valid time, transaction time or both;
3. *Database mobility*: whether the changes in cardinality or the spatial position of the data items, or both, can change over time;
4. *Data loading*: whether the data set is known a priori or not, whether only updates concerning the current state can be made or whether any state can be updated;
5. *Object representation*: which abstraction (e.g., MBRs - Minimum Bounding Rectangles) is used to represent the spatial objects.
6. *Temporal treatment*: whether it supports special actions such as packing or purging (vacuuming) spatial data as time evolves.

7. *Query support*: whether it is able to process not only pure spatial and temporal queries, but also queries which are spatiotemporal in nature.

After the directions above, and for the purposes of this paper, we assume spatiotemporal data specified as follows:

- The data set consists of two-dimensional points, which are moving in a *discrete* manner within the unit square;
- Updates are allowed only in the current state of the database;
- The timestamp of each point's version grows monotonically following a transaction time pattern, and
- The cardinality of the data set remains fixed as time evolves.

Regarding the indexing structures, no packing or purging of data is assumed. Finally they must provide support to process at least two types of queries: (1) containment queries with respect to a time point; and (2) containment queries with respect to a time interval. By containment query we mean one where, given a reference MBR, all points lying inside such MBR should be retrieved.

Hence, according to the terminology in [19], this paper considers databases of the point/transaction-time/evolving/chronological class. For simplicity, throughout the paper we assume the two-dimensional space, although extending the presented arguments for higher dimension is not problematic.

The remainder of the paper is organized as follows. In Section 2 we detail the access structures which we will compare. Next, in Section 3, the methodology used to generate spatiotemporal data is discussed. Section 4 presents and discusses the experiments we perform regarding space requirements, update and query performance. Finally, the paper is closed with a summary of our findings and directions for future research.

2 Spatiotemporal Access Structures

As mentioned earlier, we are aware of only five access structures that consider both spatial and temporal attributes of objects, namely MR-trees and RT-trees [25], 3D R-trees [22], HR-trees [13] and Overlapping Linear Quadtrees [23].

In the RT-tree the temporal information is kept inside the R-tree nodes. This is in addition to the traditional content of the R-tree nodes. On the other hand searching in the RT-tree is only guided by the spatial data, hence temporal information plays a secondary role. As such queries based solely on the temporal domain cannot be processed efficiently, as they would require a complete scan of the database. No actual performance analysis was reported in [25].

The 3D R-trees, as originally proposed in [22], use standard R-trees to index multimedia data. The scenario investigated is that of images and sound in a multimedia authoring environment. In such a scenario it is reasonable to admit that the temporal and spatial bounds of the indexed objects are known beforehand. Aware of that fact the authors proposed two approaches, called the *simple* and the *unified* scheme. In the former one, a two-dimensional R-tree indexes the spatial component of the data set, and an one-dimensional R-tree indexes the temporal component. Query processing is performed using both trees and performing the necessary operations between the two returned answer sets. The latter approach uses a single three-dimensional R-tree and treats time as another spatial dimension. The authors conclude that the advantage of using one or the other approach is a matter of trade-off based on how much often purely spatial or temporal queries are posed relatively to spatiotemporal ones.

The Overlapping Linear Quadtrees, the MR-trees and the HR-trees are all based on the concept of overlapping trees [11]. The basic idea is that, given two trees where the younger one is an evolution of the older one, the second one is represented incrementally. As such only the modified branches are actually stored, the branches that do not change are simply re-used. The Overlapping Linear Quadtrees, as the name implies are based on Quadtrees [16] and as such are not constrained to index only MBRs. The MR-trees and the HR-trees are very similar in nature and we comment on the HR-tree in more details shortly. Indeed, next we discuss the three access structures we investigate in the remainder of this paper.

2.1   3D R-tree

The structure we discuss here is based on the 3D R-tree proposed in [22]. The most straightforward way to index spatiotemporal data is to consider time to be another axis, along with the traditional spatial ones. Using this rationale, an object which lies initially at (x_i, y_i) during time $[t_i, t_j)$ and at (x_j, y_j) during $[t_j, t_k)$ can be modeled by two line segments in the three-dimensional space, namely the lines: $\overline{((x_i, y_i, t_i), (x_i, y_i, t_j))}$ and $\overline{((x_j, y_j, t_j), (x_j, y_j, t_k))}$, which can be indexed using a three-dimensional R-tree.

This idea works fine if the end time of all such lines is known. For instance consider in the above example that the object moves from its initial position to the new one but is to remain there until some time not known beforehand. All we know is that it lies in its new position until *now*, or *until changed*, no further knowledge can be assumed. The very problem of handling *now* or *until changed* is complex enough by itself (refer to [3] for a thorough discussion on the topic). To make things simpler we assume that *now* (or *until changed*) is a time point sufficiently far in the future, about which there is no further knowledge.

What matters to our discussion is that standard spatial access structures are not well suited to handle such type of "open" lines. In fact, one cannot avoid them. It is reasonable to assume that once the position of an spatial object is known, it is unknown when (and if) it is going to move. As such all current knowledge would yield such open lines, which would render known spatial access structures, e.g., R-trees, of little use. Recently, [2] investigated that problem in the context of temporal databases and proposed appropriate extensions to R*-trees. Another approach was presented in [18] where a Quadtree based index is periodically reconstructed using the current information about the objects' location. The objects' motion equations are also maintained associated to the index. Between index reconstructions, future objects positions are inferred using the indexed data and the motion equations.

One special case where one could overcome such an issue is when all movements are known *a priori*. This would cause only "closed" lines to be input, and thus the above problem would not exist. In the comparisons we make later in the paper using this structure, which we simply refer to as 3D R-tree, we shall make such an assumption. One feature that may favor such an approach is that any R-tree derivative could be used.

2.2   2+3 R-tree

One possible way to resolve the above issue is to use two R-trees, one for two-dimensional points, and another one for three-dimensional lines (hence the name 2+3 R-tree). The two-dimensional points would represent the current spatial information about the data points, whereas the three-dimensional lines would the represent (piecewise) the historical information. A similar idea has been proposed in [10] in the context of bitemporal databases. In that paper bitemporal ranges with open transaction time ranges are were kept under one R-tree (called front R-tree) as a line segment. Whenever an open transaction time range is closed it becomes a closed rectangle, which is indexed under another R-tree (called back R-tree), after removing the previously associated line segment from the front R-tree. In the 2+3 R-tree, while the end time of an object's position is unknown, it is indexed under a two-dimensional R-tree, keeping the start time of its position along with its id. Note that the original R-tree (or any of its derivatives) keep only the object's id (or a pointer to the actual data record) and its MBR in the leaf nodes. The two-dimensional R-tree used in this approach is thus minimally modified.

Once the end time of an "open" object's current state (i.e., position) is known, we proceed with (a) constructing its three-dimensional line as explained above, (b) inserting it into the three-dimensional R-tree and (c) deleting the existing entry from the two-dimensional R-tree.

Using the example from the previous section: from time t_i until the time point immediately before[1] t_j the object is indexed under the two-dimensional R-tree. At time t_j, it moves, as such, (1) the point (x_0, y_0) is deleted from the two-dimensional R-tree, (2) the line $\overline{[(x_0, y_0, t_i), (x_0, y_0, t_j)]}$ is input into the three-dimensional R-tree, and, finally, (3) the point (x_1, y_1) is input into the two-dimensional R-tree. Keep in mind that the start time of a point position is also part of the information held along with the remainder of its data.

It is important to note that both trees may need to be searched, depending on the time point with respect to which the queries are posed. of the 3D R-tree. That is to say that the two-dimensional R-tree serves the single purpose of holding the current (i.e., open) intervals. Should one know all object movements

---

[1] We assume, without loss of generality, that the time domain is isomorphic to the rationals.

a priori the two-dimensional R-tree would not be used at all, hence the 2+3 R-tree reduces to the 3D R-tree presented earlier.

2.3   HR-tree

The two approaches above have drawbacks. The first suffers from the fact that it cannot handle open-ended lines. The second, while able to overcome that problem, must search two distinct R-trees for a variety of queries. In this section we review the HR-tree [13], which is designed to index spatiotemporal data as classified earlier.

Consider again the example in Section 2.1. At time t_i one could obtain the current state (snapshot) of the indexed points, build and keep the corresponding two-dimensional R-tree, repeating this procedure for t_j and t_k. Obviously, it is not practical to keep the R-trees corresponding to all actual previous states of the underlying R-tree. On the other hand it is reasonable to expect that some (perhaps the vast majority) of the indexed points do not change their positions at every timestamp. Consequently R-trees may have some (or many) nodes identical to the previous version. The HR-tree explores this, by keeping all previous states (snapshots) of the two-dimensional R-tree only *logically*.

As an illustration consider the two consecutive (with respect to their timestamps) R-trees in Figures 1(a) and (b), which can be represented in a more compact manner as shown in Figure 1(c). Note that with the addition of an array **A** one can easily access the R-tree he/she desires. In fact, once the root node of the desired R-tree for a given timestamp is obtained, query processing cost is the *same* as if all R-trees where kept physically.

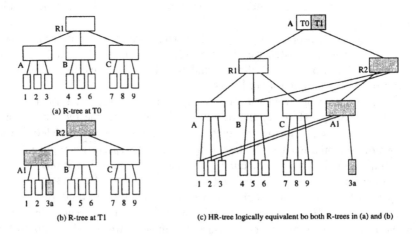

Fig. 1. Example of the HR-tree approach.

Notice however that it is desirable to keep the number of newly created branches as low as possible. For that reason some R-tree variants are not suitable to serve as HR-tree's framework, notably, the R^+-tree [17] and the R^*-tree [1]. In the former the MBRs are "clipped" and one single MBR may appear in several internal nodes, therefore increasing the number of branches to be created in each incremental R-tree. Likewise, the R^*-tree, avoids node splitting by forcing entries re-insertion, which is likely to affect several branches, hence enlarging the HR-tree.

Among the other alternatives, we have found the Hilbert R-tree [8] to be very suitable for our purposes and use it as HR-tree's baseline. From now on, unless explicitly mentioned otherwise, we use the term R-tree(s) to refer to the Hilbert R-tree(s) as originally defined. The interested reader can find all HR-tree's algorithms detailed in [12].

3 Data Generation

For the data generation itself, we have used GSTD[2] [20], a spatiotemporal data generator where the user can tune several parameters to obtain data sets which fulfill his/her needs. Some of them are: the initial data distribution, the amount of time a point is going to rest at the same location (*interval*), the distance it will move (*shift*) and where it is going to move to in the space (*direction*).

All data is initially generated assuming a two-dimensional unit square. Any point moving out of such a square has its coordinates adjusted to fit in the workspace. We also assume that the interval follows a gaussian distribution and the shift and direction follow the uniform one.

To illustrate how data is generated and how it evolves, Figure 2 (3) shows an initial data set using the gaussian (skewed) distribution, and four "snapshots" taken after 25, 50, 75 and 100 timestamps. It is easy to note that after 100 timestamps the initial distribution becomes very close to a uniform one. This feature will allow us to investigate how dependent of the initial spatial data distribution the access structures are. Naturally, data points which were initially randomly distributed, remain randomly distributed as time evolves.

Fig. 2. Evolution of gaussianly distributed data points.

---

[2] http://www.dblab.ece.ntua.gr/~theodor/GSTD (with a mirror site available at http://www.dcc.unicamp.br/~mario/GSTD).

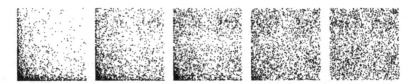

Fig. 3. Evolution of skewedly distributed data points.

4   Performance Comparison

As pointed out above our main concern is to investigate the performance yielded by the 3D R-tree, the 2+3 R-tree and the HR-tree when indexing moving points. Recall that in order to use the 3D R-tree one must know the whole history in advance. While some applications, such as digital battle field, may use *previously recorded snapshots*, others involve the *now* parameter. To overcome that problem, one may use the 2+3 R-tree approach as discussed in Section 2.2. In any case, we decided to include the 3D R-tree as a yardstick. Both the 3D and 2+3 R-trees are Hilbert R-trees in nature.

Our experiments were performed on a Pentium II 300 Mhz PC running LINUX with 64 Mbytes of core memory. The disk pages, i.e., tree nodes, use 1,024 bytes and all programs were coded using GNU's C++ compiler. No caching is explored for the investigated structures. Although it is certain that caching would improve the structures' performance we believe that different cache policies would be better suited for each of the structures. Therefore, instead of taking the risk of using a policy which could benefit of the structures in particular, we decided to leave this issue to be investigated thoroughly in the future.

Although this paper presents quantitative results using only a data set cardinality of 100,000 data points, we have also experimented with other sizes of data sets (25K, 50K and 75K) and reached to similar conclusions [12]. All objects timestamps fell within the unit time interval [0, 1] with a granularity of 0.01, i.e., 100 distinct and equally spaced timestamps could be identified. Three initial spatial distributions were investigated: uniform, gaussian and skewed. The GSTD parameters were set in such a way that the points could move randomly in the workspace and therefore the final distributions tend to the uniform one (see Figures 2 and 3). The queries were uniformly distributed, and three different area sizes were used, denoted respectively as small, medium and large MBRs (Figure 4).

Recall that we are interested in queries of the type "which are the points contained in a given region at (or during) a time point (interval)". The same set of two-dimensional queries are three-dimensionalized by "adding" a third temporal axis to make containment queries with respect to a time interval. For each time point or interval we ran 100 queries and report the averages. Next we show the obtained results regarding storage requirements, index building cost and query processing cost (measured in terms of disk I/O). Query processing

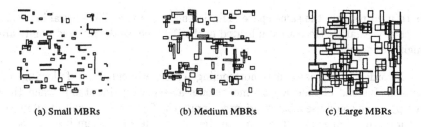

(a) Small MBRs   (b) Medium MBRs   (c) Large MBRs

Fig. 4. Query MBRs with centers uniformly distributed.

cost was measured when the database was in a static state, i.e., no updates were processed concurrently to the queries.

4.1 Storage Requirements

Figure 5 shows how large each of the structures are after indexing the initial 100,000 data points, and all their evolutions, i.e., after 100 timestamps, as a function initial spatial distribution. It is clear that the qualitative behavior of either structure does not seem to depend upon the initial distribution of the spatial data.

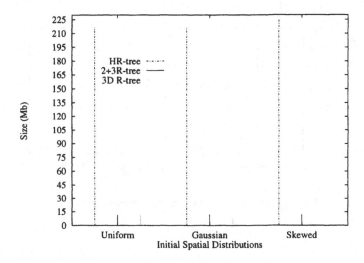

Fig. 5. Indices' sizes.

One result not shown in the figure is that, as expected, the HR-tree approach does save space when compared to the extreme case of physically storing all (100) R-trees. In fact, the average savings amounted to over 33%. On the other hand, the HR-tree is an order of magnitude larger than the 2+3 and 3D R-tree, which both used roughly the same space. This is due to the fact that several branches of the "virtual" R-trees are duplicated in the HR-tree, as the indexed points are highly dynamic.

In order to alliviate this shortcoming we experimented the following approach. Instead of indexing all movements at the very timestamp when they happen, one could use a batch-oriented approach. The idea is to collect all movements into a buffer and from time to time flush out all of them into the same virtual R-tree. For instance, consider points locations which would originally be indexed under timestamps t, $t + 1$ and $t + 2$. Using such an approach all such points could be indexed at time $t + 2$. The tradeoff in doing this is that one may not be able to query only the time point of interest. In the example just presented querying time point $t + 1$ would require retrieving the (virtual) R-tree at time $t + 2$, and consequently filter the answer properly. In other words, such batching may yield false-hits. We investigate this trade-off in more details shortly.

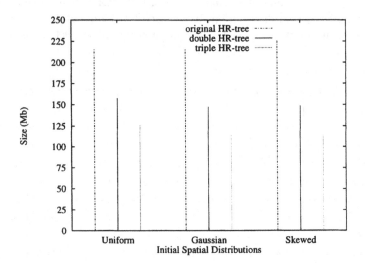

Fig. 6. HR-tree size using a batch oriented approach.

Figure 6 shows the obtained results when all movements were indexed at their exact timestamp (as in Figure 5), and at every two and three timestamps (which we refer to as double and triple approach). The gains were about 30% and 45% respectively. Note that even though the HR-tree became smaller it still remains larger than the other two structures. Fortunately, as we shall see shortly, the imposed overhead due to the false-hits is not likely to be as high the yielded gain (depending on the query size).

4.2   Index Building Cost

One interesting aspect to consider is the cost (in terms of disk I/Os) needed to construct the indices. Figure 7 shows such an information for all three initial distributions after indexing 100,000 data points and their evolutions. As expected the 2+3 R-tree is the one which takes more time (hence, I/Os) to be built. This is due to the fact that whenever a point moves, there is an insertion (of the new version) and a deletion (of the previous position) on the two-dimensional R-tree, and one insertion of a line (the previous position history) on the three dimensional R-tree. The HR-tree appears as the runner-up as at least one complete branch is updated from one timestamp to another one (assuming at least one point moved). The 3D R-tree on the other hand is the most economical alternative, given that if all point movements are known a priori only one three-dimensional line is inserted per point movement and no deletions occur.

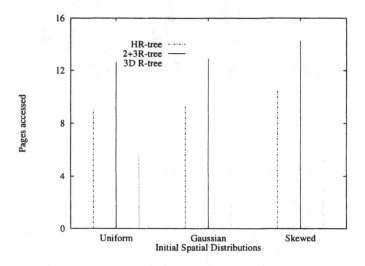

Fig. 7. Indexing building cost.

Unlike in the case for the indices sizes, the batching approach yields only some marginal improvements (when used for the HR-tree) regarding update cost.

4.3   Query Processing Cost

There are two cases to consider, one when the query is posed with respect to a specific time point and another when a time interval is considered. We consider each one in turn, starting with the case of a fixed reference time point query. The U, G and S labels in x-axis of the following figures denote the initial uniform, gaussian and skewed spatial distribution respectively. The results shown are the

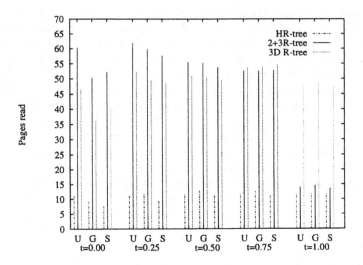

Fig. 8. Point query processing cost, small MBRs.

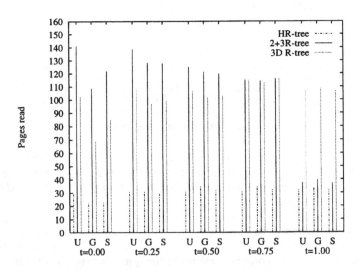

Fig. 9. Point query processing cost, large MBRs.

average number of I/Os obtained when querying time points 0, 0.25, 0.5, 0.75 and 1.

Figures 8 and 9 show the results obtained when querying each structure, at the timestamps described above, and using the small and large query MBRs respectively. The results from the medium MBRs are qualitatively the same, and quantitatively proportional to the query size (with respect the small and large MBRs), thus they are not shown for the sake of brevity.

Our conjecture that the HR-tree would require substantially smaller query processing time was shown to be true in all cases. When the temporal part of the query is a point, the tree that corresponds to that timestamp is obtained and the query processing is exactly the same one of a containment query in a single standard R-tree. On the other hand, for both the 3D and 2+3 R-tree the whole structure is involved in the query processing, thus increasing significantly the query processing cost. In general, querying the HR-tree was always 3 to 4 times cheaper than querying the 3D R-tree.

One noteworthy result is obtained when querying the 2+3 R-tree at time 1, i.e., that end of the indexed temporal window. At that time point, the three-dimensional of the two R-trees is not traversed because there is no object with an end time equal to 1, thus all the answers come from the 2D R-tree – where there is always a current version for all indexed points. In fact, when querying time point 0.99, i.e., the indexed timestamp immediately before the last one, the 2+3 R-tree would require over 130% more I/Os than necessary when querying time point 1. Therefore the good performance obtained when querying that particular timestamp is by no means typical.

Note that as time evolves the 2+3 R-tree and the 3D R-tree exchange places as the runner-up structure. After some amount of updating, having all current and historical data in a single structure yields a large overlap ratio in the tree MBRs and thus a more complex tree traversal. Finally, it also became clear that the size of the query MBR affects all structures equally.

It is now necessary to measure the trade-off posed when one used the double or triple HR-tree approach as discussed earlier (we noted earlier that such an approach was able to reduce the HR-tree's size). Figure 10 shows the results when querying large query MBRs at time points 0, 0.25, 0.5, 0.75 and 1 (the results were qualitatively the same for small and medium sized queries). The difference in the curves for the original and the double and triple approach represents the number of pages which were read due to the batching, i.e., overhead pages. The average overhead was 17% for small queries, 20% for medium queries and 30% for large queries. It is important to note that despite such overhead the HR-tree still remains the overall faster index structure (compare Figure 9 to Figure 10).

Next we proceed to investigate how the structures perform when querying a time interval instead of a point. Figures 11, and 12 illustrate the query processing cost when varying the average length of the queried time interval. Such a length is measured in number of consecutive timestamps. That is, we measured the structure's performance when the time interval was up to 10% of the total (unit) time window length. Again the results using medium query MBRs,

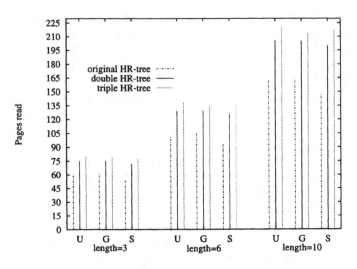

Fig. 10. Point query processing overhead using the batch oriented approach and large MBRs.

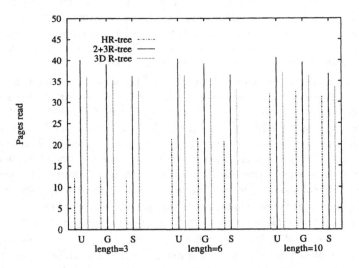

Fig. 11. Interval query processing cost, small MBRs.

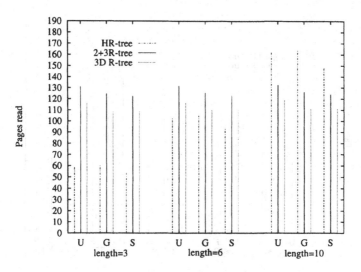

Fig. 12. Interval query processing cost, large MBRs.

were qualitatively the same. Larger intervals were not investigated as the curves shown already presented a clear trend.

While the HR-tree is well suited to search a time point, for time intervals it has to traverse as many logical R-trees as many indexed time points are covered by that interval. As a result the HR-tree loses its relative advantage relatively fast with the increase in the queried interval length. In fact, we observed this is worsened by the increase in the query MBR area.

Figure 13 shows that the overhead imposed by the batching approach is now harmful (comparing to the performance delivered by the other structures). That is, batching updates does not seem worthwhile for the case of querying time intervals.

5   Summary and Future Research

In this paper we raised the issue that despite the fact that applications dealing with spatiotemporal data are gaining strength, not much has been done regarding implementation and/or extensions of appropriate database management systems. Towards that goal our contribution was to present and investigate access structures for spatiotemporal data. To the best of our knowledge it is the first performance study for spatiotemporal access structures. We implemented three R-tree based structures: the 3D R-tree, the 2+3 R-tree and the HR-tree; and investigated several parameters that affect their performance:

- initial distribution of point data (uniform vs. gaussian vs. skewed)
- temporal extent of query windows (point vs. interval time queries)
- time snapshot of point time queries (from less to more recent)

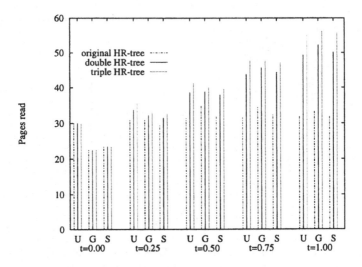

Fig. 13. Interval query processing overhead using the batch oriented approach and large MBRs.

– updating batch sizes (for the HR-tree)

After several experiments (more detailed experiments may be found in [12]), we have discovered that:

– The less dynamic the data set, the higher the storage savings yielded by the HR-tree when compared to the ideal (from the query processing perspective) but impractical (in terms of disk storage demand) solution of having all logical R-trees physically stored;
– The 3D and 2+3 R-trees tend to be much smaller than the HR-tree;
– The use of a batching approach at update time is capable of reducing substantially the HR-tree's size, yielding some overhead at query processing time.
– When querying a specific time point the HR-tree offers a much better query processing time than the 3D and 2+3 R-trees. In fact, it offers the same performance as if all logical R-trees were physically stored. The overhead imposed by the batching approach is acceptable as the HR-tree remains the best performer;
– If instead of a time point a time interval is queried, the HR-tree loses its advantage rather quickly with the increase in the length of the queried time interval. In such a case the batching approach overhead for the HR-tree is hardly worthwhile.

Considering that with current technology storage is much less of a problem than time to query data, we consider the HR-tree a good candidate access structure for spatiotemporal data when most queries are posed with respect to a time point or a very short time range. We also have to note that, unlike HR-tree and

2+3 R-tree, the 3D R-tree is not capable of supporting on-line spatiotemporal applications that involve the *now* (or *until changed*) parameter.

The present paper has not dealt specifically with how the above structures behave with respect to movement direction and speed and the use of caching structures and policies. For instance, suppose that instead of spreading in the space, all points move coordinately towards the same direction, how would each access structure support this ? Also a few points may move much faster than the others (or vice-versa), is that a feature that will affect the structures' performance ? These and several other questions are currently being investigated.

As future work, each structure's performance is planned to be analytically explored, in correspondence with the R-tree analysis for selection and join queries that appears in [21]. Both directions, extensive experimentation and analytical work, converge on building a spatiotemporal benchmarking environment consisting of real and synthetic data sets and access structures for evaluation purposes.

Acknowledgements

Mario A. Nascimento was partially supported by CNPq (process number 300208/97-9) and by the Pronex/FINEP funded project "SAI: Advanced Information Systems" (process number 76.97.1022.00), and was also with Embrapa. He is currently with the Univ. of Alberta, Canada. Jefferson R. O. Silva was supported by FAPESP (process number 97/11205-8). Yannis Theodoridis was partially supported by the EC funded TMR project "CHOROCHRONOS: A Research Network for Spatiotemporal Database Systems", contract number ERBFMRX-CT96-0056 while he was with NTU Athens. We thank Timos Sellis for fruitful discussions and comments on earlier drafts of the paper.

References

1. N. Beckmann et al. The R*-tree: An efficient and robust access method for points and rectangles. In *Proc. of the 1990 ACM SIGMOD Intl. Conf. on Management of Data*, pages 322–331, June 1990.
2. R. Bliujute et al. R-tree based indexing of now-relative bitemporal data. In *Proc. of the 24th Very Large Databases Conf.*, pages 345–356, August 1998.
3. J. Clifford et al. On the semantics of "NOW" in temporal databases. *ACM Transactions on Database Systems*, 22(2):171–214, 1997.
4. Informix Corp. Developing datablade modules for informix dynamic server with universal data option. White paper, 1998.
5. Egenhofer, M.J. and Golledge, R.G. (Eds.). *Spatial and Temporal Reasoning in Geographical Information Systems*. Oxford Univ. Press, New York, USA, 1998.
6. V. Gaede and O. Günther. Multidimensional access methods. *ACM Computing Surveys*, 30(2):123–169, 1998.
7. A. Guttman. R-trees: A dynamic index structure for spatial searching. In *Proc. of the 1984 ACM SIGMOD Intl. Conf. on Management of Data*, pages 47–57, June 1984.

8. I. Kamel and C. Faloutsos. Hilbert R-tree: An improved R-tree using fractals. In *Proc. of the 20th Very Large Databases Conf.*, pages 500–509, September 1994.
9. G. Kollios, D. Gunopulos, and V.J. Tsotras. On indexing mobile objects. In *Proc. of the 18th ACM SIGMOD-SIGACT-SIGART Symposium on Principles of Database Systems*, pages 261–272, May 1999.
10. A. Kumar, V.J. Tsotras, and C. Faloutsos. Access methods for bi-temporal databases. In *Proc. of the International Workshop on Temporal Databases*, pages 235–254, September 1995.
11. Y. Manolopoulos and G. Kapetanakis. Overlapping B^+-trees for temporal data. In *Proc. of the 5th Jerusalem Conf. on Information Technology*, pages 491–498, August 1990.
12. M. A. Nascimento, J. R. O. Silva, and Y. Theodoridis. Access structures for moving points. Technical Report 33, TimeCenter, 1998.
13. M.A. Nascimento and J.R.O. Silva. Towards historical R-trees. In *Proc. of the 1998 ACM Symposium on Applied Computing*, pages 235 – 240, February 1998.
14. D. Pfoser and C.S. Jensen. Capturing the uncertainty of moving-objects representation. In *Proc. of the 6th Intl. Symposium on Spatial Databases*, July 1999. To appear.
15. B. Salzberg and V.J. Tsotras. A comparison of access methods for time evolving data. Technical Report 18, TimeCenter, 1997. To appear at *ACM Computing Surveys*.
16. H. Samet. *The Design and Analysis of Spatial Data Strucutures*. Addison-Wesley, Reading, USA, 1990.
17. T. Sellis, N. Roussopoulos, and C. Faloutsos. The R^+-tree: A dynamic index for multidimensional objects. In *Proc. of the 13th Very Large Databases Conf.*, pages 507–518, September 1987.
18. J. Tayeb, O. Ulusoy, and O. Wolfson. A quadtree based dynamic attribute indexing method. *Computer Journal*, 41(3):185–200, 1998.
19. Y. Theodoridis et al. Specifications for efficient indexing in spatiotemporal databases. In *Proc. of the 10th IEEE Intl. Conf. on Scientific and Statistical Database Management*, pages 123 – 132, July 1998.
20. Y. Theodoridis, J.R.O. Silva, and M.A. Nascimento. On the generation of spatiotemporal datasets. In *Proc. of the 6th Intl. Symposium on Spatial Databases*, July 1999. To appear.
21. Y. Theodoridis, E. Stefanakis, and T. Sellis. Efficient cost models for spatial queries using R-trees. Technical Report CH-98-5, Chorochronos, 1998. To appear at *IEEE Transactions on Knowledge and Data Engineering*.
22. Y. Theodoridis, M. Vazirgiannis, and T. Sellis. Spatio-temporal indexing for large multimedia applications. In *Proc. of the 3rd IEEE Conf. on Multimedia Computing and Systems*, pages 441 – 448, June 1996.
23. T. Tzouramanis, M. Vassilakopoulos, and Y. Manolopoulos. Overlapping linear quadtrees: a spatio-temporal access method. In *Proc. of the 6th ACM Intl. Workshop on Geographical Information Systems*, pages 1–7, November 1998.
24. O. Wolfson et al. Moving objects databases: Issues and solutions. In *Proc. of the 10th IEEE Intl. Conf. on Scientific and Statistical Database Management*, pages 111 – 122, July 1998.
25. X. Xu, J. Han, and W. Lu. RT-tree: An improved R-tree index structure for spatiotemporal databases. In *Proc. of the 4th Intl. Symposium on Spatial Data Handling*, pages 1040 – 1049, 1990.
26. C. Zaniolo et al., editors. *Advanced Databases Systems*. Morgan Kauffman, San Francisco, USA, 1997.

Temporal Dependencies Generalized for Spatial and Other Dimensions

Jef Wijsen and Raymond T. Ng

[1] University of Antwerp, Department of Mathematics and Computer Science,
Universiteitsplein 1, B-2610 Wilrijk, Belgium
Jef.Wijsen@uia.ua.ac.be
[2] University of British Columbia, Department of Computer Science,
Vancouver, B.C. V6T 1Z4, Canada
rng@cs.ubc.ca

Abstract. Recently, there has been a lot of interest in *temporal granularity*, and its applications in temporal dependency theory and data mining. *Generalization hierarchies* used in multi-dimensional databases and OLAP serve a role similar to that of time granularity in temporal databases, but they also apply to non-temporal dimensions, like space. In this paper, we first generalize temporal functional dependencies for non-temporal dimensions, which leads to the notion of roll-up dependency (RUD). We show the applicability of RUDs in conceptual modeling and data mining. We then indicate that the notion of time granularity used in temporal databases is generally more expressive than the generalization hierarchies in multi-dimensional databases, and show how this surplus expressiveness can be introduced in non-temporal dimensions, which leads to the formalism of RUD with negation (RUD⁻). A complete axiomatization for reasoning about RUD⁻ is given.

1 Introduction

Generalization hierarchies play an important role in OLAP and data mining [5, 6, 8]. Along the spatial dimension, for example, countries are divided into states, states into cities, and so on. Each of these levels can be used to aggregate space-related data, such as census data. Recently, several database researchers have focused on one particular generalization hierarchy called *time granularity* [3]. This hierarchy captures the partitioning of years into months, months into days, and so on. Demonstrably, time granularity has useful applications in temporal dependency theory [16–18] and temporal data mining [4, 20]. This focus on temporal aspects raises some interesting and important questions concerning the peculiarity of the time dimension. Does temporal dependency theory carry over to non-temporal dimensions, like space? What is so typical about the temporal dimension that justifies its special treatment? In the literature we find some indications that part of the work on temporal databases can be generalized for other dimensions. Jensen et al. study temporal dependencies, and mention [10, page 579] that their framework can be generalized to spatial dimensions. Their work, however, does not deal with temporal or spatial granularity. Wang et al. [16, page 119] mention an approach where time is treated as a conventional attribute, and the time hierarchy is captured by FDs like DATE → MONTH and MONTH → YEAR. They give two concrete examples where this naive approach falls short. Although the examples are interesting, they are rather intricate and do not explain under which conditions the naive approach fails.

In this paper, we further explore the generalization of temporal dependency theory to non-temporal dimensions. To this extent, we introduce the notion of roll-up dependency (RUD), a natural extension of temporal functional dependency to multidimensional databases. Section 2 starts with some motivating applications for RUDs. After that, the construct of roll-up is formalized, and the notion of RUD defined. A sound and complete axiomatization for reasoning about RUDs is given. Section 3 starts by showing that the concept of time granularity used in temporal databases is generally more expressive than the information hierarchies used in OLAP. In simple words, whereas generalization hierarchies are confined to *finer-than* relationships (for example, month is finer-than year), temporal granularity also considers more complex relationships, including disjunctive ones (for example, every week is entirely contained in a year *or* a fiscal year, where a fiscal year runs from July 1 to June 30). We show how this surplus expressiveness can be generalized for non-temporal dimensions in an elegant way by allowing negation in RUDs, which leads to the formalism of RUD⁻. A sound and complete axiomatization for reasoning about RUD⁻ is given.

2   Roll-Up Dependency

2.1   Motivation

Example. Let us consider an application that stores information about hotel expenditures as a number of tuples over the schema:

$$(H : \texttt{HOTEL})(D : \texttt{DATE})(C : \texttt{CITY})(RoomCharge : \texttt{PRICE})(Tax : \texttt{PERCENT}) . \quad (1)$$

A tuple $(H : h)(D : d)(C : c)(RoomCharge : x)(Tax : y)$ over (1) expresses that on date d, a room in hotel h in city c was charged x dollar plus y percent tax. The primary key is $\{H, D\}$. The domain names HOTEL, DATE, ... are called levels, and are partially ordered by a relation $\preceq$ that expresses finer-than semantics. See Fig. 1. For example, MONTH $\preceq$ YEAR because every month belongs to a single year. We also say that a month rolls up to its year. On the other hand, WEEK and MONTH are not comparable by $\preceq$ because months do not divide evenly into weeks, nor vice versa. The level PRICE_BRACKET denotes a set of consecutive price intervals, for example, [1–10], [11–20], [21–30], and so on. We have PRICE $\preceq$ PRICE_BRACKET, and a price rolls up to its containing price bracket. Roll-up dependencies (RUDs) extend functional dependencies (FDs) by allowing attributes to be compared for equality at a specified level. For example, we may find that the tax rate does not change within a year and state, as expressed by the RUD:

$$D^{\text{YEAR}} C^{\text{STATE}} \rightarrow Tax^{\text{PERCENT}} .$$

The meaning is as follows: whenever we have two tuples t_1 and t_2 such that $t_1(D)$ and $t_2(D)$ belong to the same year, and $t_1(C)$ and $t_2(C)$ belong to the same state, then $t_1(Tax) = t_2(Tax)$. Hence, D-values are compared at the level YEAR, and C-values at the level STATE. Tax-values are compared at the level PERCENT mentioned in the underlying schema (1). For brevity, a level will be omitted in a RUD if it does not differ from the underlying schema. Hence, the RUD under consideration will be shortened as follows:

$$D^{\text{YEAR}} C^{\text{STATE}} \rightarrow Tax .$$

We next compare RUDs with temporal functional dependencies (TFDs), and then we describe the application of RUDs in data mining and conceptual modeling.

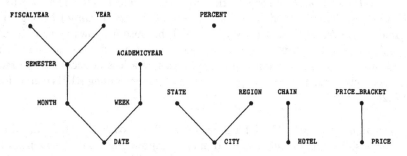

Fig. 1. Partially ordered set of levels

Comparison with TFD. RUDs extend temporal functional dependencies (TFDs) [16, 18] to non-temporal dimensions. TFDs only support roll-up for one dedicated timestamping attribute. For example, the following TFD expresses that the room charge of a hotel does not change within a week:

$$H \rightarrow_{\text{WEEK}} RoomCharge .$$

Note the special position of the time indicator WEEK. In our formalism, this constraint is expressed by the RUD:

$$H \, D^{\text{WEEK}} \rightarrow RoomCharge .$$

Only the temporal attribute (D : DATE) is subject to roll-up. RUDs, unlike TFDs, allow us to roll up any attribute. For an extensive overview of temporal dependencies in databases, see [10, 16, 17].

Data Mining. We want to know whether there are certain spatial or temporal patterns in room charges. But the database contains a large number of expenditure records, giving such a profusion of detailed information that direct comparison is impossible. This information has first to be summarized. In a first attempt, we decide that price brackets are sufficiently accurate to serve our purpose. Our aim then is to find RUDs that are highly satisfied by the data and whose fixed right-hand side is

$$RoomCharge^{\text{PRICE\_BRACKET}} \quad .$$

We fix the attribute *RoomCharge* because we are interested in finding price regularities; we fix the level PRICE_BRACKET instead of PRICE because we want to abstract from minor price changes. A data mining task may then discover the following rule:

$$H^{\text{CHAIN}} D^{\text{MONTH}} \rightarrow RoomCharge^{\text{PRICE\_BRACKET}}$$

stating that the room charges within a single chain and month are within the same price bracket. More precisely, whenever we have two tuples t_1 and t_2 such that $t_1(H)$ and $t_2(H)$ belong to the same chain, and $t_1(D)$ and $t_2(D)$ belong to the same month, then $t_1(RoomCharge)$ and $t_2(RoomCharge)$ belong to the same price bracket. This rule is very useful, because it allows us to reduce the number of price records: we only keep one record for each combination of chain and month. This data reduction is at the cost of a loss in accuracy: we record price brackets instead of exact prices. More details on mining RUDs can be found in [20].

Conceptual Modeling. There have been several proposals to extend the Entity-Relationship (ER) model to capture more temporal and spatial semantics [12]. A recent survey of temporal extensions of ER models is [7]. In [18], we use TFDs to refine the cardinality construct. Tauzovich [15] distinguishes between *snapshot cardinality* and *lifetime cardinality*. TFDs allow us to specify cardinality constraints at any granularity level, snapshot and lifetime being two extremes.

For example, over time a person can stay at several hotels. However, at any one date, a person can only stay at one place. This constraint is expressed by the cardinality "DATE : 1" in Fig. 2. Remark that the ER diagram shows the strongest cardinality constraint that applies. For example, from the diagram in Fig. 2 it is correct to conclude that a person can change hotels within a week; otherwise the diagram would have shown "WEEK : 1," or an even stronger constraint.

Collectively-Finer-Than. Significantly, Wang et al. [16] show that the notion of finer-than is generally insufficient in commonsense temporal reasoning. An example follows. Assume that a fiscal year runs from July 1 to June 30. Fiscal years, (civil) years, and weeks are not comparable by $\preceq$. In particular, some weeks span two civil years, and some other weeks span two fiscal years. See Fig. 1. But the same week cannot span two civil years and two fiscal years. In [16], this is

Fig. 2. Extending cardinality constraints in ER-diagrams

expressed by the concept *collectively-finer-than*: we say that WEEK is collectively-finer-than the set {YEAR, FISCALYEAR} because every week falls entirely within a single year or within a single fiscal year. Collectively-finer-than is a more general construct than finer-than, and plays an important role in reasoning about change, as indicated next. Consider the schema $(D : \text{DATE})(Price : \text{PRICE})$ to store a time series of prices of a particular product. The RUDs $D^{\text{YEAR}} \to Price$ and $D^{\text{FISCALYEAR}} \to Price$ state that the price does not change within a year nor within a fiscal year, respectively. It is correct to conclude from this that the price cannot change within a week. That is, $D^{\text{WEEK}} \to Price$. The extension of RUDs proposed in Sect. 3 allows us to express collectively-finer-than in our framework.

2.2 Roll-Up

The following definition, adapted from [5], defines roll-up.

Definition 1. We assume the existence of a partially ordered set $(\mathcal{L}, \preceq)$ of *levels*. Every level L of $\mathcal{L}$ has associated with it a set of values, denoted $ext(L)$.

A *roll-up instantiation* U is a set of functions as follows: for every $L_1, L_2 \in \mathcal{L}$ with $L_1 \preceq L_2$, there is a total function, denoted $U_{L_1}^{L_2}$, from $ext(L_1)$ into $ext(L_2)$, satisfying the following two conditions:

Transitivity: For every $L_1, L_2, L_3 \in \mathcal{L}$ with $L_1 \preceq L_2 \preceq L_3$, $U_{L_1}^{L_3} = U_{L_2}^{L_3} \circ U_{L_1}^{L_2}$.
Reflexivity: For every $L \in \mathcal{L}$, U_L^L is the identity on $ext(L)$.

We will write $U^L(v)$ instead of $U_{L'}^L(v)$ if L' is clear from the context. If $U^L(v) = w$, we say that v *rolls up to* w in L, where U is implicitly understood and L can be omitted if it is clear from the context.

The set $(\mathcal{L}, \preceq)$ is shown in Fig. 1. The Transitivity requirement in Definition 1 states that if month m rolls up to s in SEMESTER, and s rolls up to y in YEAR, then m rolls up to y in YEAR. Certain roll-ups will typically be stored as binary relations in a relational database. The roll-up of cities to states is an example. Other roll-ups, such as the roll-up from dates to months, will be defined by a function in some programming language.

We now introduce the notions of schema and generalization schema. For convenience, the schema (1) above will be denoted:

$$H^{\text{HOTEL}} D^{\text{DATE}} C^{\text{CITY}} RoomCharge^{\text{PRICE}} Tax^{\text{PERCENT}} . \tag{2}$$

That is, domains are typeset in superscript. A generalization schema is obtained from a schema by duplicating attributes, by omitting attributes, or by substituting superlevels for levels (we say that L is a superlevel of L' if $L' \preceq L$). For example, $D^{\text{MONTH}} C^{\text{STATE}} C^{\text{REGION}}$ is a generalization schema of the schema (2) above: the attributes H, *RoomCharge*, and *Tax* have been omitted, the attribute C has been duplicated, and superlevels have been substituted for the levels in the original schema.

Definition 2. We assume the existence of a set $\mathcal{A}$ of *attributes*. A *schema* is a set $S = \{A_1^{L_1}, \ldots, A_n^{L_n}\}$ where $n \geq 0$, and $A_1, \ldots, A_n$ are distinct attributes, and $L_1, \ldots, L_n$ are (not necessarily distinct) levels. We write $A_1^{L_1} A_2^{L_2} \ldots A_n^{L_n}$ as a shorthand for $\{A_1^{L_1}, A_2^{L_2}, \ldots, A_n^{L_n}\}$.

A *generalization schema* of the schema S is a set $P = \{A_{i_1}^{L_{i_1}}, \ldots, A_{i_m}^{L_{i_m}}\}$ where $A_{i_1}, \ldots, A_{i_m}$ are (not necessarily distinct) attributes of $\{A_1, \ldots, A_n\}$, and $L_{i_1}, \ldots, L_{i_m}$ are levels satisfying the following condition: if $A_{i_j} = A_k$ then $L_k \preceq L_{i_j}$ ($j \in [1, m]$, $k \in [1, n]$).

Let P be a generalization schema of the schema S. If $A^L \in P$ and $A^L \in S$, then we can substitute A for A^L in P. That is, we omit from P levels that are the same as in the underlying schema.

2.3   RUD

The generalization schema $D^{\text{WEEK}} C^{\text{STATE}}$ induces a partitioning of the set of tuples over the schema (2) in the following way: two tuples belong to the same partition if their D-values roll up to the same week, and their C-values roll up to the same state. A RUD $P \to Q$, where P and Q are generalization schemas, states that whenever two tuples belong to the same P-partition, then they must belong to the same Q-partition.

Definition 3. Let $S = \{A_1^{L_1}, \ldots, A_n^{L_n}\}$ be a schema. A *tuple* over S is a set $\{(A_1 : v_1), \ldots, (A_n : v_n)\}$ where $v_i \in ext(L_i)$ for each $i \in [1, n]$. A *relation* I over S is a finite set of tuples over S.

Let U be a roll-up instantiation. Let P be a generalization schema of S. Let t_1, t_2 be tuples over S. We write $t_1 \sim_{P,U} t_2$ iff for every A^L in P,

$$U^L(t_1(A)) = U^L(t_2(A)) .$$

Obviously, if I is a relation over S, then the relation $\sim_{P,U}$ on the tuples of I is an equivalence relation.

A *Roll-Up Dependency* (RUD) over S is a statement $P \to Q$ where P and Q are generalization schemas of S. Given a roll-up instantiation U, a relation I over S is said to *satisfy* $P \to Q$ iff for all tuples $t_1, t_2 \in I$, if $t_1 \sim_{P,U} t_2$ then $t_1 \sim_{Q,U} t_2$.

Logical implication is defined in the classical way. Let Σ be a set of RUDs and let σ be a single RUD (all over the same schema S). Let a roll-up instantiation U be given. Σ is said to *logically imply* σ *under* U, denoted $\Sigma \models_{RUD}^U \sigma$, iff for every relation I over S, if I satisfies every RUD of Σ, then I satisfies σ. Σ is said to *logically imply* σ, denoted $\Sigma \models_{RUD} \sigma$, iff $\Sigma \models_{RUD}^{U} \sigma$ for every roll-up instantiation U.

2.4 Reasoning about RUDs

Roll-Up Lattice. The set of generalization schemas of a given schema can be ordered by a binary relation, denoted $\trianglelefteq$, expressing the relationship less-general-than between generalization schemas. For example,

$$D^{\text{MONTH}} C^{\text{STATE}} C^{\text{REGION}} \trianglelefteq D^{\text{YEAR}} C^{\text{STATE}} \; ,$$

because for every attribute-level pair A^{L} in the second schema, there is a pair $A^{L'}$ in the first schema with $L' \preceq L$.

Definition 4. Let P and Q be generalization schemas of the schema S. P is said to be *less-general-than* Q, denoted $P \trianglelefteq Q$, iff for every A^{L} in Q, there is some $A^{L'}$ in P such that $L' \preceq L$.

The generalization schema P is called *irreducible* iff whenever P contains A^{L} and $A^{L'}$ with $L \neq L'$ then $L \parallel L'$. [1]

For example, $D^{\text{MONTH}} D^{\text{YEAR}} C^{\text{REGION}}$ is *not* irreducible, because $\text{MONTH} \preceq \text{YEAR}$; the same partitioning is defined by the irreducible generalization schema $D^{\text{MONTH}} C^{\text{REGION}}$. The proof of the following theorem can be found in [19].

Theorem 1. *Let S be a schema. The set of all irreducible generalization schemas of S, ordered by $\trianglelefteq$, is a complete lattice.*

The set of all irreducible generalization schemas of S, ordered by $\trianglelefteq$, is called the *roll-up lattice* of S. A roll-up lattice is shown in Fig. 3. Our notion of roll-up lattice extends and generalizes several earlier proposals in the literature. Our notion is more general than the one in [9], because the same attribute can appear more than once in a lattice element, as in $C^{\text{STATE}} C^{\text{REGION}}$. This extension is both natural and useful. In an OLAP application, for example, one may want to group data by state and region simultaneously. Dimensionality reduction [6] is embedded implicitly in our roll-up lattice.

Axiomatization. A sound and complete axiomatization for reasoning about RUDs is given next.

Definition 5. The axioms for reasoning about RUDs are as follows (P, Q, R are generalization schemas over a given schema):

$$\vdash_{RUD} P \to Q \text{ if } P \trianglelefteq Q \qquad (3)$$

$$P \to Q \vdash_{RUD} PR \to QR \qquad (4)$$

$$P \to Q \text{ and } Q \to R \vdash_{RUD} P \to R \qquad (5)$$

---

[1] We write $L \parallel L'$ iff neither $L \preceq L'$ nor $L' \preceq L$.

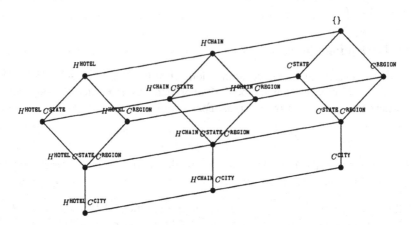

Fig. 3. The family of generalization schemas of $H^{\text{HOTEL}} C^{\text{CITY}}$ ordered by $\trianglelefteq$

In [19], we proved the following result.

Theorem 2. *Let Σ be a set of RUDs and let σ be a single RUD (all over the same schema). $\Sigma \vdash_{RUD} \sigma$ iff $\Sigma \models_{RUD} \sigma$.*

The axioms are almost Armstrong's axioms [1]. The only difference is that (3) refers to $\trianglelefteq$, whereas the corresponding Armstrong's axiom uses simple set inclusion. Following an approach stipulated in [16], we can "push" the relation $\preceq$ within the RUD formalism. If C^{CITY} is part of the database schema, we add the RUDs $C^{\text{CITY}} \to C^{\text{STATE}}$ and $C^{\text{CITY}} \to C^{\text{REGION}}$. By Armstrong's axioms, we can derive $C^{\text{CITY}} \to C^{\text{STATE}} C^{\text{REGION}}$ (this is known as the Union rule for FDs). The same RUD is derived in a different way by using the axioms of Definition 5. In particular, $C^{\text{CITY}} \trianglelefteq C^{\text{STATE}} C^{\text{REGION}}$ and hence $C^{\text{CITY}} \to C^{\text{STATE}} C^{\text{REGION}}$ follows immediately by (3). Theorem 3 generalizes the above observation.

Definition 6. *Let S be a schema. We write $S^{\mathcal{L}}$ for the smallest set of RUDs containing $A^{L_1} \to A^{L_2}$ whenever $A^L \in S$ and $L \preceq L_1 \preceq L_2$.*

Theorem 3. *Let Σ be a set of RUDs and let σ be a single RUD (all over the same schema S). $\Sigma \vdash_{RUD} \sigma$ iff $\Sigma \cup S^{\mathcal{L}} \vdash_A \sigma$, where $\vdash_A$ denotes derivability using Armstrong's axioms.*

Proof. Both directions can be proved by induction on the derivation of σ.   □

This means that, after expressing $\preceq$ by RUDs, reasoning about RUDs can be captured by Armstrong's axioms. It should be stressed, however, that there is a clear conceptual distinction between database relations and RUDs on the one hand, and roll-up instantiations and $\preceq$ on the other hand.

The RUDs of $S^{\mathcal{L}}$ express certain inherent properties of the roll-up lattice of S. Significantly, we next show that RUDs can be used in the same way to express additional properties of the roll-up lattice.

2.5 Adding Axioms to Capture More Meaning

Whenever two days fall within the same year, as well as within the same fiscal year, then these days must necessarily belong to the same semester. Semesters run from January 1 to June 30, and from July 1 to December 31. This is expressed by the RUD:

$$D^{\text{YEAR}} D^{\text{FISCALYEAR}} \to D^{\text{SEMESTER}} .$$

Significantly, the foregoing RUD is *not* implied by $S^{\mathcal{L}}$, and really imposes new constraints on the roll-up lattice. In Sect. 3, we extend RUDs to capture even more complex constraints on the roll-up lattice.

3 Adding Inequality

3.1 Introductory Examples

Recall that a fiscal year runs from July 1 to June 30. Civil and fiscal years are not comparable by $\preceq$, i.e., YEAR $\|$ FISCALYEAR. Some weeks span two civil years, and some other weeks span two fiscal years. Hence, WEEK $\|$ YEAR and WEEK $\|$ FISCALYEAR. Consider the schema $S = D^{\text{DATE}} Price^{\text{PRICE}}$ to store a time series of prices of a particular product. Consider the set of RUDs

$$\Sigma = \{ D^{\text{YEAR}} \to Price, \ D^{\text{FISCALYEAR}} \to Price \}$$

and the RUD

$$\sigma = D^{\text{WEEK}} \to Price .$$

The RUDs of Σ state that two tuples over the schema S whose D-values roll up to the same civil year or to the same fiscal year, must agree on *Price*. For a "real-life" roll-up instantiation U, we would have $\Sigma \models^U_{RUD} \sigma$, because two days of the same week cannot simultaneously belong to distinct civil years and distinct fiscal years. However, Definition 1 permits a roll-up instantiation U' with two values $d_1, d_2 \in ext(\text{DATE})$ satisfying:

$$U'^{\text{WEEK}}(d_1) = U'^{\text{WEEK}}(d_2) ,$$
$$U'^{\text{YEAR}}(d_1) \neq U'^{\text{YEAR}}(d_2) ,$$
$$U'^{\text{FISCALYEAR}}(d_1) \neq U'^{\text{FISCALYEAR}}(d_2) .$$

That is, d_1 and d_2 roll up to the same week, but to distinct years and to distinct fiscal years. Then the relation with two tuples $\{(D : d_1)(Price : 20), (D : d_2)(Price : 40)\}$ shows that $\Sigma \not\models^{U'}_{RUD} \sigma$, and hence $\Sigma \not\models_{RUD} \sigma$. Significantly, U' satisfies the definition of roll-up instantiation, but does not correspond to a "real-life" calendar. Extending RUDs with negation will allow us to exclude U'.

The foregoing example illustrates the concept *collectively-finer-than* of Wang et al. [16]. We say that WEEK is collectively-finer-than {YEAR, FISCALYEAR} meaning that every week falls entirely within a civil year, or a fiscal year, or both.

This concept turns out to be very important in temporal reasoning, and is not expressible in our formalism so far. We could introduce collectively-finer-than at the level of roll-up, as we did with finer-than ($\preceq$). However, it is clean to keep our definition of roll-up and extend RUDs so that collectively-finer-than can be expressed. The following rule expresses that, whenever two dates roll-up to the same week, then they must either roll up to the same year, or to the same fiscal year, or both:

$$D^{\text{WEEK}} \to D^{\text{YEAR}} \vee D^{\text{FISCALYEAR}} \ .$$

Using propositional calculus, we can eliminate the disjunction at the cost of introducing negation:

$$\neg D^{\text{FISCALYEAR}} \ \neg D^{\text{YEAR}} \to \neg D^{\text{WEEK}} \ .$$

The latter statement is called a RUD¬.

Significantly, the proposed extension is generic, and in no ways confined to time. Also, not only can RUD¬ impose constraints on roll-up instantiations, but also on data in relations. An example is

$$D^{\text{WEEK}} \neg D^{\text{FISCALYEAR}} C^{\text{STATE}} \to Tax$$

expressing that tax rates remain constant during weeks in which a new fiscal year starts. Hence, RUD¬ constitutes an expressive formalism, combining functional dependency, roll-up, and negation.

3.2 RUD¬

The following definition extends RUDs by allowing a negation sign in front of any attribute.

Definition 7. Let S be a schema. If S contains A^L and $L \preceq L'$, then $A^{L'}$ and $\neg A^{L'}$ are *literals* over S. A *term* over S is a set of literals over S. Let P be a term over S. Given a roll-up instantiation U, two tuples t_1 and t_2 over S are said to *satisfy* P iff

- for every positive literal A^L in P, $U^L(t_1(A)) = U^L(t_2(A))$, and
- for every negative literal $\neg A^L$ in P, $U^L(t_1(A)) \neq U^L(t_2(A))$.

A *Roll-Up Dependency with Negation* (RUD¬) over S is a statement $P \to Q$ where P and Q are terms over S such that either (i) P contains a negative literal, or (ii) Q does not contain a negative literal. Given a roll-up instantiation U, a relation I over S is said to *satisfy* $P \to Q$ iff for all tuples $t_1, t_2 \in I$, if t_1 and t_2 satisfy P, then they satisfy Q.

$\models_{RUD}$ is extended to $\models_{RUD^\neg}$ in the obvious way.

Note that we disallow expressions like $D^{\text{YEAR}} \to \neg Price$, because such an expression could not possibly be satisfied. This is because the tuples t_1 and t_2 in Definition 7 are not required to be distinct, and every individual tuple becomes a counterexample for $D^{\text{YEAR}} \to \neg Price$. Similar observations appear in [2, 14]. Every generalization schema of S is a term over S, but terms, unlike generalization schemas, do not induce a partitioning of the tuples over S.

3.3   Reasoning about RUD¬

Armstrong's axioms are no longer complete for reasoning about RUD¬s. We now give a sound and complete axiomatization for reasoning about RUD¬s.

Definition 8. The axioms for reasoning about RUD¬s are as follows (P, Q, R are terms over a given schema; p is a literal; $\neg p$ is denoted $\bar{p}$):

$$\vdash_{PC} P \to Q \text{ iff } Q \subseteq P \tag{6}$$

$$P \to Q \vdash_{PC} PR \to QR \tag{7}$$

$$P \to Q \text{ and } Q \to R \vdash_{PC} P \to R \tag{8}$$

$$pP \to Q \text{ and } \bar{p}P \to Q \vdash_{PC} P \to Q \tag{9}$$

$$\vdash_{PC} \bar{p}p \to P \tag{10}$$

It can be easily verified that the application of the above axioms can only derive RUD¬s that are syntactically correct.

Figure 4 shows a derivation for the example introduced in Sect. 3.1. The following theorem expresses that the axiomatization is sound and complete. It is the analog of Theorem 3, but is much harder to prove.

$D^{\text{YEAR}} \to Price$	given	(a)
$D^{\text{FISCALYEAR}} \to Price$	given	(b)
$\neg D^{\text{FISCALYEAR}} \neg D^{\text{YEAR}} \to \neg D^{\text{WEEK}}$	given	(c)
$D^{\text{FISCALYEAR}} D^{\text{WEEK}} \to Price\ D^{\text{WEEK}}$	from (b) by (7)	(d)
$Price\ D^{\text{WEEK}} \to Price$	by (6)	(e)
$D^{\text{FISCALYEAR}} D^{\text{WEEK}} \to Price$	from (d) and (e) by (8)	(f)
$\neg D^{\text{FISCALYEAR}} \neg D^{\text{YEAR}} D^{\text{WEEK}} \to D^{\text{WEEK}} \neg D^{\text{WEEK}}$	from (c) by (7)	(g)
$D^{\text{WEEK}} \neg D^{\text{WEEK}} \to D^{\text{YEAR}}$	by (10)	(h)
$\neg D^{\text{FISCALYEAR}} \neg D^{\text{YEAR}} D^{\text{WEEK}} \to D^{\text{YEAR}}$	from (g) and (h) by (8)	(i)
$\neg D^{\text{FISCALYEAR}} D^{\text{YEAR}} D^{\text{WEEK}} \to D^{\text{YEAR}}$	by (6)	(j)
$\neg D^{\text{FISCALYEAR}} D^{\text{WEEK}} \to D^{\text{YEAR}}$	from (i) and (j) by (9)	(k)
$\neg D^{\text{FISCALYEAR}} D^{\text{WEEK}} \to Price$	from (k) and (a) by (8)	(l)
$D^{\text{WEEK}} \to Price$	from (f) and (l) by (9)	(m)

Fig. 4. Example derivation

Theorem 4. *Let Σ be a set of RUD¬s, and let σ be a single RUD¬ (all over the same schema).*
$$\Sigma \models_{RUD¬} \sigma \text{ iff } \Sigma \cup S^{\mathcal{L}} \vdash_{PC} \sigma.$$

Proof. From Theorem 5 and Theorem 6. See Appendix A.   □

The subscript in $\vdash_{PC}$ is chosen because Appendix A also shows an equivalence between RUD¬ and positive Propositional Calculus. Undoubtedly, this equivalence can be exploited for obtaining complexity results.

4   Concluding Remarks

The concept of RUD combines functional dependency and roll-up. It has interesting applications in conceptual modeling and data mining. It allows us to express the functional determinacies present in generalization hierarchies, but cannot express certain complex relationships between levels that have been studied for temporal databases. Therefore RUDs have been extended with negation. The concept of RUD$^\neg$ expresses and generalizes these complex relationships for arbitrary levels, including spatial ones. A sound and complete axiomatization of RUD$^\neg$ is an interesting and important result.

A   Completeness Proof

To simplify the notations, the completeness proof exploits an equivalence between RUD$^\neg$ and positive propositional calculus. Similar equivalences have appeared in the literature [2, 11, 13, 14].

Definition 9. Let B be a set of *Boolean variables*. If p is a Boolean variable, then p and $\neg p$ are *literals*. For convenience, $\neg p$ can be denoted $\overline{p}$. Greek letters α and β are used to denote literals. $\overline{\overline{\alpha}}$ equals α. A set T of literals is called a *valuation* iff every Boolean variable occurs exactly once in T. Every valuation T extends uniquely to a map $\widehat{T}$ from the set of all Boolean formulas to $\{0, 1\}$ with

- $\widehat{T}(p) = 1$ if $p \in T$,
- $\widehat{T}(p) = 0$ if $\overline{p} \in T$, and
- $\widehat{T}(\varphi(p_1, \ldots, p_n)) = \varphi(\widehat{T}(p_1), \ldots, \widehat{T}(p_n))$, where $\varphi(p_1, \ldots, p_n)$ is a Boolean formula, and $\varphi(\widehat{T}(p_1), \ldots, \widehat{T}(p_n))$ is evaluated over $\{0, 1\}$ using the standard definitions of the operations $\wedge$, $\vee$, $\rightarrow$, and $\neg$.

We say that T *satisfies* φ iff $\widehat{T}(\varphi) = 1$. A Boolean formula is *satisfiable* iff there exists a valuation T satisfying φ; otherwise it is *unsatisfiable*.

A *term* is a conjunction of literals. A *Boolean rule* is a Boolean formula of the form $P \rightarrow Q$ where P and Q are terms. A Boolean rule $P \rightarrow Q$ is *positive* iff either (i) P contains a negative literal, or (ii) Q does not contain a negative literal. For convenience, sets of literals will be used for terms. That is, the set $\{\alpha_1, \ldots, \alpha_n\}$ is used for $\alpha_1 \wedge \cdots \wedge \alpha_n$. Then P is satisfied by a valuation T iff $P \subseteq T$. Logical implication is defined in the classical way and is denoted $\models_{PC}$.

Let S be the schema under consideration. We let the set B of Boolean variables coincide with $\{A^{L'} \mid A^L \in S$ and $L \preceq L'\}$.

Theorem 5. $\Sigma \models_{RUD^\neg} \sigma$ *iff* $\Sigma \cup S^{\mathcal{L}} \models_{PC} \sigma$.

Proof. A similar proof appears in [2]. $\square$

Definition 10. Let Σ be a set of Boolean rules, and let P be a term. The *closure* of P w.r.t. Σ, denoted P^+, is the smallest term containing the literal α whenever $\Sigma \vdash_{PC} P \rightarrow \alpha$.

Lemma 1. $P \to Q$ and $P \to R \vdash_{PC} P \to QR$.

Proof. $P \to PQ$ can be derived from $P \to Q$ by (7). Likewise, $PQ \to QR$ can be derived from $P \to R$ by (7). By (8), $P \to QR$. □

Lemma 2. Let Σ be a set of Boolean rules. $Q \subseteq P^+$ iff $\Sigma \vdash_{PC} P \to Q$.

Proof. $\Rightarrow$. Let $\alpha \in Q$. By the premise, $\alpha \in P^+$, hence $\Sigma \vdash_{PC} P \to \alpha$. By repeated application of Lemma 1, $\Sigma \vdash_{PC} P \to Q \Leftarrow$. Let $\alpha \in Q$. By (6), $\Sigma \vdash_{PC} Q \to \alpha$. By the premise and (8), $\Sigma \vdash_{PC} P \to \alpha$. Hence, $\alpha \in P^+$. □

Lemma 3. Let Σ be a set of Boolean rules. Let P be a set of literals. $P \subseteq P^+$.

Proof. By (6), $\vdash_{PC} P \to P$. By Lemma 2, $P \subseteq P^+$. □

Lemma 4. Let Σ be a set of Boolean rules. $(P^+)^+ \subseteq P^+$.

Proof. Let $\alpha \in (P^+)^+$. Hence $\Sigma \vdash_{PC} P^+ \to \alpha$. We have $\Sigma \vdash_{PC} P \to P^+$ as a corollary of Lemma 2. By (8), $\Sigma \vdash_{PC} P \to \alpha$. Hence, $\alpha \in P^+$. □

Lemma 5. Let P and Q be terms. If P is unsatisfiable, then $\vdash_{PC} P \to Q$.

Proof. Assume P unsatisfiable. Without loss of generality, P contains $\bar{p}p$. By (6), $\vdash_{PC} P \to \bar{p}p$. By (10) and (8), $\vdash_{PC} P \to Q$. □

Lemma 6. Let Σ be a set of Boolean rules, and let $P \to \alpha$ be a Boolean rule. If $\Sigma \nvdash_{PC} P \to \alpha$ then there exists a valuation T containing P^+ such that $\bar{\alpha} \in T$ and $T^+ = T$.

Proof. Assume $\Sigma \nvdash_{PC} P \to \alpha$. P is satisfiable, or else $\vdash_{PC} P \to \alpha$ by Lemma 5, a contradiction. Assume the desired valuation T does not exist; i.e., for every valuation T containing P^+, $\alpha \in T$ or $T^+ \neq T$. $\alpha \in T$ implies $\alpha \in T^+$ by Lemma 3. Assume $T^+ \neq T$. Since $T \subseteq T^+$ by Lemma 3, T^+ must contain a literal (say β) not in T. Since every Boolean variable occurs in T, T contains $\bar{\beta}$, and so does T^+ by Lemma 3. Hence, T^+ contains $\bar{\beta}\beta$. Hence, $\vdash_{PC} T^+ \to \alpha$ by Lemma 5, and $\alpha \in (T^+)^+$. By Lemma 4, $\alpha \in T^+$. Hence, for every valuation T containing P^+, $\Sigma \vdash_{PC} T \to \alpha$. By repeated application of (9), $\Sigma \vdash_{PC} P^+ \to \alpha$. Hence, $\alpha \in (P^+)^+$. Hence, $\alpha \in P^+$ by Lemma 4. Consequently, $\Sigma \vdash_{PC} P \to \alpha$, a contradiction. We conclude by contradiction that T exists. □

Lemma 7. Let Σ be a set of Boolean rules, and let $P \to \alpha$ be a Boolean rule. If $\Sigma \models_{PC} P \to \alpha$ then $\Sigma \vdash_{PC} P \to \alpha$.

Proof. Assume $\Sigma \nvdash_{PC} P \to \alpha$. We need to show $\Sigma \nvDash_{PC} P \to \alpha$. By Lemma 6, there exists a valuation T containing P^+ such that $\bar{\alpha} \in T$ and $T^+ = T$. Since $P \subseteq P^+ \subseteq T$ and $\alpha \notin T$, T falsifies $P \to \alpha$. Let $R \to S$ be a Boolean rule in Σ that is falsified by T. That is, $R \subseteq T$ and $S \nsubseteq T$. By (6), $\vdash_{PC} T \to R$, hence $\Sigma \vdash_{PC} T \to S$ by (8). Hence, $S \subseteq T^+$ by Lemma 2. But then $S \subseteq T$, a contradiction. We conclude by contradiction that T satisfies Σ. □

Theorem 6. Let Σ be a set of Boolean rules, and let σ be a Boolean rule. $\Sigma \models_{PC} \sigma$ iff $\Sigma \vdash_{PC} \sigma$.

Proof. $\Rightarrow$ *(Completeness)*. Follows from Lemma 7 and Lemma 1. $\Leftarrow$ *(Soundness)*. Straightforward. □

References

1. S. Abiteboul, R. Hull, and V. Vianu. *Foundations of Databases*. Addison-Wesley, 1995.
2. J. Berman and W. J. Blok. Positive boolean dependencies. *Information Processing Letters*, 27:147–150, 1988.
3. C. Bettini, C. Dyreson, W. Evans, R. Snodgrass, and X. Wang. A glossary of time granularity concepts. In O. Etzion, S. Jajodia, and S. Sripada, editors, *Temporal Databases: Research and Practice*, number 1399 in LNCS State-of-the-art Survey, pages 406–413. Springer-Verlag, 1998.
4. C. Bettini, X. Wang, and S. Jajodia. Testing complex temporal relationships involving multiple granularities and its application to data mining. In *Proc. ACM SIGACT-SIGMOD-SIGART Symposium on Principles of Database Systems*, pages 68–78, Montreal, Canada, June 1996. ACM Press.
5. L. Cabibbo and R. Torlone. Querying multidimensional databases. In *Sixth Int. Workshop on Database Programming Languages*, pages 253–269, 1997.
6. J. Gray, S. Chaudhuri, A. Bosworth, A. Layman, D. Reichart, M. Venkatrao, F. Pellow, and H. Pirahesh. Data cube: A relational aggregation operator generalizing group-by, cross-tab, and sub-totals. *Data Mining and Knowledge Discovery*, 1:29–53, 1997.
7. H. Gregersen and C. S. Jensen. Temporal Entity-Relationship models—a survey. Technical Report TR-3, TimeCenter, 1997.
8. J. Han. OLAP mining: An integration of OLAP with data mining. In *Proceedings of the 7th IFIP 2.6 Working Conference on Database Semantics (DS-7)*, pages 1–9, 1997.
9. V. Harinarayan, A. Rajaraman, and J. Ullman. Implementing data cubes efficiently. In *Proc. ACM SIGACT-SIGMOD-SIGART Symposium on Principles of Database Systems*, pages 205–216, Montreal, Canada, 1996.
10. C. Jensen, R. Snodgrass, and M. Soo. Extending existing dependency theory to temporal databases. *IEEE Trans. on Knowledge and Data Engineering*, 8(4):563–582, 1996.
11. R. Khardon, H. Mannila, and D. Roth. Reasoning with examples: Propositional formulae and database dependencies. To appear, 1999.
12. C. Parent, S. Spaccapietra, and E. Zimanyi. Spatio-temporal information systems: a conceptual perspective. Tutorial at ER'98, 1998.
13. Y. Sagiv, C. Delobel, D. S. Parker, Jr., and R. Fagin. An equivalence between relational database dependencies and a fragment of propositional logic. *Journal of the ACM*, 28(3):435–453, 1981.
14. Y. Sagiv, C. Delobel, D. S. Parker, Jr., and R. Fagin. Correction to "An equivalence between relational database dependencies and a fragment of propositional logic". *Journal of the ACM*, 34(4):1016–1018, 1987.
15. B. Tauzovich. Towards temporal extensions to the Entity-Relationship model. In *Proc. 10th. Int. Conf. on Entity-Relationship Approach*, pages 163–179. ER Institute, 1991.
16. X. Wang, C. Bettini, A. Brodsky, and S. Jajodia. Logical design for temporal databases with multiple granularities. *ACM Trans. on Database Systems*, 22(2):115–170, 1997.
17. J. Wijsen. Reasoning about qualitative trends in databases. *Information Systems*, 23(7):469–493, 1998.

18. J. Wijsen. Temporal FDs on complex objects. To appear in the March, 1999 issue of *ACM Trans. on Database Systems*, 1999.
19. J. Wijsen and R. Ng. Discovering roll-up dependencies. Technical report, The University of British Columbia, Dept. of Computer Science, 1998. Also available at http://www.uia.ua.ac.be/u/jwijsen/.
20. J. Wijsen, R. Ng, and T. Calders. Discovering roll-up dependencies. In *Proc. ACM SIGKDD Int. Conf. Knowledge Discovery and Data Mining*, San Diego, CA, 1999.

Tractable Query Answering in Indefinite Constraint Databases: Basic Results and Applications to Querying Spatiotemporal Information[*]

Manolis Koubarakis[1] and Spiros Skiadopoulos[2]

[1] Dept. of Informatics, University of Athens
Panepistimioupolis, TYPA Buildings
157 81 Athens, Greece
manolis@di.uoa.gr,
WWW home page: www.di.uoa.gr/~manolis
[2] Dept. of Electrical and Computer Engineering
National Technical University of Athens
Zographou 157 73 Athens, Greece
spiros@dbnet.ece.ntua.gr

Abstract. We consider the scheme of indefinite constraint databases proposed by Koubarakis. This scheme can be used to represent indefinite information arising in temporal, spatial and truly spatiotemporal applications. The main technical problem that we address in this paper is the discovery of tractable classes of databases and queries in this scheme. We start with the assumption that we have a class of constraints C with satisfiability and variable elimination problems that can be solved in PTIME. Under this assumption, we show that there are several general classes of databases and queries for which query evaluation can be done with PTIME data complexity. We then search for tractable instances of C in the area of temporal and spatial constraints. Classes of constraints with tractable satisfiability problems can be easily found in the literature. The largest class that we consider is the class of Horn disjunctive linear constraints over the rationals. Because variable elimination for Horn disjunctive linear constraints cannot be done in PTIME, we try to discover subclasses with tractable variable elimination problems. The class of UTVPI$^{\neq}$ constraints is the largest class that we show to have this property. Finally, we restate the initial general results with C ranging over the newly discovered tractable classes. Tractable query answering problems for indefinite temporal and spatial constraint databases are identified in this way.

[*] This research has been partially supported by European project CHOROCHRONOS (funded under Framework IV) and by a grant from the Greek Secretariat for Research and Technology. Spiros Skiadopoulos has also been supported by a postgraduate fellowship from NATO.

A   Introduction

Linear constraints have recently been used by constraint database researchers to represent temporal, spatial and spatiotemporal information [22, 13, 14, 37, 24, 31, 4, 12, 33]. The information represented by linear constraints can be of type *absolute* (e.g., the explosion occured at 3:30 a.m. yesterday), *relative* (e.g., point A is north of point B), *indefinite* or *indeterminate* (e.g., the course lasted between 1 and 2 hours), and combination of these types (e.g., point A is north or west of point B).

Query evaluation in the presence of indefinite information is a hard problem even in the case of relational databases [47, 1, 11]. This tells us that the situation will probably be much worse for the case of indefinite information in spatiotemporal databases. This remark can be contrasted with reality: indefinite information is crucial for some applications of spatiotemporal databases e.g., Geographic Information Systems [34] or image and video database systems [42]. It is therefore important to determine whether there exist interesting cases where query evaluation in indefinite spatiotemporal databases can be done in PTIME.

In this paper we consider the scheme of indefinite constraint databases proposed by Koubarakis [25, 26, 31]. This scheme can be used to represent indefinite information arising in temporal, spatial and truly spatiotemporal applications (e.g., moving objects [40, 16]). The main technical problem that we address is the discovery of tractable classes of databases and queries in this scheme. Our results are original and can be summarized as follows:

1. We start with the assumption that we have a class of constraints C with satisfiability and variable elimination problems that can be solved in PTIME. Under this assumption, we demonstrate several general classes of databases and queries for which query evaluation can be done with PTIME data complexity.
2. We then try to find useful instances of C from the area of temporal and spatial constraints. Classes with tractable satisfiability problems can be easily found in the literature. The largest class that we consider is the class of Horn disjunctive linear constraints over the rationals[1] [21, 29]. A *Horn disjunctive linear constraint* is a disjunction of weak linear inequalities (e.g., $x_1 + x_2 + 3x_3 \leq 4$) and linear disequations (e.g., $x_1 - 4x_4 + 5x_3 \neq 6$) such that the number of inequalities does not exceed one.

   Because variable elimination for Horn disjunctive linear constraints cannot be done in PTIME [29], we try to discover subclasses with tractable variable elimination problems. The class of UTVPI$^{\neq}$ constraints is the largest class that we show to have this property. A *UTVPI constraint* is a linear constraint $\pm x_1 \leq c$ or $\pm x_1 \pm x_2 \leq c$ where x_1, x_2 are variables and c is a rational number. The class of UTVPI$^{\neq}$ *constraints* also includes disequations of the form $\pm x_1 \neq c$ or $\pm x_1 \pm x_2 \neq c$.

---

[1] All the results of this paper still hold if our constraints are taken over the set of real numbers.

Our results on UTVPI$^{\neq}$ constraints are original and extend the results of [28, 30]. In the full paper we also provide efficient algorithms for consistency checking and global consistency enforcement for UTVPI and UTVPI$^{\neq}$ constraints.

3. Finally, we restate the results of Item 1 with $\mathcal{C}$ ranging over the newly discovered tractable classes. Tractable query answering problems for indefinite temporal and spatial constraint databases are identified in this way. Two of them are significant extensions of tractable problems identified previously by [5, 43] while all others are new.

Our results will be of interest to spatiotemporal database researchers, constraint database researchers but also people working on traditional constraint satisfaction problems. The methodology of this paper has also been applied to the problem of querying temporal constraint networks in [32].

The paper is organized as follows. The next section reviews the scheme of indefinite constraint databases and a method for query evaluation. In Section C we identify tractable cases of query evaluation. Section D presents subclasses of linear constraints with a satisfiability problem and a variable elimination problem that can be solved in PTIME. Section E uses the results of Sections C and D to identify tractable query answering problems in temporal and spatial domains. This section also discusses some questions left open by our analysis. All proofs are omitted and can be found in the full version of the paper.

B   The Scheme of Indefinite Constraint Databases

In this section we present the scheme of indefinite $\mathcal{L}$-constraint databases [31] where $\mathcal{L}$ is a many-sorted first order constraint language and $\mathbf{M}_{\mathcal{L}}$ is its intended $\mathcal{L}$-structure (i.e., the structure that gives the intended interpretation of the symbols of $\mathcal{L}$). In this paper we only use the following first-order constraint languages: the language of linear inequalities $\mathcal{L}_{LIN}$ and the language of polynomial inequalities $\mathcal{L}_{POLY}$. A *polynomial inequality* is an expression of the form $\Sigma_{i=1}^{n} a_i \Pi_{j=1}^{m} x_j^{k_j} \sim 0$ where the a_i's are integer coefficients, the x_j's are variables ranging over the rational numbers, the k_j's are natural numbers and $\sim$ is $<$ or $=$. A *linear inequality* is an expression of the form $\Sigma_{i=1}^{n} a_i x_i \sim c$ where the a_i's are integer coefficients, the x_i's are variables ranging over the rational numbers, $\sim$ is $<$ or $=$ and c is an integer. The language $\mathcal{L}_{POLY}$ (and its sublanguage $\mathcal{L}_{LIN}$) will be interpreted over the set of rational numbers $\mathcal{Q}$ with the obvious denotations for their symbols.

In a constraint database model with constraint language $\mathcal{L}$, we usually distinguish a class of formulas of $\mathcal{L}$ and call it the class of $\mathcal{L}$-*constraints*. In the examples of this section linear inequalities and polynomial inequalities form the classes of $\mathcal{L}_{LIN}$-constraints and $\mathcal{L}_{POLY}$-constraints respectively. Section D considers more specific classes of $\mathcal{L}_{LIN}$-constraints. In this paper we only consider $\mathcal{L}$-constraint classes that *admit variable elimination* and are *weakly closed under negation* (i.e., the negation of every $\mathcal{L}$-constraint is equivalent to a disjunction of

$\mathcal{L}$-constraints). Many interesting constraint classes have this property (e.g., the class of polynomial or linear inequalities).

For each sort $s \in sorts(\mathcal{L})$, let U_s be a countably infinite set of *attributes* of sort s. The set of all attributes, denoted by $\mathcal{U}$, is $\bigcup_{s \in sorts(\mathcal{L})} U_s$. The sort of attribute A will be denoted by $sort(A)$. With each $A \in \mathcal{U}$ we associate a set of values $dom(A) = dom(s, \mathbf{M}_{\mathcal{L}})$ called the *domain* of A.[2] A *relation scheme* R is a finite subset of $\mathcal{U}$ (R will be called the *name* of the scheme).

For every $s \in sorts(\mathcal{L})$, we assume the existence of two disjoint countably infinite sets of *variables*: the set of *u-variables* $UVAR_{\mathcal{L}}^s$ and the set of *e-variables* $EVAR_{\mathcal{L}}^s$. Let $UVAR_{\mathcal{L}}$ and $EVAR_{\mathcal{L}}$ denote $\bigcup_{s \in sorts(\mathcal{L})} UVAR_{\mathcal{L}}^s$ and $\bigcup_{s \in sorts(\mathcal{L})} EVAR_{\mathcal{L}}^s$ respectively. The intersection of the sets $UVAR_{\mathcal{L}}$ and $EVAR_{\mathcal{L}}$ with the domains of attributes is empty.

U-variables are like the variables in the constraint database scheme of [23]. E-variables are exactly like the marked nulls of [19]. U-variables will be denoted by letters of the English alphabet, usually x, y, z, t, possibly subscripted. E-variables will be denoted by letters of the Greek alphabet, usually $\omega, \lambda, \zeta, \nu$, possibly subscripted.

Definition 1. *Let R be a relation scheme. An* indefinite $\mathcal{L}$-constraint tuple t *over scheme R is a mapping from $R \cup \{CON\}$ to $UVAR_{\mathcal{L}} \cup WFF(\mathcal{L})$[3] such that (i) $t(A) \in UVAR_{\mathcal{L}}^{sort(A)}$ for each $A \in R$, (ii) $t(A_i)$ is different than $t(A_j)$ for all distinct $A_i, A_j \in R$, (iii) $t(CON)$ is a conjunction of $\mathcal{L}$-constraints and (iv) the free variables of $t(CON)$ are included in $\{t(A) : A \in R\} \cup EVAR_{\mathcal{L}}$. $t(CON)$ is called the* local condition *of the tuple t while $t(R)$ is called the* proper part *of t.*

Definition 2. *Let R be a relation scheme. An* indefinite $\mathcal{L}$-constraint relation *over scheme R is a finite set of indefinite $\mathcal{L}$-constraint tuples over R.*

Definition 3. *An $\mathcal{L}$-constraint rule is an expression of the form*

$$R_0(t_{01}, \ldots, t_{0k_0}) \leftarrow R_1(t_{11}, \ldots, t_{1k_1}), \ldots, R_n(t_{n1}, \ldots, t_{nk_n}), c_1, \ldots, c_m$$

where $R_0, R_1, \ldots, R_n$ are relation scheme names, $c_1, \ldots, c_m$ are $\mathcal{L}$-constraints and each t_{ij} is a term of $\mathcal{L}$ (i.e., a variable, a constant or a function term). An $\mathcal{L}$-constraint rule of the above form is recursive iff R_0 is one of $R_1, \ldots, R_n$. For the purposes of this paper $\mathcal{L}$-constraint rules are assumed to be non-recursive.[4]

Definition 4. *A database scheme $\tilde{R}$ is a sequence $(R_1, \ldots, R_n)$ where each R_i is a relation scheme.*

---

[2] If s is a sort and $\mathbf{M}$ is a structure then $dom(s, \mathbf{M})$ denotes the domain of s in structure $\mathbf{M}$.

[3] $WFF(\mathcal{L})$ denotes the set of quantifier-free well-formed formulas of $\mathcal{L}$.

[4] Let us notice that the indefinite constraint database scheme of [31] does not contain $\mathcal{L}$-constraint rules. The introduction of rules in the present paper is done simply for convenience so that new relations can be defined from existing ones. Since rules are assumed to be non-recursive, no expressive power with respect to querying is added to the scheme.

Definition 5. *An* indefinite $\mathcal{L}$-constraint database DB over scheme $\widetilde{R} = (R_1, \ldots, R_n)$ *is a triple* $(\widetilde{r}, RS, CS)$ *where* $\widetilde{r} = (r_1, \ldots, r_n)$ *is a sequence of indefinite $\mathcal{L}$-constraint relations (the scheme of r_i is R_i), RS is a set of $\mathcal{L}$-constraint rules and CS is a conjunction of $\mathcal{L}$-constraints over $EVAR_{\mathcal{L}}$. $\widetilde{r}$ is called the* relational part *of DB, RS is called the* rule set *and CS is called the* constraint store.

The above definitions extend the constraint database scheme of Kanellakis, Kuper and Revesz [22] by introducing an additional kind of variables called *e-variables*. E-variables have the semantics of marked nulls of [19]. As in [11], the possible values of the e-variables can be constrained by a *constraint store*. The semantics of our scheme are the usual *closed-world* semantics discussed in [11]. The interested reader can consult [25,31] for details.

The following example from [31] shows the power of the scheme for the representation of *temporal* information.

Example 1. Let us consider a planning database used by a medical laboratory for keeping track of patient appointments for the year 1996. The set of rationals Q will be our time line. The year 1996 is assumed to start at time 0 and every interval $[i, i+1)$ represents a day (for $i \in \mathcal{Z}$ and $i \geq 0$). Time intervals will be represented by their endpoints. They will always be assumed to be of the form $[B, E)$ where B and E are the endpoints.

The following is an indefinite $\mathcal{L}_{LIN}$-constraint database for this application domain.[5] The implicit constraint language is the union of two simpler languages: the first order language of linear constraints (for temporal data), and a first order language with equality and an infinite number of constants (for administrative data).

APPOINTMENT

PATIENT	TREATMENT	BEGIN	END	CON
Smith	Chemotherapy1	ω_1	ω_2	*true*
Smith	Chemotherapy2	ω_3	ω_4	*true*
Smith	Radiation	ω_5	ω_6	*true*

CONSTRAINT_STORE :

$$\omega_1 \geq 0, \ \omega_2 \geq 0, \ \omega_3 \geq 0, \ \omega_4 \geq 0, \ \omega_5 \geq 0, \ \omega_6 \geq 0,$$
$$\omega_2 = \omega_1 + 1, \ \omega_4 = \omega_3 + 1, \ \omega_6 = \omega_5 + 2, \ \omega_2 \leq 91, \ \omega_3 \geq 91, \ \omega_4 \leq 182,$$
$$\omega_3 - \omega_2 \geq 60, \ \omega_5 - \omega_4 \geq 20, \ \omega_6 \leq 213$$

The above database represents the following information. There are three scheduled appointments for patient Smith. This is represented by three tuples in relation APPOINTMENT. Chemotherapy appointments must be scheduled for a single day. Radiation appointments must be scheduled for two consecutive

---

[5] We do not follow strictly the definition of an $\mathcal{L}$-constraint tuple for reasons of economy of expression and clarity. These examples can easily be made to conform with Definition 1 by introducing u-variables and adding equality constraints in the local condition of each tuple.

days. This information is represented by constraints $\omega_2 = \omega_1 + 1$, $\omega_4 = \omega_3 + 1$, and $\omega_6 = \omega_5 + 2$. There is also more information about individual appointments. E.g., the first chemotherapy appointment for Smith should take place in the first three months of 1996 (i.e., days 0-91) etc.

The following example shows that *truly spatiotemporal information* can also be captured in our scheme. The example has been motivated by the work of [40, 41].

Example 2. Let us consider an object moving on a straight line in Q^2 with motion vector $d = (d_1, d_2)$ and speed v. Let us also assume that its initial position at time t_0 is $(x(t_0), y(t_0))$. The position $(x(t), y(t))$ of the object at future time t can be computed using the following equations:

$$x(t) = x(t_0) + v(t - t_0)d_1 \text{ and } y(t) = y(t_0) + v(t - t_0)d_2$$

Let us now consider a concrete example and assume that we have an indefinite $\mathcal{L}_{POLY}$-constraint database containing information about the moving object $Car1$:

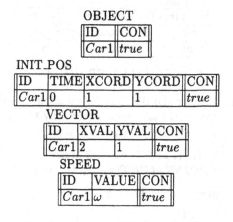

OBJECT

ID	CON
$Car1$	$true$

INIT_POS

ID	TIME	XCORD	YCORD	CON
$Car1$	0	1	1	$true$

VECTOR

ID	XVAL	YVAL	CON
$Car1$	2	1	$true$

SPEED

ID	VALUE	CON
$Car1$	ω	$true$

$$CONSTRAINT\_STORE : 40 \leq \omega \leq 50$$

$FUTURE\_POS(o, t, x_0 + v(t - t_0)d_1, y_0 + v(t - t_0)d_2) \leftarrow OBJECT(o),$
$INIT\_POS(o, t_0, x_0, y_0),$
$VECTOR(o, d_1, d_2),$
$SPEED(o, v).$

The only relation with truly indefinite information is $SPEED$. The speed of $Car1$ is not known precisely: all we know is that it is between 40 and 50 miles per time unit. The future position of any object is computed using the $\mathcal{L}_{POLY}$-constraint rule which defines the relation $FUTURE\_POS$. Later in this section, we will pose queries to the above database to compute the position of object $Car1$ at times other than 0.

B.1   Query Evaluation

In [25, 27, 31] Koubarakis defined *modal relational calculus with $\mathcal{L}$-constraints* as a declarative query language for indefinite $\mathcal{L}$-constraint databases. This modal calculus is essentially relational calculus with $\mathcal{L}$-constraints plus the modal operator $\Diamond$ or $\Box$ appended in front of relational calculus expressions. Therefore modal queries can be distinguished between *possibility* queries and *necessity* (or *certainty*) queries. A model-theoretic semantics for our query language has been given in [25, 27, 31]. The query evaluation procedure sketched below gives an equivalent proof-theoretic semantics.

Example 3. Let us consider the database of Example 1 and the query "Find all appointments for patients that possibly start at the 92th day of 1996". This query can be expressed as follows:[6]

$$\{\ APP\_S92(PATIENT, TREATMENT), x, y/\mathcal{D}: $$
$$\Diamond(\exists t_1, t_2/\mathcal{Q})(APPOINTMENT(x, y, t_1, t_2) \wedge t_1 = 92)\ \}$$

The answer to this query is the following:

APP_S92

PATIENT	TREATMENT	CON
Smith	Chemotherapy2	*true*
Smith	Radiation	*true*

$CONSTRAINT\_STORE : true$

Example 4. Let us consider the database of Example 1 and the query "Find all appointments for patients that should necessarily take place in the first six months of 1996". This query can be expressed as follows:

$$\{\ APP(PATIENT, TREATMENT), x, y/\mathcal{D}: $$
$$\Box(\exists t_1, t_2/\mathcal{Q})(APPOINTMENT(x, y, t_1, t_2) \wedge t_1 \geq 0 \wedge t_2 \leq 182)\ \}$$

The answer to this query is the following:

APP

PATIENT	TREATMENT	CON
Smith	Chemotherapy1	*true*
Smith	Chemotherapy2	*true*

$CONSTRAINT\_STORE : true$

Example 5. Consider the database of Example 2 and the query "What are the possible future positions of object $Car1$ at time 5". This query can be expressed as follows:

$$\{\ POS\_AT\_5(XCORD, YCORD), x, y/\mathcal{Q}: \ \Diamond FUTURE\_POS(Car1, 5, x, y)\ \}$$

The above query has the following answer:

---

[6] $\mathcal{D}$ is the *data sort*.

POS_AT_5

XCORD	YCORD	CON
x	y	$401 \leq x \leq 501, \; y = \frac{1}{2}x + \frac{1}{2}$

$CONSTRAINT\_STORE:$ *true*

Because the database does not contain definite information about the speed of $Car1$, a line segment in $\mathcal{Q}^2$ is returned as the answer to the query.

In our scheme we can express many of the queries on moving points discussed in [40, 41, 16]. We can not express queries involving special functions (e.g., aggregates) since we have not introduced them in our framework. Queries on moving regions can also be expressed. However as shown in [4, 12] spatial regions can be represented more gracefully in a constraint database model based on nested relations with one level of nesting. Extending our scheme in this direction is a topic of current research.

As in the definite information case [22], query evaluation over indefinite $\mathcal{L}$-constraint databases can be viewed as quantifier elimination in the theory $Th(\mathbf{M}_{\mathcal{L}})$ [25, 27, 31]. Quantifier elimination is always possible in our framework since $Th(\mathbf{M}_{\mathcal{L}})$ admits quantifier elimination. If q is a possibility query with free variables $\overline{x}$ over database $DB = (\tilde{r}, RS, CS(\overline{\omega}))$ then query evaluation is equivalent to quantifier elimination from a formula of the form $(\exists \overline{\omega}/\overline{s'})(CS(\overline{\omega}) \wedge \psi(\overline{x}, \overline{\omega}))$ where $\overline{s'}$ is a vector of sorts and ψ is a formula of $Th(\mathbf{M}_{\mathcal{L}})$ which depends on q and DB. Similarly, if q is a certainty query with free variables $\overline{x}$ then query evaluation is equivalent to quantifier elimination from a formula of the form $(\forall \overline{\omega}/\overline{s'})(CS(\overline{\omega}) \Rightarrow \psi(\overline{x}, \overline{\omega}))$.

Example 6. Let us consider the query of Example 3 over the database of Example 1. This query can be evaluated by eliminating quantifiers from the following formula:

$(\exists \omega_1, \omega_2, \omega_3, \omega_4, \omega_5, \omega_6/\mathcal{Q})$
$((\omega_1 \geq 0 \wedge \omega_2 \geq 0 \wedge \omega_3 \geq 0 \wedge \omega_4 \geq 0 \wedge \omega_5 \geq 0 \wedge \omega_6 \geq 0 \wedge$
$\omega_2 = \omega_1 + 1 \wedge \omega_4 = \omega_3 + 1 \wedge \omega_6 = \omega_5 + 2 \wedge \omega_2 \leq 91 \wedge \omega_3 \geq 91 \wedge$
$\omega_4 \leq 182 \wedge \omega_3 - \omega_2 \geq 60 \wedge \omega_5 - \omega_4 \geq 20 \wedge \omega_6 \leq 213) \wedge$
$(\exists t_1, t_2/\mathcal{Q})((x = Smith \wedge y = Chemotherapy1 \wedge t_1 = \omega_1 \wedge t_2 = \omega_2) \vee$
$(x = Smith \wedge y = Chemotherapy2 \wedge t_1 = \omega_3 \wedge t_2 = \omega_4) \vee$
$(x = Smith \wedge y = Radiation \wedge t_1 = \omega_5 \wedge t_2 = \omega_6)) \wedge t_1 = 92).$
The result of the elimination is

$(x = Smith \wedge y = Chemotherapy2) \vee (x = Smith \wedge y = Radiation)$

and it is shown as a relation in Example 3.

Example 7. Let us now consider the query of Example 5 over the database of Example 2. First of all notice that the instance of relation $FUTURE\_POS$ derived from the instances of relations $OBJECT, INIT\_POS, VECTOR$ and $SPEED$ after applying the given rule contains only the tuple

$(Car1, \; t, \; 1 + 2\omega t, \; 1 + \omega t).$

Therefore our query can be evaluated by eliminating quantifiers from the following formula:

$$(\exists \omega / \mathcal{Q})(40 \le \omega \le 50 \, \land \, x = 1 + 10\omega \, \land \, y = 1 + 5\omega)$$

The result of the elimination is

$$401 \le x \le 501 \, \land \, y = \frac{1}{2}x + \frac{1}{2}$$

and it is shown as a relation in Example 5.

C   Tractable Query Evaluation in Indefinite Constraint Databases

The complexity of database query evaluation is usually measured using the notion of data complexity introduced in [46, 6].[7] When we use data complexity, we measure the complexity of query evaluation as a function of the database size only; the query and the schema are considered *fixed*. In our case we also assume that the size of any integer constant in the database is *logarithmic* in the size of the database.[8]

Assuming the data complexity measure, is it easy or hard to answer a query over an indefinite constraint database? Not surprisingly, the answer depends primarily on the type of constraints involved and secondarily on the type of the database and the query.

In previous research, Koubarakis [26, 31] has provided upper bounds for modal calculus queries over indefinite point constraint databases where point constraints have been restricted to inequalities of the form $t_1 - t_2 \le c$ interpreted over the rationals or the integers. [45] has done very good work on lower bounds and PTIME cases for indefinite order databases.

In the Artificial Intelligence literature, [43] has exhibited a class of indefinite interval constraint databases and a class of conjunctive possibility queries with a query answering problem that can be done with PTIME data complexity. [5] has a very similar result for indefinite point constraint databases where the point constraints considered are as in [26, 31].

In this paper we start with the assumption that we have an arbitrary class of constraints $\mathcal{C}$ with an "easy" satisfiability problem and variable elimination problem. Under this assumption, we show that there are several classes of databases and modal queries involving $\mathcal{C}$-constraints, for which query evaluation can be done with PTIME data complexity.

We will reach tractable cases of query evaluation by restricting the classes of constraints, databases and queries we allow in our framework. We introduce the concepts of query type and database type to make these distinctions.

---

[7] There is also *expression complexity* and *combined complexity* but we will not deal with them in this paper.

[8] When a database is viewed as a formula in some constraint language, this is equivalent to assuming that any integer constant in a formula ϕ is assumed to have size $O(\log |\phi|)$. This assumption has also been made in [22] and [38].

C.1   Query Types

A *query type* is a tuple of the following form:

$Q(Open/Closed, Modality, PositiveExistential/SingleRelation, Constraints)$

The first argument of a query type distinguishes between *closed* and *open* queries. A query is *open* when it has free variables and it is *closed* (or *yes/no*) when it has no free variables. The argument *Modality* can be $\Diamond$ or $\Box$ representing possibility or necessity queries respectively.

The third argument can be *PositiveExistential* or *SingleRelation*. We use *PositiveExistential* to denote that the relational calculus expression in the query is a positive existential one i.e., it is of the form $(\exists \overline{x}/\overline{s})\phi(\overline{x})$ where ϕ involves only the logical symbols $\wedge$ and $\vee$.

We use *SingleRelation* to denote that the query is of the form $\overline{u}/\overline{s}_1 : OP\ (\exists \overline{t}/\overline{s}_2)p(\overline{u}, \overline{t})$ where $\overline{u}$ and $\overline{t}$ are vectors of variables, $\overline{s}_1$, $\overline{s}_2$ are vectors of sorts, p is a relation name and OP is a modal operator.

The fourth argument *Constraints* denotes the class of constraints that is used as query conditions. For example consider a database DB with two binary relations r and p. The query

$$: \Box(\exists x, y, t, u/Q)((r(x,t)\ \vee\ p(y,u))\ \wedge\ 2t + 3u \leq 4\ \wedge\ x = u + 1)$$

belongs to the query class

$$Q(Closed, \Box, PositiveExistential, Linear).$$

C.2   Database Types

We can characterise an indefinite constraint database according to the arity of its predicates, the class of constraints of its constraint store, and the class of local conditions in the database:

$$DB(Arity, LocalCondition, ConstraintStore)$$

The attribute *Arity* can have values *N-ary* and *Monadic* and gives the arity of the predicates in the database. The attribute *LocalCondition* gives the constraint class of the local condition of every tuple in the database. The attribute *ConstraintStore* gives the constraint class of the database constraint store.

For instance, a database having:

– *N*-ary predicates with local condition a conjunction of linear constraints.
– A constraint store which is a set of linear constraints.

can be represented by type $DB(N\text{-}ary, Linear, Linear)$.

In one of our results we consider the type of a database which consists of a *single N*-ary relation, the constraints in the constraint store belong to some class $\mathcal{C}$, and all local conditions of tuples consist of a *single* constraint from class $\mathcal{C}$. This database type is represented by

$$SingleRelDB(N\text{-}ary, Single\text{-}\mathcal{C}, \mathcal{C}).$$

C.3   Results

The following definitions are useful in the rest of this section.

Definition 6. *If C is a class of constraints then $\vee \overline{C}$ is a new class of constraints defined as follows. A constraint c is in $\vee \overline{C}$ iff c is a disjunction of negations of C-constraints.*

Definition 7. *Let C be a class of constraints. The problem of deciding whether a given set of constraints from C is satisfiable will be denoted by $SAT(C)$. The problem of eliminating an arbitrary number of variables from a given set of constraints from class C will be denoted by $VAR\text{-}ELIM(C)$. If the number of variables is fixed then the problem will be denoted by $FVAR\text{-}ELIM(C)$.*

Let us now present our results assuming the data complexity measure. We first consider closed queries. In the rest of this section sorts in query variables are omitted for brevity. If C is a class of constraints then the members of C will be referred to as C-constraints.

Lemma 1. *Let C be a class of constraints. Evaluating a query of the class*

$$Q(Closed, \Diamond, PositiveExistential, C)$$

over an indefinite constraint database $\tilde{r}$ of the class $DB(N\text{-}ary, C, C)$ is equivalent to deciding the consistency of a set of m formulas of the form

$$CS(\overline{\omega}) \wedge \theta_i(\overline{\omega}), \ i = 1, \ldots, m$$

where CS and θ_i are conjunctions of C-constraints, and m is a polynomial in the size of $\tilde{r}$.

Theorem 1. *Let C be a class of constraints such that $SAT(C)$ and $FVAR\text{-}ELIM(C)$ can be solved in PTIME. Let $\tilde{r}$ be an indefinite constraint database of the class*

$$DB(N\text{-}ary, C, C)$$

and f be a query of the class

$$Q(Closed, \Diamond, PositiveExistential, C)$$

The problem of deciding whether $f(\tilde{r}) = yes$ can be solved with PTIME data complexity.

Lemma 2. *Let $\mathcal{E}, C$ be two classes of constraints such that $\mathcal{E} \subseteq C$ and $\vee \overline{\mathcal{E}} \subseteq C$. Evaluating a query of the class $Q(Closed, \square, PositiveExistential, \mathcal{E})$ over an indefinite constraint database $\tilde{r}$ of the class $DB(N\text{-}ary, \mathcal{E}, C)$ is equivalent to deciding the consistency of a formula of the form*

$$CS(\overline{\omega}) \wedge \theta_1(\overline{\omega}) \wedge \ldots \wedge \theta_m(\overline{\omega})$$

where CS is a conjunction of C-constraints, θ_i, $1 \leq i \leq m$ are C-constraints, and m is a polynomial in the size of $\tilde{r}$.

Theorem 2. *Let $\mathcal{E}, \mathcal{C}$ be two classes of constraints such that $\mathcal{E} \subseteq \mathcal{C}$, $\vee \overline{\mathcal{E}} \subseteq \mathcal{C}$ and $SAT(\mathcal{C})$ and $FVAR\text{-}ELIM(\mathcal{E})$ can be solved in PTIME. Let $\tilde{r}$ be an indefinite constraint database of the class*

$$DB(N\text{-}ary, \mathcal{E}, \mathcal{C})$$

and f be a query of the class

$$Q(Closed, \Box, PositiveExistential, \mathcal{E}).$$

The problem of deciding whether $f(\tilde{r}) = yes$ can be solved with PTIME data complexity.

We now turn our attention to tractable query evaluation for open queries.

Lemma 3. *Let $\mathcal{C}$ be a class of constraints. Evaluating a query of the class*

$$Q(Open, \Diamond, PositiveExistential, \mathcal{C})$$

over an indefinite constraint database $\tilde{r}$ of the class $DB(N\text{-}ary, \mathcal{C}, \mathcal{C})$ is equivalent to eliminating quantifiers from a set of m formulas of the form

$$(\exists \overline{\omega})(CS(\overline{\omega}) \wedge \theta_i(\overline{u}, \overline{\omega})), \quad i = 1, \ldots, m$$

where CS and θ_i are conjunctions of $\mathcal{C}$-constraints, $\overline{u}$ is the vector of free variables of the query, and m is a polynomial in the size of $\tilde{r}$.

Theorem 3. *Let $\mathcal{C}$ be a class of constraints such that $VAR\text{-}ELIM(\mathcal{C})$ can be done in PTIME. Let $\tilde{r}$ be an indefinite constraint database of the class*

$$DB(N\text{-}ary, \mathcal{C}, \mathcal{C})$$

and f be a query of the class

$$Q(Open, \Diamond, PositiveExistential, \mathcal{C}).$$

The problem of evaluating $f(\tilde{r})$ can be solved with PTIME data complexity.

Lemma 4. *Let $\mathcal{C}$ be a class of constraints which is closed under negation. Evaluating a query of the class*

$$Q(Open, \Box, SingleRelation, None)$$

over an indefinite constraint database $\tilde{r}$ of the class $SingleRelDB(N\text{-}ary, Single\text{-}\mathcal{C}, \mathcal{C})$ is equivalent to eliminating quantifiers from a formula of the form

$$CS(\overline{\omega}) \wedge \theta_1(\overline{u}, \overline{\omega}) \wedge \ldots \wedge \theta_m(\overline{u}, \overline{\omega})$$

where CS is a conjunction of $\mathcal{C}$-constraints, θ_i, $1 \leq i \leq m$ are $\mathcal{C}$-constraints, $\overline{u}$ is the vector of free variables of the query and m is the number of tuples of the single relation referred in the query.

Theorem 4. *Let C be a class of constraints such that C is closed under negation and $VAR\text{-}ELIM(C)$ can be done in PTIME. Let $\tilde{r}$ be an indefinite constraint database of the class*

$$SingleRelDB(N\text{-}ary, Single\text{-}C, C)$$

and f be a query of the class

$$Q(Open, \square, SingleRelation, None).$$

The problem of evaluating $f(\tilde{r})$ can be solved with PTIME data complexity.

This section presented some results on tractable query answering problems for the scheme of indefinite $\mathcal{L}$-constraint databases. Let us now see how these results are specialized for the model of indefinite $\mathcal{L}_{LIN}$-constraint databases. The first thing that we have to do is find subclasses of linear constraints that have the nice properties assumed by the theorems of this section.

D   The Class of UTVPI$^{\neq}$ Constraints

Linear constraints and their subclasses have been studied in many areas of computer science, and more recently in temporal and spatial reasoning. The following is an interesting class of linear constraints with good computational properties.

Definition 8 ([29, 21]). *A Horn disjunctive linear constraint is a disjunction $d_1 \vee \dots \vee d_n$ where each d_i, $i = 1, \dots, n$ is a weak linear inequality or a linear disequation and the number of inequalities among d_1, ..., d_n does not exceed one.*

[21, 29] have shown that Horn disjunctive linear constraints subsume many interesting classes of temporal and spatial constraints.

Example 8. The following is a set of Horn disjunctive linear constraints:

$$3x_1 + x_5 - 3x_4 \leq 10, \quad x_1 + x_3 + x_5 \neq 7, \quad 4x_1 + x_3 \neq 3 \vee 5x_2 + 3x_5 + x_4 \neq 5$$

$$3x_1 + x_5 - 3x_4 \leq 10 \vee 2x_1 + 3x_2 - 4x_3 \neq 4 \vee x_1 + x_3 + x_5 \neq 7$$

Theorem 5 ([29, 21]). *The satisfiability of a set of Horn disjunctive linear constraints can be decided in PTIME.*

Unfortunately we do not have a nice theorem like the above concerning variable elimination for Horn disjunctive linear constraints. In fact, variable elimination cannot be done in PTIME even for sets of linear inequalities. If we have a set C of linear inequalities, it might not be possible to describe the result of a variable elimination operation on C by a set of linear inequalities with size less than exponential in the number of eliminated variables [50]. The following is a weaker result which considers Horn disjunctive linear constraints and a fixed number of variables.

Theorem 6 ([29]). *We can eliminate a fixed number of variables from a set of Horn disjunctive linear constraints in PTIME.*

Luckily there are *subclasses* of linear constraints where variable elimination can be done in PTIME. Let us consider them in turn.

Definition 9 ([28, 30]). *A* DIFF$^{\neq}$ *constraint is a linear constraint of the form $t_1 \sim c$ or $t_1 - t_2 \sim c$ where t_1, t_2 are variables, c is a constant and $\sim$ is $\leq$ or $\neq$.*

The above constraint class extends the class of *difference constraints* or *DIFF constraints* studied in temporal reasoning [8] by adding disequations of the form $x_1 - x_2 \neq c$ or $x_1 \neq c$.

Theorem 7 ([28, 30]). *Let C be a set of* DIFF$^{\neq}$ *constraints. The consistency of C can be decided in $O(n^3)$ time where n is the number of variables in C. We can eliminate any number of variables from C in $O(dn^4)$ time where d is the number of disequations and n is the number of variables in C.*

Can we extend the class of DIFF (resp. DIFF$^{\neq}$) constraints without sacrificing its nice computational properties? The first natural extension that comes to mind is the class of UTVPI (resp. UTVPI$^{\neq}$) constraints.[9]

Definition 10. *A* UTVPI *constraint is a linear constraint of the form $\pm x_1 \leq c$ or $\pm x_1 \pm x_2 \leq c$ where x_1, x_2 are variables and c is a constant. If we also allow disequations, we have the class of* UTVPI$^{\neq}$ *constraints.*

Example 9. Below we give some examples of UTVPI$^{\neq}$ constraints:

$$-x_1 \leq 12, \ x_1 + x_2 \leq 2, \ x_3 - x_2 \leq 0.5, \ x_3 + x_2 \neq 6$$

UTVPI$^{\neq}$ constraints are an interesting subclass of linear constraints for spatial databases over $\mathcal{Q}^2$. They are more expressive than dense order constraints [23, 9, 10], and thus they allow more precise approximations of arbitrary regions of $\mathcal{Q}^2$ traditionally approximated by bounding boxes. The disequations present in this class allowe a limited form of negative information (e.g., they can be used to *remove* points and straight lines from polygons).[10]

The following theorem is the main result of this section. It shows that UTVPI$^{\neq}$ constraints can give us more expressive power than DIFF$^{\neq}$ constraints without sacrificing none of their nice computational properties.

Theorem 8. *Let C be a set of* UTVPI$^{\neq}$ *constraints. The consistency of C can be decided in $O(n^3)$ time where n is the number of variables in C. We can eliminate any number of variables from C in $O(dn^4)$ time where d is the number of disequations and n is the number of variables in C.*

---

[9] UTVPI is an acronym for linear inequalities with *U*nit coefficients and at most *T*wo *V*ariables *P*er *I*nequality.

[10] UTVPI constraints *over the integers* have also been studied [20, 17]. [17] presents a constraint logic programming system with UTVPI constraints and several applications that would otherwise be solved using finite domain constraints.

It is natural now to ask the following question. Can we extend the above theorem to the class of *two-variables-per-inequality* or *TVPI* constraints (i.e., linear constraints of the form $ax + by \leq c$ where x, y are variables and a, b are rational constants)? TVPI constraints have previously been considered in several papers including [39, 18, 9, 10]. It is currently an open problem whether variable elimination for TVPI constraints can be done in PTIME. [9, 10] has considered *monotone* TVPI constraints (i.e., TVPI constraints of the form $x \leq by + c$ with $b \geq 0$) and showed that under a condition involving the graph representation of the constraints, variable elimination can be done in strongly polynomial time (i.e., where the polynomials do not depend on the coefficient sizes).

E   Tractable Query Answering with Indefinite Information in Temporal and Spatial Domains

Let us recall that a query type is a tuple of the form

$$Q(Open/Closed, Modality, PositiveExistential/SingleRelation, Constraints)$$

and a database type is a tuple of the form

$$DB(Arity, LocalCondition, ConstraintStore).$$

The arguments *Constraints* or *LocalCondition* vary over constraint classes. For the purposes of this section, these classes can be *HornDisjLinear*, *Linear*, *LinearEquality*, UTVPI$^{\neq}$, *DIFF* (with obvious meaning). We will also encounter the classes *Single*-UTVPI$^{\neq}$ and *None*. In the former case the local condition in every tuple of the database consists of a single UTVPI$^{\neq}$ constraint. In the latter case we have no constraints (equivalently, all constraints are *true*).

We will also have the following new classes of temporal and spatial constraints:

- **IA.** This is the Interval Algebra of Allen [2].
- **SIA.** This is the subalgebra of **IA** which includes only interval relations that can be translated into conjunctions of order constraints $x \leq y$ or $x \neq y$ on the endpoints of intervals [44].
- **ORDHorn.** This is the subalgebra of **IA** which includes only interval relations that can be translated into conjunctions of ORD-Horn constraints on the endpoints of intervals [35]. An *ORD-Horn constraint* is a disjunction of weak inequalities of the form $x \leq y$ and disequations of the form $x \neq y$ with the additional constraint that the number of inequalities should not exceed one [35].
- **2d-IA** and **2d-OrdHorn.**
  2d-IA is a generalization of **IA** in two dimensions and it is based on the concept of *rectangle* in $\mathcal{Q}^2$ [15, 36, 3]. Every rectangle r can be defined by a 4-tuple $(L_x^r, L_y^r, U_x^r, U_y^r)$ that gives the coordinates of the lower left and upper right corner of r. There are 13^2 basic relations in **2d-IA** describing all possible configurations of 2 rectangles in $\mathcal{Q}^2$ [36].

2d-OrdHorn is the subalgebra of **2d-IA** which includes only these relations R with the property $r_1 \ R \ r_2 \equiv \phi(r_1, r_2) \wedge \psi(r_1, r_2)$ where ϕ is a conjunction of ORD-Horn constraints on variables L_x^r and U_x^r, and ψ is a conjunction of ORD-Horn constraints on variables L_y^r and U_y^r.

– **PA** and **CPA**. **PA** is the Point Algebra of [48]. **CPA** is the subalgebra of **PA** which does not include the relation $\neq$ [49].

The following theorem uses the results of Sections C and D to identify tractable query answering problems in indefinite linear constraint databases.

Theorem 9. *Evaluation of*

1. $Q(Closed, \diamondsuit, PositiveExistential, HornDisjLinear)$ *queries over* $DB(N\text{-}ary, HornDisjLinear, HornDisjLinear)$ *databases,*
2. $Q(Closed, \square, PositiveExistential, LinearEquality)$ *queries over* $DB(N\text{-}ary, LinearEquality, HornDisjLinear)$ *databases,*
3. $Q(Open, \diamondsuit, PositiveExistential, UTVPI^{\neq})$ *queries over* $DB(N\text{-}ary, UTVPI^{\neq}, UTVPI^{\neq})$ *databases and*
4. $Q(Open, \square, SingleRelation, None)$ *queries over* $SingleRelDB(N\text{-}ary, Single\text{-}UTVPI^{\neq}, UTVPI^{\neq})$ *databases*

can be performed in PTIME (using the data complexity measure).

The first part of Theorem 9 is a significant extension of the PTIME result of [5] on possibility queries over conjunctions of DIFF constraints.

Theorem 9 does not mention constraints on higher-order objects (e.g., intervals, rectangles) explicitly so one might think that it useful only for one-dimensional databases. Luckily this is not true. For example, results for interval constraint databases can be deduced immediately by taking into account the subsumption relations between classes of interval and point constraints. For example, the first part of Theorem 9 implies that evaluating

$$Q(Closed, \diamondsuit, PositiveExistential, \mathbf{ORDHorn})$$

queries over $DB(N\text{-}ary, None, \mathbf{ORDHorn})$ databases can be done with PTIME data complexity. This is a significant extension of the PTIME result of [43] on possibility queries over conjunctions of **SIA** constraints.

The first part of Theorem 9 also implies that evaluating

$$Q(Closed, \diamondsuit, PositiveExistential, \mathbf{2d\text{-}ORDHorn})$$

queries over $DB(N\text{-}ary, None, \mathbf{2d\text{-}ORDHorn})$ databases can be done with PTIME data complexity. This is an interesting result for spatial databases with indefinite information over $\mathcal{Q}^2$. This result can be generalized to $\mathcal{Q}^n$ if one defines an appropriate algebra **nd-ORDHorn**.

Theorem 9 does not constrain the arity of database predicates. The following is a result by van der Meyden [45] which constrains the database to consist of monadic predicates only. In this way van der Meyden has discovered a tractable query answering problem that allows a certainty query to contain order constraints (compare with the second result of Theorem 9).

Theorem 10. *Evaluating* $Q(Closed, \square, Conjunctive, \mathbf{CPA})$ *queries over* $DB(Monadic, None, \mathbf{CPA})$ *databases can be done in PTIME (using the data complexity measure).*

If we move to databases with binary predicates, the corresponding query answering problem becomes NP-complete [45].

Unlike [45], we have not proven any lower bound results that show where the boundary is between tractable and hard query answering problems with respect to the classes of queries and databases considered. The boundary can sometimes be identified easily with respect to the constraint class considered. For example, when we go from Horn disjunctive constraints to a constraint class with an intractable consistency checking problem (e.g., **IA** constraints) then the first tractability result of Theorem 9 is invalidated. In general more research is necessary for drawing an informative picture of tractable vs. intractable query answering problems.

We do not deal with *expression complexity* and *combined complexity* at all in this paper. Query anwering problems like the ones considered in Theorems 9 and 10 can be shown to be very hard in the combined complexity measure [45]. [45] has introduced several additional restrictions on queries and databases to arrive at query answering problems with PTIME combined complexity (but only the simple case of **PA** constraints is considered). A similar detailed study of expression/combined complexity of query answering in our framework is left to further research.

Finally let us mention the work of [7] who consider tractable temporal reasoning in a framework similar to ours. A detailed comparison of our work with [7] is not very easy at this stage because the formalism of [7] allows several kinds of deductive rules that cannot be encoded in our model.

References

1. S. Abiteboul, P. Kanellakis, and G. Grahne. On the Representation and Querying of Sets of Possible Worlds. In *Proceedings of the ACM SIGMOD International Conference on Management of Data*, pages 34–48, 1987.
2. J.F. Allen. Maintaining Knowledge about Temporal Intervals. *Communications of the ACM*, 26(11):832–843, November 1983.
3. P. Balbiani, J.-F. Condotta, and L.F. del Cerro. Bidimensional Temporal Relations. In *Proceedings of KR'98*, June 1998.
4. E. Bertino, A. Belussi, and B. Catania. Manipulating Spatial Data in Constraint Databases. In M. Scholl and A. Voisard, editors, *Proc. of the Fifth Int. Symp. on Spatial Databases*, number 1262 in Lecture Notes in Computer Science, pages 115–140, Berlin, Germany, July 1997. Springer Verlag, Berlin.
5. V. Brusoni, L. Console, and P. Terenziani. On the computational complexity of querying bounds on differences constraints. *Artificial Intelligence*, 74(2):367–379, 1995.
6. A. Chandra and D. Harel. Structure and Complexity of Relational Queries. *Journal of Computer and System Sciences*, 25:99–128, 1982.
7. T. Dean and M. Boddy. Reasoning About Partially Ordered Events. *Artificial Intelligence*, 36:375–399, 1988.

8. R. Dechter, I. Meiri, and J. Pearl. Temporal Constraint Networks. In R. Brachman, H. Levesque, and R. Reiter, editors, *Proceedings of 1st International Conference on Principles of Knowledge Representation and Reasoning*, pages 83–93, Toronto, Ontario, 1989.
9. D.Q. Goldin. *Constraint Query Algebras*. PhD thesis, Dept. of Computer Science, Brown University, 1997.
10. D.Q. Goldin and P. Kanellakis. Constraint Query Algebras. *Constraints*, 1(1):45–83, 1997.
11. G. Grahne. The Problem of Incomplete Information in Relational Databases. Technical Report Report A-1989-1, Department of Computer Science, University of Helsinki, Finland, 1989. Also published as Lecture Notes in Computer Science 554, Springer Verlag, 1991.
12. S. Grumbach, P. Rigaux, and L. Segoufin. The DEDALE system for complex spatial queries. In *Proceedings of ACM SIGMOD International Conference on Management of Data*, pages 213–224, 1998.
13. S. Grumbach and J. Su. Finitely representable databases. In *Proceedings of the 13th ACM SIGACT-SIGMOD-SIGART Symposium on Principles of Database Systems*, pages 289–300, 1994.
14. S. Grumbach, J. Su, and C. Tollu. Linear constraint databases. In D. Leivant, editor, *Proceedings of the Logic and Computational Complexity Workshop*, Indianapolis, 1994. Springer Verlag. To appear in LNCS.
15. H.-W. Guesgen. Spatial reasoning based on Allen's temporal logic. Technical Report TR-89-094, ICSI, 1989.
16. R.H. Gueting, M.H. Bohlen, M. Erwing, C.S. Jensen, N.A. Lorentzos, M. Schneider, and M. Vazirgiannis. A Foundation for Representing and Querying Moving Objects. Technical Report 238-9, Informatik, FernUniversitat, 1998.
17. W. Harvey and P. Stuckey. A unit two variable per inequality integer constraint solver for constraint logic programming. In *Proceedings of Australian Computer Science Conference (Australian Computer Science Communications)*, pages 102–111, 1997.
18. D.S. Hochbaum and J. Naor. Simple and fast algorithms for linear and integer programs with two variables per inequality. *SIAM Journal of Computing*, 23(6):1179–1192, 1994.
19. T. Imielinski and W. Lipski. Incomplete Information in Relational Databases. *Journal of ACM*, 31(4):761–791, 1984.
20. Joxan Jaffar, Michael J. Maher, Peter Stuckey, and Ronald Yap. Beyond Finite Domains. In A. Borning, editor, *Proceedings of PPCP'94*, volume 874 of *Lecture Notes in Computer Science*, pages 86–94. Springer Verlag, 1994.
21. Jonsson, P. and Bäckström, C. A Linear Programming Approach to Temporal Reasoning. In *Proceedings of AAAI-96*, 1996.
22. P.C. Kanellakis, G.M. Kuper, and P.Z. Revesz. Constraint Query Languages. In *Proceedings of the 9th ACM SIGACT-SIGMOD-SIGART Symposium on Principles of Database Systems*, pages 299–313, 1990.
23. P.C. Kanellakis, G.M. Kuper, and P.Z. Revesz. Constraint Query Languages. *Journal of Computer and System Sciences*, 51:26–52, 1995.
24. M. Koubarakis. Database Models for Infinite and Indefinite Temporal Information. *Information Systems*, 19(2):141–173, March 1994.
25. M. Koubarakis. Foundations of Indefinite Constraint Databases. In A. Borning, editor, *Proceedings of the 2nd International Workshop on the Principles and Practice of Constraint Programming (PPCP'94)*, volume 874 of *Lecture Notes in Computer Science*, pages 266–280. Springer Verlag, 1994.

26. M. Koubarakis. *Foundations of Temporal Constraint Databases.* PhD thesis, Computer Science Division, Dept. of Electrical and Computer Engineering, National Technical University of Athens, February 1994. Available electronically from http://www.co.umist.ac.uk/~manolis.

27. M. Koubarakis. Databases and Temporal Constraints: Semantics and Complexity. In J. Clifford and A. Tuzhilin, editors, *Recent Advances in Temporal Databases (Proceedings of the International Workshop on Temporal Databases, Zürich, Switzerland, September 1995)*, Workshops in Computing, pages 93–109. Springer, 1995.

28. M. Koubarakis. From Local to Global Consistency in Temporal Constraint Networks. In *Proceedings of the 1st International Conference on Principles and Practice of Constraint Programming (CP'95)*, volume 976 of *LNCS*, pages 53–69, Cassis, France, September 1995.

29. M. Koubarakis. Tractable Disjunctions of Linear Constraints. In *Proceedings of the 2nd International Conference on Principles and Practice of Constraint Programming (CP'96)*, Boston, MA, August 1996. 297-307.

30. M. Koubarakis. From Local to Global Consistency in Temporal Constraint Networks. *Theoretical Computer Science*, 173:89–112, February 1997. Invited submission to the special issue dedicated to the 1st International Conference on Principles and Practice of Constraint Programming (CP95), Editors: U. Montanari and F. Rossi.

31. M. Koubarakis. The Complexity of Query Evaluation in Indefinite Temporal Constraint Databases. *Theoretical Computer Science*, 171:25–60, January 1997. Special Issue on Uncertainty in Databases and Deductive Systems, Editor: L.V.S. Lakshmanan.

32. M. Koubarakis and S. Skiadopoulos. Querying Temporal Constraint Networks in PTIME. In *Proceedings of AAAI-99*, 1999. Forthcoming.

33. G.M. Kuper, S. Ramaswamy, K. Shim, and J. Su. A Constrint-Based Spatial Extension to SQL. In *Proceedings of ACM-GIS98*, pages 112–117, 1998.

34. R. Laurini and D. Thompson. *Fundamentals of Spatial Information Systems.* Academic Press, 1992.

35. Bernhard Nebel and Hans-Jürgen Bürckert. Reasoning about temporal relations: A maximal tractable subclass of Allen's interval algebra. *Journal of the ACM*, 42(1):43–66, January 1995.

36. D. Papadias, Y. Theodoridis, T. Sellis, and M. Egenhofer. Topological Relations in the World of Minimum Bounding Rectangles: A Study with R-trees. In *Proceedings of the 1995 ACM SIGMOD International Conference on Management of Data*, pages 92–103, 1995.

37. J. Paredaens. Spatial Databases: the Final Frontier. In *Proceedings of ICDT-95*, pages 14–32, 1995.

38. P.Z. Revesz. A Closed Form for Datalog Queries with Integer Order. In *Proceedings of the 3rd International Conference on Database Theory*, pages 187–201, 1990.

39. Robert Shostak. Deciding Linear Inequalities by Computing Loop Residues. *Journal of the ACM*, 28(4):769–779, 1981.

40. A.P. Sistla, O. Wolfson, S. Chamberlain, and S. Dao. Modeling and Querying Moving Objects. In *Proceedings of ICDE-97*, 1997.

41. A.P. Sistla, O. Wolfson, S. Chamberlain, and S. Dao. Querying the uncertain position of moving objects. In *Temporal Databases: Research and Practice*, volume 1399, pages 310–337. Springer Verlag, 1998.

42. V.S. Subrahmanian. *Principles of Multimedia Database Systems.* Morgan Kaufmann, 1998.

43. Peter van Beek. Temporal Query Processing with Indefinite Information. *Artificial Intelligence in Medicine*, 3:325–339, 1991.
44. Peter van Beek and Robin Cohen. Exact and Approximate Reasoning about Temporal Relations. *Computational Intelligence*, 6:132–144, 1990.
45. R. van der Meyden. The Complexity of Querying Indefinite Data About Linearly Ordered Domains (Preliminary Version). In *Proceedings of the 11th ACM SIGACT-SIGMOD-SIGART Symposium on Principles of Database Systems*, pages 331–345, 1992. Full version appears in JCSS, 54(1), pp. 113-135, 1997.
46. M. Vardi. The Complexity of Relational Query Languages. In *Proceedings of ACM SIGACT/SIGMOD Symposium on Principles of Database Systems*, pages 137–146, 1982.
47. M. Vardi. Querying Logical Databases. *Journal of Computer and System Sciences*, 33:142–160, 1986.
48. Marc Vilain and Henry Kautz. Constraint Propagation Algorithms for Temporal Reasoning. In *Proceedings of AAAI-86*, pages 377–382, 1986.
49. Marc Vilain, Henry Kautz, and Peter van Beek. Constraint Propagation Algorithms for Temporal Reasoning: A Revised Report. In D.S. Weld and J. de Kleer, editors, *Readings in Qualitative Reasoning about Physical Systems*, pages 373–381. Morgan Kaufmann, 1989.
50. M. Yannakakis. Expressing Combinatorial Optimization Problems by Linear Programs. In *Proc. of ACM Symposium on the Theory of Computing*, pages 223–288, 1988.

Animating Spatiotemporal Constraint Databases

Jan Chomicki[1], Yuguo Liu[2], and Peter Revesz[2]

[1] Monmouth University, West Long Branch, NJ 07764, USA
chomicki@monmouth.ed,
WWW home page: http://www.monmouth.edu/~chomicki
[2] University of Nebraska-Lincoln, Lincoln, NE 68588, USA
revesz@cse.unl.edu,
WWW home page: http://cse.unl.edu/~revesz

Abstract. Constraint databases provide a very expressive framework for spatiotemporal database applications. However, animating such databases is difficult because of the cost of constructing a graphical representation of a single snapshot of a constraint database. We present a novel approach that makes the efficient animation of constraint databases possible. The approach is based on a new construct: *parametric polygon*. We present an algorithm to construct the set of parametric polygons that represent a given linear constraint database. We also show how to animate objects defined by parametric polygons, analyze the computational complexity of animation, and present empirical data to demonstrate the efficiency of our approach.

A   Introduction

Spatiotemporal databases have recently begun to attract broader interest [10, 12, 27]. While the temporal [4, 23, 24] and spatial [14, 28] database technologies are relatively mature, their combination is far from straightforward. In this context, the constraint database approach [15] appears to be very promising. Constraint databases provide a uniform framework for modeling arbitrarily high dimensional data, they are thus naturally suited for temporal, spatial, and spatiotemporal database applications. Constraint databases are similar to relational databases: They enjoy formal, model-theoretic semantics and support a variety of well-established query languages like relational algebra, relational calculus, and variants of Datalog.

Spatiotemporal databases applications, like modelling continuous evolution or change in natural and social phenomena, lead to a new mode of user interaction. The user would like to be able to *animate* the spatiotemporal objects present in the database by viewing their consecutive snapshots. The need to support animation efficiently adds new requirements to the underlying database engine. Snapshots of spatiotemporal objects have to be displayed quickly. That's where the constraint database technology falls somewhat short. In that approach, a snapshot of a spatiotemporal object is a spatial object, represented *implicitly* using a conjunction of inequalities (for polyhedral objects the inequalities are linear). Such a representation cannot be immediately displayed on computer screen: It has first to be converted to an *explicit* boundary representation. The conversion is relatively time-consuming. It has also to be repeated for every time instant in the animation. As a result, animation with a fine time granularity becomes slow and the ability to do real-time animation is limited.

To make the animation of spatiotemporal objects more efficient, we propose to use a separate data model just for the display purposes (the decoupling of retrieval and display was postulated in the context of spatial query languages by Egenhofer [8,9]). For linear constraint databases, this model is a natural generalization of the spaghetti data model [18], called the *parametric spaghetti data model* (introduced in [5]). The basic modelling construct of the latter model is a *parametric polygon*. Using parametric polygons the conversion from an implicit constraint representation to an explicit display representation is broken into two stages: the construction of parametric polygons and their instantiation with consecutive time instants followed by display. The first stage, responsible for the bulk of the conversion, is now done only once, which leads to very substantial time savings and makes animation much more efficient. In this paper, we describe the mapping from linear constraint databases to parametric polygons and show using empirical data the superiority of this approach.

The plan of the paper is as follows. In section B we introduce the basic notions of linear constraint databases and the parametric spaghetti data model. In section C we present the mapping used for the construction of parametric polygons. In section D we show two basic animation algorithms for spatiotemporal objects and compare them empirically. We also discuss the issue of efficient display of snapshots. In section E we discuss related work and in section F we present conclusions and speculate about future work.

B Basic Concepts

B.1 The Linear Constraint Data Model

In the *linear constraint data model* [15,18,25] each database consists of a finite set of *constraint relations*. Each constraint relation consists of a finite set of constraint tuples. Each constraint tuple is a conjunction of linear constraints over the attribute variables of the relation. For example, suppose that *desert* is the following constraint relation:

```
Desert(x, y, t) :- x >= 0, y >= 0,
                   x - t <= 10, x + y <= 20,
                   t >= 0, t <= 10.

Desert(x, y, t) :- x >= 0, y >= 0,
                   x + y + t <= 30,
                   t >= 10, t <= 20.
```

The intended meaning of each of the above constraint tuples is a set of polygons, with one polygon for each time instance satisfying the inequalities on

t. In this way, one can represent, for example, how the boundaries of a desert area are changing over time. For example, at times $0, 10$ and 20 the desert area would look as shown in Figure B.1. At time 0 the area is the polygon shown in solid lines. Between time 0 and 10 the right side of the desert extends until at time 10 the area becomes a triangle. Then the shape remains a triangle but it expands further until at time 20 the hypotenuse becomes the dotted line shown in the figure.

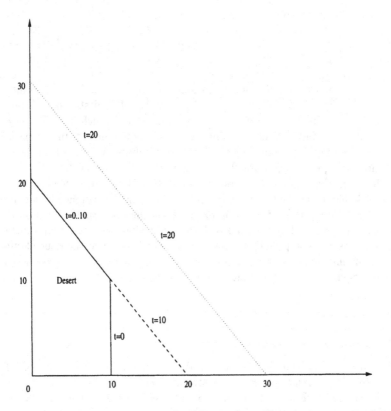

Fig. 1. An Example of Desert Area Changing

A more complex example with many constraint tuples is a relation *City* that describes the expansion of the area of a city over time. Each constraint tuple represents one small region of the city. We created such a constraint relation that approximates the area of the city of Lincoln, Nebraska for the years between 1950 and 1990. The snapshot of the city for year 1990 is shown in Figure B.1.

Although the linear constraint data model allows any number of attribute variables to be constrained by conjunctions of linear constraints, in this paper we assume that three distinguished variables are linearly dependent only on

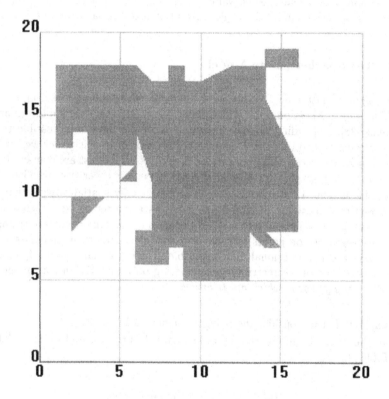

Fig. 2. City Area Snapshot at t = 1990

each other, namely x and y for the dimensions in the plane and t for time. Other attribute variables may be present and dependent on each other but must be independent of x, y and t. The animation algorithm refers only to those three variables and therefore, for simplicity, we assume that they are the only variables in constraint tuples. As we are dealing with continuous movement in the Euclidean plane, we fix the domain of all the variables to be the set of real numbers.

A *snapshot* of a constraint tuple over x, y and t is obtained by instantiating the variable t to some specific value t_0. A snapshot of a constraint relation consists of snapshots of all the tuples instantiated to the same value t_0.

B.2   The Spaghetti Data Model

The spaghetti data model [18] is a very popular model for representing spatial databases for CAD (Computer Aided Design) and GIS (Geographic Information Systems)[28]. Depending on the dimension K of the data it is possible to be more specific and to talk the K-spaghetti data model. In this paper we assume that $K = 2$, because in GIS applications the objects of interest are planar. Hence we in our paper spaghetti will mean 2-spaghetti unless otherwise specified.

In the spaghetti data model we can represent only spatial objects that are composed of a finite set of closed polygons. As a matter of fact, each spatial object can be decomposed into a set of triangles (some are degenerate triangles like line segments or points) where each triangle is represented by its three corners in a single relational database table. There are many good algorithms from computational geometry for triangulating polygons [1]. In this paper, we consider *only polygons which are triangles*.

Example 1. Let us consider the polygonal figure in Figure 1.

In the spaghetti model the figure in Figure 1 is represented by the relation in Table 1.

Table 1. Triangular Representation

ID	x	y	x'	y'	x''	y''
p1	10	4	10	4	10	4
l1	5	10	9	6	9	6
l1	9	6	9	3	9	3
t1	2	3	2	7	6	3
r1	1	2	1	11	11.5	11
r1	11.5	11	11.5	2	1	2
p2	3	5	3	8	4	9
p2	4	9	7	6	3	8
p2	3	5	7	6	3	8

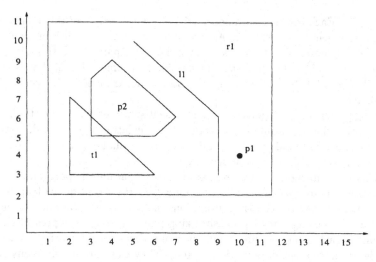

Fig. 3. A polygonal figure

Note that the rectangle is represented by two and the pentagon by three triangles.

The abstract semantics of a spaghetti data model is for each object the set of points (in two dimensions) that belong to the area of the plane that is within any of the triangles associated with that object.

B.3   The Parametric Spaghetti Data Model

The *parametric spaghetti data model* provides an alternative representation of linear constraint databases. The parametric spaghetti data model uses *parametric polygons*. For example, the constraint tuple for the *desert* relation (Figure B.1) can be represented in the parametric spaghetti data model as the table in Table 2.

Table 2. Parametric Spaghetti Data Representation of the Desert Tuple

x	y	x'	y'	x''	y''	$FROM$	TO
0	0	0	20	10+t	10-t	0	10
0	0	10+t	0	10+t	10-t	0	10
0	0	10+t	0	0	10+t	10	20

The parametric spaghetti model extends with a temporal parameter t the spaghetti model. The range of the parameter t is given for each row of the above table. Each row is a parametric triangle. The vertices of this triangle are defined as linear functions of t. A parametric polygon can be represented by a number of parametric triangles. A snapshot of a parametric triangle is the triangle obtained by instantiating the variable t to some value t_0 that is in the interval $(FROM, TO)$. The meaning of a parametric triangle is the set of all its snapshots.

Using parametric polygons one can represent spatiotemporal objects that are defined using linear arithmetic constraints [5]. The latter objects need, however, to satisfy an additional condition: all of their snapshots have to be bounded. The objects may still be unbounded in time.

What kind of change can be represented using parametric polygons? Due to the restrictions to *linear* functions of t, only *fixed-speed* continuous transformations can be modeled. The transformations include translation and scaling, so continuously moving, growing, or shrinking polygons may be represented. Objects may appear and disappear finitely many times (each incarnation will be modeled as a different parametric polygon). They can also finitely many times change their attributes like color or shading. However, only spatial extents can change continuously in this model.

To implement parametric polygons, one does not need to extend the relational data model. Each linear function of t can be represented using exactly two coefficients. If *pair* is not available as a data type, one simply doubles the number of attributes holding spatial data.

C   Constructing the parametric representation

In this section we show how to construct a representation in the parametric spaghetti model of a spatiotemporal object defined using linear arithmetic constraints over x, y, and t.

Let $w(x, y, t)$ be a generalized tuple over x, y, and t. It represents a polyhedron P with finitely many extreme points. In order to be able to construct an equivalent parametric representation, we require that $w(x, y, t_0)$ describes a closed bounded polygon for every time instant t_0. Otherwise, the snapshot cannot be represented in the parametric spaghetti model. Note that a spatiotemporal object can be unbounded but only in one dimension: t.

Mapping Algorithm:

1. Determine the extreme points and the faces of P [22].
2. Determine all the intersections of the faces of P. Each such intersection is a line and can be described as a system of two linear equations in x, y, and t (the faces are described by single linear equations). From this system obtain the equation relating x and t (eliminate y) and the one relating y and t (eliminate x). We will call those equations the *characteristic equations* of the line. For each line, determine which extreme points lie on it (there may be 1 or 2).
3. Let $t_0, \ldots, t_k$ be the time coordinates of the extreme points of P, sorted in ascending order. Duplicates are ignored. If there is a point in P whose

t-coordinate is greater than t_k, then P is unbounded in the t-dimension and all extreme points with $t = t_k$ are marked "right special". Symmetrically, if there is a point in P whose t-coordinate is less than t_0, all extreme points with $t = t_0$ are called "left special".

4. For every left-open interval $I = (t_i, t_{i+1}]$, repeat the following:

   (a) Denote by P_I the slice of P that contains all the points of P whose time coordinates are in I. P_I is a polytope, possibly with some vertices that were not among the extreme points of P. The vertices of P_I are obtained by substituting t_i (or t_{i+1}) in the characteristic equations of each line of P to obtain the x and y coordinates and checking whether the resulting point is in P. The lines for which the check is positive for both t_i and t_{i+1} are marked as "relevant to P_I". All the vertices of P_I have t-coordinates equal to t_i or t_{i+1} (by construction).

   (b) Among the edges of P_I pick those that lie on lines that are relevant to P_I (those edges will connect a vertex with $t = t_i$ with one that has $t = t_{i+1}$). For each such edge the characteristic equations of the corresponding line give a representation of one vertex of a parametric polygon.

   (c) Triangulate the obtained parametric polygon, for example by picking an arbitrary order of parametric vertices $v_0, v_1, v_2, v_3, \ldots$ and forming the triangulation $(v_0, v_1, v_2), (v_0, v_2, v_3), \ldots$. No new triangulation points are created. Each obtained triangle defines a parametric row T with $T.FROM = t_i$ and $T.TO = t_{i+1}$.

5. If there are any right special points, define $I = [t_k, +\infty)$ and:

   (a) Denote by P_I the slice of P that contains all the points of P whose time coordinates are in I. This is still a polyhedron but no longer bounded. The vertices of P_I are obtained by substituting t_k in the characteristic equations of each edge of P to obtain the x and y coordinates and checking whether the resulting point is in P and whether the line contains a point with $t > t_k$ (to exclude lines connecting two vertices with the same t).The lines for which both checks are positive are marked as "relevant to P_I".

   (b) The relevant lines of P_I do not contain edges but rather extreme rays of P_I (they are also extreme rays of P). For each such ray the characteristic equation of the corresponding line gives a representation of one vertex of a parametric polygon.

   (c) Triangulation is done is in the previous case. The attributes $T.FROM = t_k$, $T.TO = +\infty$.

6. The left-special points are treated symmetrically to right-special points.

Example 2. We apply the above construction to the constraint relation representing Figure B.1. We obtain the following extreme points (x, y, t):

$$(0,0,0), (10,0,0), (10,10,0), (0,20,0), (0,0,10), (20,0,10), (0,20,10), (0,0,20),$$

$$(30,0,20), (0,30,20).$$

None of them is special. We obtain two slices: $(0, 10]$ and $(10, 20]$. Some of the faces are: $x + t = 10$ and $x + y = 20$. From the intersection of those two faces we obtain two characteristic equations $x = 10 + t$ and $y = 10 - t$ that describe one vertex of a parametric polygon. The remaining vertices are determined in a similar way. For the slice $(0, 10]$ we obtain a parametric quadrangle which is then triangulated into two triangles (in a time-independent way). Those triangles are represented by the first two rows in Table 2. The last row in this table represents the second slice $(10, 20]$.

D   Naive and Parametric Animation

By the *animation* of a linear constraint database relation R we mean the sequential display of its snapshots or spatial extents (the set of (x, y) points) at times $t_0, t_1, \ldots, t_n$ at the user's request. The user specifies the initial time t_0, the time period Δ and the number of steps n, with the implicit condition that $t_i = t_{i-1} + \Delta$ for each $1 \leq i \leq n$.

In this section we describe and compare two methods for the animation of linear constraint databases. These two methods are called the naive and the parametric animation methods.

D.1   Animation Methods

Naive animation method. The naive animation method works directly on linear constraint databases. It finds for each time instance t_i, by instantiating the variable t to t_i, a linear constraint database relation that has only two spatial variables, namely x and y. Each constraint tuple of this relation defines a convex polygon. The naive method finds a triangulation of each polygon and the vertices of each triangle. Finally, it displays the set of triangles.

Parametric animation method. The parametric animation method has a *preprocessing* step and a *display* step. In the preprocessing step it constructs a parametric spaghetti database representation of the linear constraint database using the algorithm outlined in section C. This construction needs to be done only once, before any user requests. The construction also finds for each parametric triangle p a beginning time $t_{p.from}$ and an ending time $t_{p.to}$. Before $t_{p.from}$ or after $t_{p.to}$ the parametric triangle has no spatial extent and does not need to be displayed.

During the display step, which is done at the user's request, for each consecutive time instant t_i and for each parametric triangle it is checked first that t_i is between $t_{p.from}$ and $t_{p.to}$. Corresponding to the parametric triangles whose range includes t_i, the parametric method finds, by instantiating the variable t to t_i, a set of triangles defined by their corner vertices. Then it displays the set of triangles.

Both animation methods assume that the computer system used provides in its graphics library as a primitive a display module for triangles defined by their corner vertices. Such a primitive is common in computer systems. The two animation methods are summarized in Figure 4.

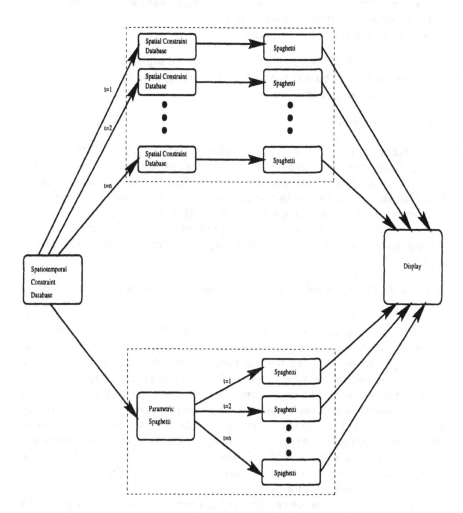

Fig. 4. Two Methods for the Animation of Spatiotemporal Databases

D.2   Computational Complexity

To compare the time complexity of both animation methods, we restrict ourselves to constraint relations consisting of single generalized tuples and their parametric representations. As each tuple is processed independently, the time of animating a constraint relation is then obtained in a straightforward way. Also, we assume that all processing is done in main memory.

We define first the following parameters:

- m - the number of constraints in the generalized tuple,
- k - the number of parametric tuples representing the generalized tuple,
- n - the number of animation steps.

Lemma 1. $k \in \theta(m^2)$.

Proof. From the description of the mapping in section C, it is clear that $k \in O(m^2)$. To see that this bound is actually achieved, consider a family of pyramids whose "bottom" side is an m-gon and the remaining sides are isosceles triangles. Now take the intersection of this solid with a half-space whose bounding plane cuts across the solid by meeting its bottom side at an angle α, $0 < \alpha < \pi/2$. The result can be represented as a constraint tuple with $m + 2$ linear arithmetic constraints but the conversion produces a representation with $O(m^2)$ parametric tuples.

Lemma 2. *For any given time t, the number of parametric tuples containing t is in $O(m)$.*

The naive approach requires no preprocessing. Each snapshot can be constructed and displayed in $O(m \log m)$ time [19]. Thus the entire animation requires $O(nm \log m)$ time. In the parametric approach, a polyhedral representation of the generalized tuple (step 1 of the mapping) can be constructed in $O(m \log m)$ time [19]. The entire preprocessing thus takes $O(\max(k, m \log m))$ time, due to the size of the parametric representation. Displaying all the snapshots takes $O(nk)$ time. In the worst case ($k \in O(m^2)$), the total time required by parametric animation is $O(nm^2)$, compared to $O(nm \log m)$ for the naive one. However, this was a rather artificial example. We have found that in practice $k \in O(m)$, and then the parametric approach requires $O(m \log m + nm)$ time, compared to $O(nm \log m)$ for the naive one.

Parametric animation can be further improved. For example, relations with parametric triangles can be indexed using one of the interval-indexing methods like interval or priority search trees [19]. Triangles to be displayed at a given time can then be quickly retrieved (in time $O(\log k + m)$ which by Lemma 1 is $O(m)$). In this approach, the display time can thus be reduced to $O(nm)$ even when $k \in O(m^2)$. This is optimal. However, building of the index takes $O(k \log k)$ time. This cost can be amortized over multiple runs if the parametric representation is built once and animated several times. (Notice that such amortization is not possible in the naive approach.)

Another possible optimization that does not use an index consists of keeping track during the animation of the set of "live" parametric triangles (those whose interval (FROM,TO) contains the current time). If the number of "live" triangles at any given time is small (and thus one avoids having to look at the many triangles that are not "live"), the savings may be significant. Lemma 2 says that the size of the set of live triangles is in $O(m)$. This approach could be implemented by creating two copies of the parametric table: one sorted on the FROM column (the *FROM table*) and the other on the TO column (the *TO* table). The copies are then merged. When a *FROM* tuple is encountered during the merge, the parametric triangle is added to "live" set, otherwise (a *TO* tuple) the corresponding triangle is removed from this set. In addition, one needs to keep track of the current time and at every consecutive time instant instantiate all the "live" parametric triangles. This approach adds $O(k \log k)$ time to preprocessing. Now display consists of n display events and $O(k)$ interval endpoint events. Each of the latter involves insertion or deletion in a structure of size $O(m)$. Each of the former involves retrieving all objects in this structure. Thus display now takes $O(nm + k \log m)$ time. If the number of "live" triangles at any time can be bounded by a constant, this approach takes $O(n + k)$ time, as compared to $O(n \log k)$ using interval indexing.

D.3   Implementation Results

We implemented both animation methods in Microsoft Visual C++ on top of MLPQ (Management of Linear Programming Queries), a system developed and used at the University of Nebraska for querying linear constraint databases [21, 17]. The animation system is named ASTD (Animation of Spatiotemporal Databases).

The main library routines that we implemented include an $O(m^2)$-time routine to convert a linear constraint database with only x, y special variables into a set of triangles, and a separate routine to convert linear constraint databases with x, y and t special variables into a set of parametric triangles. No optimizations of the parametric approach were used. We implemented the animation routines that use the conversion routines and the Visual C++ MFC class library function for displaying triangles given their corner vertices.

We also implemented a graphical user interface module through which a user can call the ASTD system and specify the following parameters: the animation method to be used, the name of the linear constraint database relation to be animated, the initial time, the time period, and the number of time steps. ASTD also allows the setting of another parameter, namely the minimum delay time $d_{\min}$. The minimum delay time controls the speed of the animation in the sense that there must be at least $d_{\min}$ time between the issue of two commands to display a set of triangles. In our execution experiments the minimum delay time was set to be very small. Hence each snapshot was essentially displayed as soon as the animation algorithm calculated the corner vertices of the set of triangles to be displayed.

We measured the execution times for the animation of the two examples (desert, city area) described in section B using the same parameters. In addition, we have experimented with an even more complex example: a spatiotemporal representation of the geographic range of California gull. Two snapshots of this representation are shown in Figure D.3.

The ASTD system ran on a 266 MHz Pentium II with 64M memory in a Windows NT environment. Table 3 compares the execution times (in milliseconds) of the two animation methods on the above three examples. For all examples, the parametric animation method was much faster. The missing entry in the last row is due to the fact that the computation ran out of available memory.

Table 3. Naive vs. Parametric Animation (Time in Millisecond)

Example	Number of Tuples/ Number of Time Points	Without Parametric Representations	With Parametric Representations
Desert	2 / 20	2,980	480
City	17 /20	17,860	1,680
Gull	131 / 60	-	12,470

D.4   Time Series

For completeness, we mention another possible approach to the problem of animating spatiotemporal databases. In this approach the time series of all the snapshots is precomputed and stored in a relational database. During the animation, consecutive snapshots are retrieved and displayed. This approach suffers from the fact that time granularity has to be fixed in advance. More significantly, the amount of data required by this approach is considerably higher than in the approaches described in the present paper. As a result, the animation data may have to be stored on disk, significantly increasing animation time.

E   Related work

Spatiotemporal data models and query languages. Spatiotemporal data models and query languages are a topic of growing interest. The paper [27] presents one of the first such models. In [10] the authors define in an abstract way moving points and regions. Apart from moving points, no other classes of concrete, database-representable spatiotemporal objects are defined. In that approach continuous movement (but not growth or shrinking) can be modeled using linear interpolation functions. In [12] the authors propose a formal spatiotemporal data model based on constraints in which, like in [27], only discrete change can be modeled. An SQL-based query language is also presented. We have proposed

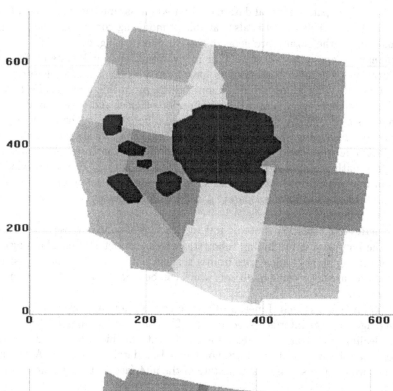

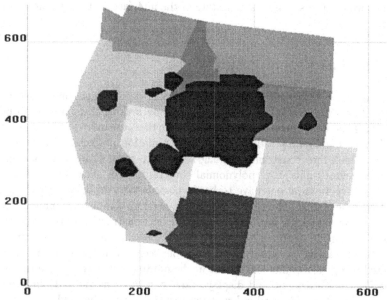

Fig. 5. California gull at t=0 (top) and t=31 (bottom).

elsewhere [7] a spatiotemporal data model based on parametric mappings of geometric objects. This model is also capable of modeling continuous change and avoids some of the closure problems of the parametric spaghetti model.

Computer animation. In this area many formalisms and systems for the specification of graphical animations have been proposed, including scripting languages [13]. The issues include, among others, producing realistic effects, animation language design, and making animation efficient and easy to build. The animations can typically be specified in several different ways (the following list is based on the system Maya (`http://www.aw.sgi.com`): by key frames with interpolation between them, procedurally, by inter-object constraints or by motion path (the path is specified by the user as a NURBS curve). To our knowledge, the work on computer animation has so far concentrated solely on the display level and the need to have a separate database representation of animations has not been identified.

Robotics and vision. Spatiotemporal applications abound in those areas. However, the emphasis is on finding robot trajectories (robot motion planning) or reconstructing object trajectories from a sequence of images (computer vision). Trajectories are not treated as objects which can be stored in a database, queried, or animated.

User interface design. Linear arithmetic constraints have been proposed as a language for user interface specification [2]. The main emphasis of this work is on dealing with constraint relationships (constraint hierachies) and efficient constraint solving. Constraints are not treated as database objects. Also, constraints are used to specify a single state of the interface, not a sequence of such states.

F   Conclusions and Future Work

We have shown that defining a separate display data model enhances the usability of spatiotemporal constraint databases by making their animation more efficient. This work opens many avenues for further research.

Computer animation. For more serious animation projects, it may be necessary to look into constraint languages that are more expressive than linear arithmetic constraints, e.g., polynomial constraints. For such constraints, new parametric representations have to be developed. We also believe that our approach can be further enhanced using techniques from computer graphics, animation, and computational geometry (more efficient construction of the parametric representation, more efficient display). In computer graphics, it is common to animate scenes with thousands of polygons per scene. If such animations are represented using constraints and stored in the database, it may become infeasible to perform preprocessing and display entirely in main memory. Then external memory algorithms [26] and index structures [16] need to be used.

Two-tiered data model. If the parametric 2-spaghetti data model is more suitable than the linear constraint database model, then perhaps the latter may be abandoned altogether? In fact, the parametric model can express some spatiotemporal objects which are not definable using linear constraints [5, 6]. However, the parametric model lacks important closure properties, e.g., it is not closed with respect to intersection [6]. This means that relations containing parametric polygons cannot be joined, although other operations like selection or projection can easily be supported. Therefore, we believe that the constraint model remains more suitable for querying. However, one should explore the option of storing the parametric polygons in a database and providing necessary indexing mechanisms. In this way *content-based* retrieval of animations can be supported.

Higher dimension. In this paper, we focused on two dimensional spatiotemporal problems which only had x, y and t as linearly dependent variables. However, many real-life spatiotemporal problems are three dimensional, that is, involve three spatial and one temporal variables that are linearly dependent on each other [20]. We need to develop a three-dimensional parametric representation and study translations of three-dimensional constraint databases to this representation. Also, the display of three dimensional parametric spaghetti databases on two dimensional computer screens has to be studied.

Multiple time granularities. It is natural to allow multiple time granularities: years, months, days, etc. To represent them in a constraint database one can use complex values in the time domain or multiple temporal attributes. The parametric representation would have to be suitably extended and the mapping from constraint databases to the parametric representation generalized.

Rotation. Neither the linear constraint data model nor the parametric spaghetti data model can describe rotation of objects. Since rotation is a fairly common movement of spatiotemporal objects, an extension has to be found of both data models that can describe rotational movements. We are currently investigating data models that add rotation without having to deal with general polynomial constraint databases.

General continuous change. It is natural to allow other attributes, apart from the spatial ones, to change continuously. For an example, consider continuous picture shading. To represent it, one would define the shade attribute as a (linear) function of time. No extension of the constraint data model is necessary to represent such an attribute. The parametric spaghetti model is easy to extend in this direction by allowing linear functions of time in non-spatial attributes. The change to the display algorithm is also minor. However, the mapping (section C) from linear constraint databases to the parametric representation continues to work only under the assumption that spatial and non-spatial attributes are independent [3]. In practical terms, it means that all the points of a polygon have to change in exactly the same way.

Acknowledgments

The work of the first author was supported by NSF grant IRI-9632870. The work of the second and third authors was supported by NSF grants IRI-9632871 and IRI-9625055, and by a Gallup Research Professorship. The first author thanks

Anna Lipka of Alias/Wavefront for the information about Maya and Vassilis Tsotras for the references to the literature on interval indexing. The authors are grateful to the anonymous reviewers for their helpful comments.

References

1. M. Bern. Triangulations. In Goodman and O'Rourke [11], chapter 22, pages 413–428.
2. A. Borning, K. Marriott, P. Stuckey, and Y. Xiao. Solving linear arithmetic constraints for user interface applications. In *ACM Symposium on User Interface Software and Technology*, 1997.
3. J. Chomicki, D. Goldin, and G. Kuper. Variable Independence and Aggregation Closure. In *ACM Symposium on Principles of Database Systems*, pages 40–48, Montréal, Canada, June 1996.
4. J. Chomicki. Temporal Query Languages: A Survey. In D. M. Gabbay and H. J. Ohlbach, editors, *Temporal Logic, First International Conference*, pages 506–534. Springer-Verlag, LNAI 827, 1994.
5. J. Chomicki and P. Z. Revesz. Constraint-Based Interoperability of Spatiotemporal Databases. In *International Symposium on Large Spatial Databases*, pages 142–161, Berlin, Germany, July 1997. Springer-Verlag, LNCS 1262.
6. J. Chomicki and P. Z.. Revesz. Constraint-Based Interoperability of Spatiotemporal Databases. *Geoinformatica*, 3(3), September 1999.
7. J. Chomicki and P. Z. Revesz. A Geometric Framework for Specifying Spatiotemporal Objects. In *International Workshop on Time Representation and Reasoning*, Orlando, Florida, May 1999.
8. M. Egenhofer. Why not SQL! *International Journal of Geographic Information Systems*, 6(2):71–85, 1992.
9. M. Egenhofer. Spatial SQL: A Query and Presentation Language. *IEEE Transactions on Knowledge and Data Engineering*, 6(1), 1994.
10. M. Erwig, R.H. Güting, M. M. Schneider, and M. Vazirgiannis. Spatio-Temporal Data Types: An Approach to Modeling and Querying Moving Objects in Databases. In *ACM Symposium on Geographic Information Systems*, November 1998.
11. Jacob E. Goodman and Joseph O'Rourke, editors. *Handbook of Discrete and Computational Geometry*. CRC Press, 1997.
12. S. Grumbach, P. Rigaux, and L. Segoufin. Spatio-Temporal Data Handling with Constraints. In *ACM Symposium on Geographic Information Systems*, November 1998.
13. M. Gervautz and D. Schmalstieg. Integrating a scripting language into an interactive animation system. In *Computer Animation*, pages 156–166, Geneva, Switzerland, 1994.
14. R. H. Güting. An Introduction to Spatial Database Systems. *VLDB Journal*, 3(4):357–400, October 1994.
15. P. C. Kanellakis, G. M. Kuper, and P. Z. Revesz. Constraint Query Languages. *Journal of Computer and System Sciences*, 51(1):26–52, August 1995.
16. P. C. Kanellakis, S. Ramaswamy, D. E. Vengroff, and J. S. Vitter. Indexing for Data Models with Constraints and Classes. *Journal of Computer and System Sciences*, 52(3):589–612, 1996.

17. P. Kanjamala, P.Z. Revesz, and Y. Wang. MLPQ/GIS: A Geographic Information System using Linear Constraint Databases. In *9th COMAD International Conference on Management of Data*, pages 389–393, Hyderabad, India, December 1998. Tata McGraw Hill.

18. J. Paredaens. Spatial Databases, The Final Frontier. In *International Conference on Database Theory*, pages 14–32, Prague, Czech Republic, January 1995. Springer-Verlag, LNCS 893.

19. F. Preparata and M. Shamos. *Computational Geometry*. Springer-Verlag, 1985.

20. J.. Raper. *Three Dimensional Applications in Geographical Information Systems*. Taylor & Francis, 1989.

21. P. Z. Revesz and Y. Li. MLPQ: A Linear Constraint Database System with Aggregate Operators. In *International Database Engineering and Applications Symposium*, pages 132–137. IEEE Press, 1997.

22. R. Seidel. Convex Hull Computations. In Goodman and O'Rourke [11], chapter 19, pages 361–375.

23. R. T. Snodgrass. Temporal Databases. In *Theories and Methods of Spatio-Temporal Reasoning in Geographic Space*, pages 22–64. Springer-Verlag, LNCS 639, 1992.

24. A. Tansel, J. Clifford, S. Gadia, S. Jajodia, A. Segev, and R. T. Snodgrass, editors. *Temporal Databases: Theory, Design, and Implementation*. Benjamin/Cummings, 1993.

25. L. Vandeurzen, M. Gyssens, and D. Van Gucht. On the Desirability and Limitations of Linear Spatial Database Models. In *International Symposium on Large Spatial Databases*, pages 14–28, 1995.

26. J.S. Vitter. External Memory Algorithms and Data Structures. In J. Abello and J.S. Vitter, editors, *External Memory Algorithms and Visualization*, DIMACS Series on Discrete Mathematics and Theoretical Computer Science. American Mathematical Society, 1999.

27. M. F. Worboys. A Unified Model for Spatial and Temporal Information. *Computer Journal*, 37(1):26–34, 1994.

28. Michael F. Worboys. *GIS: A Computing Perspective*. Taylor&Francis, 1995.

Author Index

Lecture Notes in Computer Science

For information about Vols. 1–1594
please contact your bookseller or Springer-Verlag

Vol. 1631: P. Narendran, M. Rusinowitch (Eds.), Rewriting Techniques and Applications. Proceedings, 1999. XI, 397 pages. 1999.

Vol. 1632: H. Ganzinger (Ed.), Automated Deduction – Cade-16. Proceedings, 1999. XIV, 429 pages. 1999. (Subseries LNAI).

Vol. 1633: N. Halbwachs, D. Peled (Eds.), Computer Aided Verification. Proceedings, 1999. XII, 506 pages. 1999.

Vol. 1634: S. Džeroski, P. Flach (Eds.), Inductive Logic Programming. Proceedings, 1999. VIII, 303 pages. 1999. (Subseries LNAI).

Vol. 1636: L. Knudsen (Ed.), Fast Software Encryption. Proceedings, 1999. VIII, 317 pages. 1999.

Vol. 1637: J.P. Walser, Integer Optimization by Local Search. XIX, 137 pages. 1999. (Subseries LNAI).

Vol. 1638: A. Hunter, S. Parsons (Eds.), Symbolic and Quantitative Approaches to Reasoning and Uncertainty. Proceedings, 1999. IX, 397 pages. 1999. (Subseries LNAI).

Vol. 1639: S. Donatelli, J. Kleijn (Eds.), Application and Theory of Petri Nets 1999. Proceedings, 1999. VIII, 425 pages. 1999.

Vol. 1640: W. Tepfenhart, W. Cyre (Eds.), Conceptual Structures: Standards and Practices. Proceedings, 1999. XII, 515 pages. 1999. (Subseries LNAI).

Vol. 1641: D. Hutter, W. Stephan, P. Traverso, M. Ullmann (Eds.), Applied Formal Methods – FM-Trends 98. Proceedings, 1998. XI, 377 pages. 1999.

Vol. 1642: D.J. Hand, J.N. Kok, M.R. Berthold (Eds.), Advances in Intelligent Data Analysis. Proceedings, 1999. XII, 538 pages. 1999.

Vol. 1643: J. Nešetřil (Ed.), Algorithms – ESA '99. Proceedings, 1999. XII, 552 pages. 1999.

Vol. 1644: J. Wiedermann, P. van Emde Boas, M. Nielsen (Eds.), Automata, Languages, and Programming. Proceedings, 1999. XIV, 720 pages. 1999.

Vol. 1645: M. Crochemore, M. Paterson (Eds.), Combinatorial Pattern Matching. Proceedings, 1999. VIII, 295 pages. 1999.

Vol. 1647: F.J. Garijo, M. Boman (Eds.), Multi-Agent System Engineering. Proceedings, 1999. X, 233 pages. 1999. (Subseries LNAI).

Vol. 1648: M. Franklin (Ed.), Financial Cryptography. Proceedings, 1999. VIII, 269 pages. 1999.

Vol. 1649: R.Y. Pinter, S. Tsur (Eds.), Next Generation Information Technologies and Systems. Proceedings, 1999. IX, 327 pages. 1999.

Vol. 1650: K.-D. Althoff, R. Bergmann, L.K. Branting (Eds.), Case-Based Reasoning Research and Development. Proceedings, 1999. XII, 598 pages. 1999. (Subseries LNAI).

Vol. 1651: R.H. Güting, D. Papadias, F. Lochovsky (Eds.), Advances in Spatial Databases. Proceedings, 1999. XI, 371 pages. 1999.

Vol. 1652: M. Klusch, O.M. Shehory, G. Weiss (Eds.), Cooperative Information Agents III. Proceedings, 1999. XI, 404 pages. 1999. (Subseries LNAI).

Vol. 1653: S. Covaci (Ed.), Active Networks. Proceedings, 1999. XIII, 346 pages. 1999.

Vol. 1654: E.R. Hancock, M. Pelillo (Eds.), Energy Minimization Methods in Computer Vision and Pattern Recognition. Proceedings, 1999. IX, 331 pages. 1999.

Vol. 1656: S. Chatterjee, J.F. Prins, L. Carter, J. Ferrante, Z. Li, D. Sehr, P.-C. Yew (Eds.), Languages and Compilers for Parallel Computing. Proceedings, 1998. XI, 384 pages. 1999.

Vol. 1661: C. Freksa, D.M. Mark (Eds.), Spatial Information Theory. Proceedings, 1999. XIII, 477 pages. 1999.

Vol. 1662: V. Malyshkin (Ed.), Parallel Computing Technologies. Proceedings, 1999. XIX, 510 pages. 1999.

Vol. 1663: F. Dehne, A. Gupta. J.-R. Sack, R. Tamassia (Eds.), Algorithms and Data Structures. Proceedings, 1999. IX, 366 pages. 1999.

Vol. 1664: J.C.M. Baeten, S. Mauw (Eds.), CONCUR'99. Concurrency Theory. Proceedings, 1999. XI, 573 pages. 1999.

Vol. 1666: M. Wiener (Ed.), Advances in Cryptology – CRYPTO '99. Proceedings, 1999. XII, 639 pages. 1999.

Vol. 1668: J.S. Vitter, C.D. Zaroliagis (Eds.), Algorithm Engineering. Proceedings, 1999. VIII, 361 pages. 1999.

Vol. 1671: D. Hochbaum, K. Jansen, J.D.P. Rolim, A. Sinclair (Eds.), Randomization, Approximation, and Combinatorial Optimization. Proceedings, 1999. IX, 289 pages. 1999.

Vol. 1672: M. Kutylowski, L. Pacholski, T. Wierzbicki (Eds.), Mathematical Foundations of Computer Science 1999. Proceedings, 1999. XII, 455 pages. 1999.

Vol. 1673: P. Lysaght, J. Irvine, R. Hartenstein (Eds.), Field Programmable Logic and Applications. Proceedings, 1999. XI, 541 pages. 1999.

Vol. 1674: D. Floreano, J.-D. Nicoud, F. Mondad a(Eds.), Advances in Artificial Life. Proceedings, 1999. XVI, 737 pages. 1999. (Subseries LNAI).

Vol. 1677: T. Bench-Capon, G. Soda, A M. Tjoa (Eds.), Database and Expert Systems Applications. Proceedings, 1999. XVIII, 1105 pages. 1999.

Vol. 1678: M.H. Böhlen, C.S. Jensen, M.O. Scholl (Eds.), Spatio-Temporal Database Management. Proceedings, 1999. X, 243 pages. 1999.

Vol. 1684: G. Ciobanu, G. Păun (Eds.), Fundamentals of Computation Theory. Proceedings, 1999. XI, 570 pages. 1999.

Vol. 1685: P. Amestoy, P. Berger, M. Daydé, I. Duff, V. Frayssé, L. Giraud, D. Ruiz (Eds.), Euro-Par'99. Parallel Processing. Proceedings, 1999. XXXII, 1503 pages. 1999.

Vol. 1688: P. Bouquet, L. Serafini, P. Brézillon, M. Benerecetti, F. Castellani (Eds.), Modeling and Using Context. Proceedings, 1999. XII, 528 pages. 1999. (Subseries LNAI).

Vol. 1689: F. Solina, A. Leonardis (Eds.), Computer Analysis of Images and Patterns. Proceedings, 1999. XIV, 650 pages. 1999.

Vol. 1690: Y. Bertot, G. Dowek, A. Hirschowitz, C. Paulin, L. Théry (Eds.), Theorem Proving in Higher Order Logics. Proceedings, 1999. VIII, 359 pages. 1999.

Vol. 1694: A. Cortesi, G. Filé (Eds.), Static Analysis. Proceedings, 1999. VIII, 357 pages. 1999.